P9-CFA-428

821.09 HOP

Gerard Manley Hopkins

GERARD MANLEY HOPKINS

Modern Critical Views

Henry Adams
Edward Albee
A. R. Ammons
Matthew Arnold
John Ashbery
W. H. Auden
Jane Austen
James Baldwin
Charles Baudelaire
Samuel Beckett
Saul Bellow
The Bible
Elizabeth Bishop
William Blake
Jorge Luis Borges
Elizabeth Bowen
Bertolt Brecht
The Brontës
Robert Browning
Anthony Burgess
George Gordon, Lord
  Byron
Thomas Carlyle
Lewis Carroll
Willa Cather
Cervantes
Geoffrey Chaucer
Kate Chopin
Samuel Taylor Coleridge
Joseph Conrad
Contemporary Poets
Hart Crane
Stephen Crane
Dante
Charles Dickens
Emily Dickinson
John Donne & The
  Seventeenth-Century
  Metaphysical Poets
Elizabethan Dramatists
Theodore Dreiser
John Dryden
George Eliot
T. S. Eliot
Ralph Ellison
Ralph Waldo Emerson
William Faulkner
Henry Fielding
F. Scott Fitzgerald
Gustave Flaubert
E. M. Forster
Sigmund Freud
Robert Frost

Robert Graves
Graham Greene
Thomas Hardy
Nathaniel Hawthorne
William Hazlitt
Seamus Heaney
Ernest Hemingway
Geoffrey Hill
Friedrich Hölderlin
Homer
Gerard Manley Hopkins
William Dean Howells
Zora Neale Hurston
Henry James
Samuel Johnson and
  James Boswell
Ben Jonson
James Joyce
Franz Kafka
John Keats
Rudyard Kipling
D. H. Lawrence
John Le Carré
Ursula K. Le Guin
Doris Lessing
Sinclair Lewis
Robert Lowell
Norman Mailer
Bernard Malamud
Thomas Mann
Christopher Marlowe
Carson McCullers
Herman Melville
James Merrill
Arthur Miller
John Milton
Eugenio Montale
Marianne Moore
Iris Murdoch
Vladimir Nabokov
Joyce Carol Oates
Sean O'Casey
Flannery O'Connor
Eugene O'Neill
George Orwell
Cynthia Ozick
Walter Pater
Walker Percy
Harold Pinter
Plato
Edgar Allan Poe

Poets of Sensibility & the
  Sublime
Alexander Pope
Katherine Anne Porter
Ezra Pound
Pre-Raphaelite Poets
Marcel Proust
Thomas Pynchon
Arthur Rimbaud
Theodore Roethke
Philip Roth
John Ruskin
J. D. Salinger
Gershom Scholem
William Shakespeare
  (3 vols.)
  Histories & Poems
  Comedies
  Tragedies
George Bernard Shaw
Mary Wollstonecraft
  Shelley
Percy Bysshe Shelley
Edmund Spenser
Gertrude Stein
John Steinbeck
Laurence Sterne
Wallace Stevens
Tom Stoppard
Jonathan Swift
Alfred, Lord Tennyson
William Makepeace
  Thackeray
Henry David Thoreau
Leo Tolstoi
Anthony Trollope
Mark Twain
John Updike
Gore Vidal
Virgil
Robert Penn Warren
Evelyn Waugh
Eudora Welty
Nathanael West
Edith Wharton
Walt Whitman
Oscar Wilde
Tennessee Williams
William Carlos Williams
Thomas Wolfe
Virginia Woolf
William Wordsworth
Richard Wright
William Butler Yeats

These and other titles in preparation

Modern Critical Views

GERARD MANLEY HOPKINS

Edited and with an introduction by
Harold Bloom
Sterling Professor of the Humanities
Yale University

CHELSEA HOUSE PUBLISHERS ◇ 1986
New York ◇ New Haven ◇ Philadelphia

© 1986 by Chelsea House Publishers, a division of Chelsea House
Educational Communications, Inc.
  133 Christopher Street, New York, NY 10014
  345 Whitney Avenue, New Haven, CT 06511
  5014 West Chester Pike, Edgemont, PA 19028

Printed and bound in the United States of America

∞ The paper used in this publication meets the minimum re-
quirements of the American National Standard for Permanence of
Paper for Printed Library Materials, Z39.48−1984.

Library of Congress Cataloging-in-Publication Data
Main entry under title:

Gerard Manley Hopkins.

  (Modern critical views)
  Bibliography; p.
  Includes index.
    1. Hopkins, Gerard Manley, 1844−1889—Criticism
and interpretation—Addresses, essays, lectures.
I. Bloom, Harold. II. Series.
PR4803.H44Z6434 1986   821'.8   85-29964
ISBN 0-87754-691-6 (alk. paper)

Contents

CONTENTS

Editor's Note

This volume gathers together a representative selection of the best criticism available upon the poetry of Gerard Manley Hopkins, arranged in the chronological order of its publication. I am grateful to Eden Quainton for his erudition and judgment in helping to edit this book.

The introduction attempts to correct anachronistic views of Hopkins as a modernist poet, rather than as the High Victorian ephebe of Keats, and pupil of Walter Pater, that he actually was. Austin Warren's superb overview of Hopkins's achievement begins the chronological sequence, and needs no correction, recognizing as it does that the poet's mind was "first aesthetic, then technical."

A remarkable reading of "The Windhover" by Geoffrey H. Hartman emphasizes that "in Hopkins the figurative sense is always derived from physical phenomena," while showing also that the complexity of the figurations inheres in their "aesthetic surface." The analysis of *The Wreck of the Deutschland* by Elisabeth W. Schneider ranks it among the great odes of the language. A similarly high estimate is maintained by Paul L. Mariani in his spirited exegesis of the Terrible Sonnets, a veritable descent into that state named by St. John of the Cross as the Dark Night of the Soul.

Few poets are as original in their diction as Hopkins was, an originality that is the subject of James Milroy's investigation. Related to this complex question of vocabulary is the parallel study by Ellen Eve Frank, which examines Hopkins's concerns in the *Note-Books* both with architecture and with etymology, linked by an obsession with "fineness, proportion of feature."

Marylou Motto sensitively formulates some of the complex ways in which Hopkins mingles sacred and secular senses of time, as he works out the status of his poems as fictions of duration. In this book's final essay, J. Hillis Miller offers a distinguished instance of Deconstructive criticism, in which the poet's "linguistic moments" are seen as instances of the realization that "language is a medium of separation, not of reconciliation." By returning us to Pater, the poet's tutor, as well as to Hegel and Nietzsche, Miller reminds us again that Hopkins was very much a poet of his age as well as a seer of timeless moments.

Introduction

Of all Victorian poets, Hopkins has been the most misrepresented by modern critics. He has been discussed as though his closest affinities were with Donne on one side, and T. S. Eliot on the other. Yet his poetry stems directly from Keats and the Pre-Raphaelites, and the dominant influences upon his literary thought came from Ruskin and Pater. A disciple of Newman, he is as High Romantic as his master, and his best poetry, with all its peculiarities of diction and metric, is perhaps less of a departure from the Victorian norm than Browning's, or Swinburne's, or even Patmore's. His case is analogous to Emily Dickinson's. Published out of their own century, they became for a time pseudocontemporaries of twentieth-century poets, but perspectives later became corrected, and we learned to read both poets as very much involved in the literature and thought of their own generations. Hopkins was, in many of his attitudes, a representative Victorian gentleman; indeed he was as much a nationalistic jingo as Tennyson or Kipling, and his religious anguish is clearly related to a characteristic sorrow of his age. His more properly poetic anguish is wholly Romantic, like Arnold's, for it derives from an incurably Romantic sensibility desperately striving not to be Romantic, but to make a return to a lost tradition. Hopkins quested for ideas of order that were not available to his poetic mind, and as a poet he ended in bitterness, convinced that he had failed his genius.

Hopkins was born on July 28, 1844, at Stratford in Essex, the eldest of nine children, into a very religious High Anglican family, of comfortable means. He did not enjoy his early school years, but flowered at Balliol College, Oxford, where he studied Classics from 1863 to 1867, and became a student of Walter Pater, who corrected his essays. In the atmosphere of the continuing Oxford Movement, Hopkins underwent a crisis, which came in March 1865 and partly resulted from meeting an enthusiastic, young, religious poet, Digby Dolben, who was to drown in June 1867 at the age of nineteen.

1

In 1866, under Newman's sponsorship, Hopkins was received into the Roman Catholic Church. Two years later, he began his Jesuit novitiate, and continued faithful to the Order until he died. Ordained a priest in 1877, he preached in Liverpool, taught at Stonyhurst, a Jesuit seminary, and from 1884 until his death in 1889 served as Professor of Greek at the University College in Dublin. Though perfectly free to write poems and paint pictures, so far as his superiors in the Society of Jesus were concerned, Hopkins was a congenital self-torturer, and so much a Romantic that he found the professions of priest and poet to be mutually exclusive.

Austin Warren, one of Hopkins's best and most sympathetic critics, justly remarked that in Hopkins's most ambitious poems there is "a discrepancy between texture and structure: the copious, violent detail is matched by no corresponding intellectual or mythic vigor." Following Keats's advice to Shelley, that an artist must serve Mammon by loading every rift of his poem with ore, Hopkins sometimes went too far, and even a sympathetic reader can decide that the poems are overloaded.

What then is Hopkins's achievement as poet? It remains considerable, for the original, almost incredible, accomplishment of Hopkins is to have made Keatsian poetry into a devotional mode, however strained. In the "Subtle Doctor," the Scottish Franciscan philosopher Duns Scotus (1265 – 1308), also an Oxonian, Hopkins found doctrine to reconcile a concern for individual form, for the "thisness" of people and natural things, with the universal truths of the church. Following his own understanding of Scotus, Hopkins coined the word "inscape" for every natural pattern he apprehended. "Instress," another coinage, meant for him the effect of each pattern upon his own imagination. Taken together, the terms are an attempt at scholasticizing Keats's fundamental approach to perception: detachment, the poet's recourse to nonidentity, Negative Capability.

Hopkins remained unpublished until his friend, the poet Robert Bridges, brought out a first edition of the poems in 1918, nearly thirty years after Hopkins's death. By chance, this first publication almost coincided with the start of the aggressive literary modernism that dominated British and American poetry until the 1950s, and Hopkins was acclaimed by poets and critics as the true continuator of English poetry in the otherwise benighted nineteenth century, and as a precursor who could help justify modern experiments in diction, metrics, and imagistic procedure.

Hopkins's diction adds to its Keatsian and Pre-Raphaelite base a large stock of language derived from his study of Welsh and Old English, and from an amorphous group of Victorian philologists who sought a "pure English," less contaminated by the Latin and French elements that are incurably part of the language. Hopkins's metric was based, as he said, upon nursery rhymes, the choruses of Milton's *Samson Agonistes*, and Welsh poetry. Against what he called the "running" or "common" rhythm of nineteenth-century poetry, Hopkins espoused "sprung rhythm," which he insisted was inherent in the English language, the older, purely accentual meter of Anglo-Saxon verse. Evidently, Hopkins read Keats's odes as having this rhythm, despite Keats's Spenserian smoothness.

Though Hopkins came to the study of Old English late, his essential metrical achievement was to revive the schemes of Old English poetry. But the main traditions of English poetic rhythm go from Chaucer to Spenser and Milton and on to the major Romantics, and Hopkins's archaizing return to Cynewulf and Langland, though influential for a time, now seems an honorable eccentricity. Nevertheless, its expressive effectiveness is undeniable. The metrical basis of many of Hopkins's poems is a fixed number of primary-stressed syllables, surrounded by a variable number of unstressed ones, or "outrides" as he called them. The alliterations of early Germanic poetry also work powerfully to recast the poetic line into a chain of rhythmic bursts. Thus, in "The Windhover," the first two lines each have five of Hopkins's beats (as opposed to five regularized, alternating, accentual-syllabic ones):

I caúght this mórning, mórning's minión, kíng-
dom of dáylight's daúphin, dapple-dáwn-drawn Fálcon, in his ríding . . .

But the first line has ten syllables, and might be mistaken for an iambic pentameter, while the second has sixteen; and we realize as we read through the poems that what is common to them, their *meter* rather than their individual rhythms, is the sequence of five major stresses. Moreover, the phrase "dapple-*dawn*-drawn" is so accented as to preserve the meaning "drawn by dappled dawn" through its interior rhyme and alliterative clusters. Hopkins's own invented metrical terminology is, like his other philosophical vocabulary, highly figurative: "hangers" or "outrides," "sprung rhythm," "counterpointing" (or superposition of rhythmic schemes), even the blended emotive-linguistic meanings of "stress" itself, all invoke the imagery of his poems, and are as subjective as are his metaphysical concepts, but like those concepts constitute an extraordinary approach to a Catholic poetic transcendentalism.

AUSTIN WARREN

Instress of Inscape

The early Hopkins follows Keats and the "medieval school" (as he called the Pre-Raphelites). The latest Hopkins, who wrote the sonnets of desolation, was a poet of tense, economic austerity. Their nearest parallel I can call would be Donne's "holy sonnets": "Batter my heart" and "If poisonous minerals." For mode in "Andromeda" and the later sonnets (1885−9), Hopkins himself projected "a more Miltonic plainness and severity": he is thinking of Milton's sonnets and the choruses of *Samson*. In 1887 he invoked another name: "my style tends always more towards Dryden."

The middle period, which opens with the *The Wreck of the Deutschland* (1875) and closes with "Tom's Garland" and "Harry Ploughman," both written in 1885, is the period of experiment. But it is also the most Hopkinsian,—the most markedly and specially his.

Middle Hopkins startles us by its dense rich world, its crowded Ark, its plentitude and its tangibility, its particularity of thing and word. There is detailed precision of image ("rose moles all in stipple upon trout that swim"). The poet is enamored of the unique, the "abrupt self."

The exploration of Middle Hopkins,—its style, the view of life and art implicit in its style,—may well start from the institutions and movements from which the poet learned, in which he participated. The motifs are the Ritualistic Movement, Pre-Raphaelitism, Aestheticism, linguistic renovation, England, the Catholic Church. In Hopkins' celebration of the sensuous, the concrete, the particular—his "instress of the inscapes"—all of these converge.

From *Gerard Manley Hopkins* by the Kenyon Critics. © 1944 by The Kenyon Review, © 1945 by New Directions.

As a Catholic, Hopkins was an incarnationist and a sacramentalist: the sacraments are the extensions of the incarnation. As a Catholic, he believed that man is a compound of matter and form, and that his body, resurrected, will express and implement his soul through all eternity. "Man's spirit will be flesh-bound when found at best. But unencumbered." Like all Catholic philosophers, he believed in an outer world independent of man's knowing mind—he was, in the present sense of the word, a "realist."

Hopkins was an Englishman, of a proud and patriotic sort. This is not always remembered, partly because he became the priest of a Church viewed by his compatriots as Continental, or Italian, or international. But there is an English way of being Catholic. Hopkins was not an "old Catholic" of the sturdy, unemotional variety nourished on Challoner's *Garden of the Soul;* no convert could be that. But, like his admired Newman, and unlike Manning and Faber (also converts), he was "Gallican" not Ultramontane, British not Italian in his devotional life and rhetoric. He remembers when England was Catholic, when the pilgrims frequented the shrine of our Lady of Walsingham.

> Deeply surely, I need to deplore it,
> Wondering why my master bore it,
> The riving off that race
> So at home, time was, to his truth and grace
>
> That a starlight-wender of ours would say
> The marvelous Milk was Walsingham Way
>   And one—but let be, let be;
> More, more than was will yet be.

The four real shapers of Hopkins' mind were all Britons; we might go further and say, all were British empiricists—all concerned with defending the ordinary man's belief in the reality and knowability of things and persons.

Two of them were encountered at Oxford. Pater, who remained his friend, was one of his tutors. In the abstractionist academic world, Pater boldly defended the concrete—of the vital arts and music of perception, of the unique experience. "Every moment some form grows perfect in hand or face, some tone on the hills or the sea is choicer than the rest." Though Hopkins could not conceivably have written so representatively, abstractly " . . . hills . . . sea . . . choicer," the text pleads for a stressing of the inscapes. Hopkins followed some lectures by Pater on Greek philosophy: perhaps he heard, in an earlier version, Pater's lectures on Plato and Platonism, in which,

with monstrous effrontery, the Doctrine of Ideas was praised as giving con-
textual interest to the concrete.

With Ruskin, whose *Modern Painters* he read early and admiringly,
Hopkins shared the revolt against that neoclassical grandeur of generality
praised by Johnson and expounded by Reynolds. The influence of Ruskin—art
medievalist, devout student of clouds, mountains, trees—is pervasive in
Hopkins' sketches (five of which are reproduced in the *Note-Books*) and in his
journalizing—his meticulously technical descriptions of church architecture
(often neo-Gothic) and scenery.

Hopkins follows the general line of Ruskin in more than art. Remote
from him is the old "natural theology" which finds the humanly satisfactory
and well furnished world such an effect of its Creator as the watch of the
watchmaker. Nor does he, after the fashion of some mystics and Alexandrians,
dissolve Nature into a system of symbols translating the real world of the
spirit. Like Ruskin, he was able to recover the medieval and Franciscan joy in
God's creation. And like Ruskin he protested against an England which is
"seared with trade . . . and wears man's smudge." His political economy, as
well as it can be construed, was Ruskinian; what may be called Tory Socialist
or Distributist.

It was to Newman, his great predecessor, that Hopkins wrote when he
decided to become a Roman Catholic. And Newman's closest approach to a
philosophical work, his *Grammar of Assent* (1870), interested Hopkins so far
that in 1883 he planned to publish (should Newman agree) a commentary on
it. There were marked temperamental and intellectual differences between the
men. Newman, much the more complex and psychologically subtle, could feel
his way into other men's minds as Hopkins could not. Hopkins was the closer
dialectician and scholar. He did not share Newman's distrust of metaphysics,
including the scholastic, his tendency to fideism; but he was, like Newman (in
words the latter used of Hurrell Froude), "an Englishman to the backbone in
his severe adherence to the real and the concrete."

The great medieval thinker who most swayed Hopkins' spirit to peace,
Duns Scotus, was also a Briton, had been an Oxford professor. He was "Of
reality the rarest-veinéd unraveler": he was able to analyze, disengage from the
complex in which they appear, the thinnest, most delicate strands ("vein" may
be either anatomical or geological). Perhaps "rarest-veinéd unraveler" is a kind
of *kenning* for the philosopher's epithet, the Subtle Doctor. Scotus, the Franciscan critic of the Dominican Thomas Aquinas, was centrally dear to Hopkins
by virtue of his philosophical validation of the individual. St. Thomas held
that, in the relation of the individual to his species, the "matter" individuates,

while the "form" is generic: that is, that the individuals of a species re-productively multiply their common originative pattern. Scotus insisted that each individual has a distinctive "form" as well: a *haecceitas*, or thisness, as well as a generic *quidditas*, or whatness.

After meeting with this medieval Franciscan, Hopkins, taking in "any inscape of sky or sea," thought of Scotus. The word, of Hopkins' coinage, occurs already in his Oxford note-books. Suggested presumably by "land-scape": an "inscape" is any kind of formed or focussed view, any pattern discerned in the natural world. Being so central a word in his vocabulary and motif in his mental life, it moves through some range of meaning: from sense-perceived pattern to inner form. The prefix seems to imply a contrary, an outer-scape—as if to say that an "inscape" is not mechanically or inertly present, but requires personal action, attention, a seeing and *seeing into*.

The earliest "Notes for Poetry" cite "Feathery rows of young corn. Ruddy, furred and branchy tops of the elms backed by rolling clouds." "A beautiful instance of inscape *sided* on the *slide*, that is successive sidings on one inscape, is seen in the behavior of the flag flower." In 1873, two years before the *Deutschland*, he "Saw a shoal of salmon in the river and many hares on the open hills. Under a stone hedge was a dying ram: there ran slowly from his nostrils a thick flesh-coloured ooze, scarlet in places, coiling and roping its way down so thick that it looked like fat."

He made notes on ancient musical instruments and on gems and their colors: "beryl—watery green; carnelian—strong flesh red, Indian red." His love of precise visual observation never lapsed. Nor did his taste for research. Like Gray, he had a scholarly, fussy antiquarianism, adaptable to botany or archaeology. He liked "Notes and Queries," details, studies in place-names, amateur etymologies.

What is perhaps his most brilliant prose celebrates the self and its wonders: "That taste of myself, of I and me above and in all things, which is more distinctive than the taste of ale or alum." Other selves were mysterious. As a shy man, he found it easier to reach natural "inscapes" than to know other selves. He hadn't Newman's psychological finesse; wrote no psychic portraits matching by their sharpness and delicacy his notations of ash-trees. The men in his poems are seen as from a distance—sympathetically but generically.

But he gloried in the range and repertory of mankind. Like Chesterton, who was concerned that, in lying down with the lamb, the lion should "still retain his royal ferocity," Hopkins wanted monks to be mild and soldiers to be pugnacious. He imagined Christ incarnate again as a soldier. He didn't want other men to be like himself—scholarly, aesthetic, neurotic: he was drawn to soldiers, miners, Felix Randall the Blacksmith and Harry the Ploughman, to the rough and manly manual laborers. And each of these selves he wished to be functioning not only characteristically but intensely, violently, dangerously—on their mettle, like the Windhover, like Harry Ploughman, like the "Eurydice's" sailor who, "strung by duty, is strained to beauty."

In poetry, he desired both to record inscapes and to use words so that they would exist as objects. His was a double particularity.

Poetry, he wrote, shortly before the *Deutschland*, is "speech framed to be heard for its own sake and interest even over and above its interest of meaning. Some [subject] matter and meaning is essential to it but only as an element necessary to support and employ the shape which is contemplated for its own sake. Poetry is in fact speech for the inscape's sake—and therefore the inscape must be dwelt on."

In 1862, he was already collecting words—particularistic, concrete words. The earliest entries in the *Note-Books* are gritty, harshly tangy words, "running the letter," "grind, gride, grid, grit, groat, grate" and "crock, crank, kranke, crick, cranky." He is also aroused by dialectal equivalents which he encounters: *whisket* for *basket, grindlestone* for *grindstone*. He notes linguistic habits: an observed laborer, when he began to speak "quickly and descriptively, . . . dropped or slurred the article." He attends to, and tries to define, the sundry schools of Latin pronunciation—this while the priests say mass. He inquires concerning the character of the Maltese language; wants to learn Welsh—not primarily in order to convert the local Wesleyans back to their ancestral faith.

As a beginning poet, Hopkins followed Keats and the "medieval school." Even in his middle style, there remain vestiges of the earlier decorative diction, frequent use of "beauty," "lovely," "dear," "sweet" ("that sweet's sweeter ending"). But already in 1866, "The Habit of Perfection," though dominantly "medieval," anticipates the later mode:

> This ruck and reel which you remark
> Coils, keeps, and teases simple sight.

The Wreck of the Deutschland (1875) inaugurates Hopkins' middle period (his first proper mastery). The diction is as remarkable as the rhythm. Characteristic are homely dialectal words, words which sound like survivors from Anglo-Saxon, and compound epithets. From the concluding stanzas of the *Deutschland* come these lines:

> Mid-numbered He in three of the thunder-throne!
> Not a dooms-day dazzle in his coming nor dark as he came;

and

> Dame, at our door
> Drowned, and among our shoals,
> Remember us in the roads, the heaven-haven of the
> Reward:

From "The Bugler's First Communion":

> Forth Christ from cupboard fetched, how fain I of feet
> To his youngster take his treat!
> Low-latched in leaf-light housel his too huge godhead.

Modern readers take it for granted that Hopkins was influenced by Old English poetry. In his excellent *New Poets from Old: A Study in Literary Genetics*, Henry Wells notes that all the technical features representative of that poetry appear conspicuously in Hopkins; judges him far nearer to Cynewulf than to Chaucer; finds a plausible parallel to a passage in *Beowulf*. But by his own statement, Hopkins did not learn Anglo-Saxon till 1882, and seems never to have read either *Beowulf* or Cynewulf. There need of course be no pedantic mystery here. Hopkins knew something of *Piers Plowman* and is likely to have known some specimens of Old English versification.

In any case, Hopkins was already a student of Welsh poetry and an attentive reader of linguistic monographs; and he belongs among the poets who can be incited to poetry by scholars' prose.

In 1873−4, he taught "rhetoric" at Manresa House, wrote the observations on that subject collected in the *Note-Books*. His notes lead us to the *Lectures on the English Language*, published in 1859 by the versatile American scholar, George P. Marsh. This book is full of matter calculated to excite a poet, for Marsh has a real interest in the future (as well as the past) of the language and a real interest in the literary (as well as the pragmatic) use of words. The whole direction of his book suggests that literary experiment can find much in its purpose in literary history, that new poetry can come from old. Ending his lecture on "Accentuation and Double Rhymes," he urges: "We must enlarge our stock [of rhyming words] by the revival of obsolete words and inflections from native sources," or introduce substitutes for rhyme; in the following, the 25th Chapter, he incitingly discusses alliteration (with illustrations from *Piers Plowman*), consonance—e.g., "bad, led"; "find, band" (with illustrations from Icelandic poetry and invented English examples), and assonance (with illustrations from the Spanish). Hopkins' quotations from *Piers* are Marsh's; only in 1882 did he study *Piers*, and then without admiration, regarding its verse as a "degraded and doggrel" form of Anglo-Saxon sprung rhythm.

To both Bridges and Dixon, curious concerning the new poetic method of the *Deutschland*, Hopkins says nothing of Old English nor of *Piers Plowman* but speaks of nursery rhymes, the choruses of *Samson*, and of his reading in Welsh poetry (which he began studying in 1875). "The chiming of the consonants I got in part from the Welsh, which is very rich in sound and imagery." H. I. Bell, a recent student of Welsh poetry, distinguishes four types of *cynghanedd*—two offering consonantal sequences (like "Nigh*t* may *d*are / *not* my *d*eares*t*"), another with a pattern of internal rhyme ("If to the *grove* she *rove*th"), and a fourth combining internal rhyme and alliteration ("Daisies *b*loom, and roses *b*low"). Traits common to Old English and Middle Hopkins (scant use of articles, prepositions and pronouns; constant use of compound words) are shared by both with Welsh poetry.

Then there is a third line for Hopkins' diction. He derives, through Barnes and Furnivall at least, from an imprecisely defined group of historians and philologists who may be called Teutonizers and who challenged the dominance of the Latin and Romance—the "civilized," learned, and abstract elements in our language. These linguistic protestants were motivated by nationalist or regionalist feeling or by anti-intellectualism or both.

One of these protestants was the Oxford historian, E. A. Freeman, who chronicled the Norman Conquest and himself resisted it. As early as 1846, he was praising the Teutonic part of our language as affording "expression mostly of greater strength than their romance synonyms for all purposes of general literature"; and he used the phrase "pure English" for a diction purged of these synonyms. Later, he purged and prodded. In 1872 he writes to a disciple on style: "Don't be afraid . . . I find that fifteen or sixteen years back, I talked of 'commencement,' 'conclusion,' and 'termination.' I really believe that, in these times, simplicity of style comes only by long practice." Another Anglicizer was F. J. Furnivall, a founder, in 1864, of the Early English Text Society, and a constant editor of texts, for which he wrote Forewords (not prefaces) and Afterwords. He began his intellectual career under the influence of Ruskin and Maurice, was active in the Working Men's College, and protested that his interest in early literature was not linguistic but social.

Another founder of the EETS, R. C. Trench, published in 1855 his engaging *English, Past and Present*. The second lecture considers "English as it might have been" had the Normans not invaded. Admitting that there have been gains in the mixture of linguistic stocks, Trench is concerned with defining the losses. He argues that, while our present cerebral and technical words derive from the classical languages, the Anglo-Saxon might have developed—chiefly by compounding, as German has done—such a vocabulary. Even *impenetrability* could have been matched, by *unthoroughfaresomeness*, an ungraceful word but an accurate equivalent. Theological language would be intelligible to farmhand as well as scholar if we said *again-buying* for *redemption*, *middler* for *mediator*, "Christ fellow-feels for His people" instead of "He sympathizes."

In the tradition of Trench, but much more violent, William Barnes lamented the linguistic Conquest of English and declared the old stock still capable of extension by compounding. Instead of *photograph*, we should say *sunprint* or *flameprint*. Indeed, all our current Latinisms we should replace out of the "wordstores of the landfolk." Barnes's nominations are all flavorsome; samples are *wordrich* (copious of speech), *overyearn* (commiserate), *gleecraft* (music), *outclear* (elucidate), *faithheat* (enthusiasm), *footkeys* (pedals), *with-wrinkling* (spiral), *sleepstow* (dormitory), and *craftly* (technical). He regretted the loss of *inwit* in place of *conscience*; and to serve instead of *subjective* and *objective* (those psychological-philosophical terms which Coleridge introduced from Germany) he suggested *inwoning* and *outwoning*.

Barnes had something of a following among literary people; was publicly praised by Patmore, Gosse, Bridges, Hardy. His poetry, early read, Hopkins preferred to Burns's—liked its "West country instress"; but he learned most from the prose. Barnes's *Speechcraft* [i.e., Grammar], says Hopkins in 1882, is "written in an unknown tongue, a soul of modern Anglosaxon, beyond all that Furnival in his wildest Forewards ever dreamed. . . . [Evidently Hopkins was familiar with the publications of the Early English Text Society.] It makes one weep to think what English might have been, for in spite of all that Shakespeare and Milton have done with the compound ["impure" English] I cannot doubt that no beauty in a language can make up for want of purity. In fact, I am learning Anglosaxon and it is a vastly superior thing to what we have." He cites Barnes's wondrous "pitches of suchness" (for "degrees of comparison"): "We *ought* to call them so, but alas!"

Hopkins' characteristic critical and philosophical terminology follows closely the counsel of Trench and Barnes: that is, it is a compounding of Old English roots and suffixes to suit new needs and to replace Latinic terms. *Inwit* (for *conscience*) and Barnes's *inwoning* (*subjective*) suggest *instress* and *inscape*. Hopkins explains his special use of *sake* (the being a thing has outside itself) by analytic parallel of the compounds *forsake, namesake, keepsake*. The terminology of the *Comments on the Spiritual Excercises* (1880) is particularly Hopkinsian (e.g., *pitch, stress, burl*). Says Pick, "He uses almost a new language and doesn't provide a dictionary." To Bridges, Hopkins wrote of his manuscript book on rhythm, "It is full of new words, without which there can be no new science."

His doctrine of the language for poetry, nowhere exposited, was assuredly different. Archaism—the use of obsolete words for literary effect—he repudiated. His oddities (like "pashed," "fashed," "tucked," "degged") are generally dialectal; and it is safe to assume that his words of Old English lineage were collected and used by him as dialectal, still spoken, English: not "inkhorn" terms but folkspeech. Even when he thought he was improvising he was—at least in one instance—remembering: his alleged coinage, "louched" (slouched, slouching), was, as Bridges observed, to be found in Wright's Dialect Dictionary.

Whenever Hopkins explains his words (as he stands always ready to do to his friends), the particularity of the words, their compactness and detail, is made manifest. "Stickles—Devonshire for the foamy tongues of water below falls."

He defends "bole" thus: "It is not only used by poets but seems technical and *proper* [i.e., exactly belonging to] and in the mouth of timber merchants and so forth." Of "flit," called into question by a correspondent, he writes: "I myself always use it and commonly hear it used among our people. I think it is at least a North Country word, used in Lancashire, for instance."

His compoundings are another matter. Though analogues can be offered from Browning, Hopkins came to them (I suppose) by way of medieval poetry, English and Welsh, and by way of Marsh, Trench and Barnes. Here the vindication would be that to compound freely was to restore to the English language that power it once had possessed: the words compounded, or the root and suffix or prefix, were separately familiar and oral. He writes "spendsavour salt" (the salt which is spending its savour and on its way to being the Biblical salt which has lost its savour), *bloomfall, trambeam, backwheels*, "Though worlds of *wanwood* [dark or pale trees] *leafmeal* [cf. "piecemeal": the suffix means "by bits," "by portions"] lie."

Judged by its effect and its internal intent, Hopkins' poetry finds partial parallels in Holst, Delius and Vaughan Williams. As (without the precise imitation of Warlock or the archaism of Dolmetsch) they sought to resume "English" music where its genuine succession was interrupted, at the Restoration, and to go creatively back to the English glory of folksong, madrigal, the modes, to Dowland, Bull and Byrd—so Hopkins seems to be reaching back, while he reached forward, to an "English" poetry. Probably we may add, to an English Catholic poetry; and suppose that his pushing back of the Elizabethans had some incentive in his desire to get back of the Reformation to the day when all England was at once Catholic and English.

Like the poetry of the bards and the scops, Hopkins' poetry was to be oral but not conversational, formal and rhetorical without being bookish. It used dialectal words without attempting, like Barnes's *Poems of Rural Life*, to be local and homely; it uses folk-words in "serious" poetry. Hopkins' poems intend, ideally, an audience never actually extant, composed of literarily alert countrymen and linguistically adept, folk-concerned scholars; he had to create by artifice what his poetry assumed as convention. *The Wreck* and "Tom's Garland" suggest, adumbrate, a greater poetry than they achieve.

To create an English and Catholic convention of poetry and poetic language: this was too grand an order for one Victorian poet. The experiments are yet more important than the achievement; the comparative failures more interesting than the good whole poems.

The ideal of poetry must be to instress the inscapes without splintering the fabric of the universe, and, expressionally, to make every word rich in a way compatible with the more than additively rich inclusive structure of the whole poem.

In Hopkins' poems, the word, the phrase, the local excitement, often pulls us away from the poem. And in the more ambitious pieces, the odes as we may call them (*The Wreck*, "Spelt from Sibyl's Leaves," "Nature is a Heraclitean Fire"), there is felt a discrepancy between texture and structure: the copious, violent detail is matched by no corresponding mythic or intellectual vigor. Indeed, both the Wrecks are "occasional," commissioned pieces which Hopkins works at devotedly and craftfully, as Dryden did at his *Annus Mirabilis*, but which, like Dryden's poem, fail to be organisms. Hopkins wasn't a storyteller, and he was unable to turn his wrecks into myths of Wreck: they remain historical events enveloped in meditations. "The Bugler-Boy" and other poems suffer from the gap between the psychological *naïveté* and the purely literary richness. To try prose paraphrases of the middle poems is invariably to show how thin the thinking is. Hopkins' mind was first aesthetic, then technical: he thought closely on metaphysical and prosodic matters: his thinking about beauty, man and Nature is unimpressive.

The meaning of the poems hovers closely over the text, the linguistic surface of the poems. The rewarding experience of concern with them is to be let more and more into words and their linkages, to become absorbed with the proto-poetry of derivation and metaphorical expansion, to stress the inscapes of our own language.

GEOFFREY H. HARTMAN

The Dialectic of Sense-Perception

The windhover takes its name from its abilty to hover steady over one spot in the face of the wind. The subject of the poem is, in the octave, the poet's admiration for a balance achieved in the face of violent motion by counter-motion; in the sestet, the sacrifice of both admiration and admired ideal to the transcendent example of Christ. The poem's argument thus turns on Hopkins' interpretation of Christ and Christian action, and will be discussed in detail later on.

The immediate difficulty of "The Windhover" lies less in the complexity of its ideas than in its aesthetic surface. Hopkins tends to use rather simple ideas without theological complication, as if his purpose were confined to the medieval *manifestatio*—an illustration, not argumentation, of sacred doctrine. But his poems do not seem to progress by thought to which word and image are subordinate, rather by word and image distilling thought. Where another poet might use statement, elaboration, suggestion, or grammatical emphasis, Hopkins will use word on word, image on image, as if possessed with a poetic kind of *horror vacui*. Consciousness of the word is so strong in "The Wind-hover" that the poem's very continuity seems to derive from an on-the-wing multiplication of the sound of one word in the next, like a series of accelerating explosions: "morning" to "morning's" to "minion"; "king" takes the *in*, "daylight" picks up the *d* of *dom* and "dauphin" the *in*, as well as an echo of the *au* from "caught"; a sort of climax is reached in the triple adjective before the main noun with its repeated *d* and *aw*. In the next lines the *r* is multigraphed and combined with the dominant nasal glides of "striding," "rung," "rein,"

From *Hopkins: A Collection of Critical Essays.* © 1966 by Geoffrey H. Hartman. Prentice-Hall, Inc., 1966.

falling away into the *in* and *im* before the movement is broken to a new direction with the wheeling of the bird in the fifth line, where a fresh beat of the wing is felt ("then off, off forth on swing"). Moreover, the clash of words is hardened, not softened, by every kind of alliterative and assonantal device, and the poem from the first line on is marked by an excitedness of individual perception ("caught" is an intensive verb, hinting the swift, empathic, mastering glance of the observer) that omits the smoothing article and relative pronoun.

Every means is used to gain an asyndetic style with a minimum of grammatical subordination. Hopkins is a master of extreme suspension (hyperbaton) but not for the sake of subordinating one word or thought to another. The two main objects of the first three verses, falcon and air, are strongly suspended by apposition and adjective- noun- verb- qualifiers, but only to crowd each line with an asyndetic rush-of-breath movement, maximizing the density of the verse. Just as windhover, air and dawn are seen not as three separate elements, but as one whirl of action, so noun, verb and modifier are similarly viewed as one massed element with minimized grammatical distinctions. Hopkins favors the verbal noun (of which he constructs new examples: "the hurl," "the achieve") because it brings out the freshness of a verbal root at the expense of a purely linguistic form having no direct source in sense perception. What, we can imagine Hopkins asking, corresponds in my sense-seizure of this bird to noun, verb, adjective and the rest? Grammatical distinctions have no intrinsic value, and become subordinate to word-painting. Thus such images as bow-bend (line 6) make evident the indifference of linguistic form. "Bow" is an Anglo-Saxon equivalent of "bend," and adds no element of meaning to "bend" that might not have been rendered by "bend" alone; both words refer equally well to a curve or to the flexing of the knee necessary in skating or taking a curve. Yet these meanings, common to either word, might not have been conveyed by either in isolation with the exact physical stress. Hopkins, aware of the atrophied or simplified sense-root of words, combines them to suggest their original identity in a physical percept.

The physical nature of sight, sound, and movement are vividly rendered in "The Windhover." Hopkins is much aware of spatial position and angles of sight ("I caught . . . "). Rarely do we find such awareness of air as a medium, actively affecting vision, distributing light, lighted in return, inseparable from the object it surrounds. The notebooks are full of fine observations wherein sight is conceived as a physically near, self-conscious gathering in and going out: "Cups of the eyes, Gathering back the lightly hinged eyelids. Bows of the eyelids." Hopkins has written a poem to compare the Blessed Virgin to the air we breathe ("Wild air, world-mothering air . . . "). But air is also a field of sound. The "whorled ear" corresponds to the "cup" of the eye. Sound and sight are combined in "The Wind-hover" by such words as "rolling," "rung," "the hurl," where an act and its echo appear as simultaneous. Air is a true theater of action, dense with event. The density of space and the physical nature of sound and sight are found in all of Hopkins' poetry. We may add this passage from the poem "Spring" where the thrush (itself a sight-sound image) "through the echoing timber does so rinse and wring/the ear, it strikes like lightnings to hear him sing."

The rhythm of the poem moves against a like density. In the first eight lines of "The Windhover" only two connectives are found, both more ecstatic than conjunctive. The poet employs a system of hard fillings which, on the level of meter, forces weak words into a position of emphasis and, on the level of syntax, jams a group of grammatically assorted words before the suspended noun ("Of the rolling level underneath him steady air"). A counterpoint rhythm evolves that respects the abrupt and singular nature of each word, while emphasizing the one-breath swing of every line, hovering at the repeated end-rhyme, moving forward in a series of glissando movements, but never receding from the forward surge.

While rhythm is not necessarily imitative of a physical movement, with Hopkins it is. The hurl and gliding of his verse render the "hurl and gliding" of "The Windhover." We do find a similar rhythm in some other poems (e.g., "Look at the stars! look, look up at the skies! . . . Down in dim woods the diamond delves! the elves'-eyes!") and this makes us suspect that the thrust and glide of his verse is descriptive of more than the particular motion of the windhover, that the windhover's motion is only a type of a more fundamental rhythm. But the rhythm, in any case, has a physical basis, and many comments could be added to show that Hopkins conceived his words and technique in terms of physical imitation. Of his use of the rather ugly "back" in "The Leaden and the Golden Echo" he writes, "*Back* is not pretty, but it gives that feeling of physical constraint which I want."

There is, even in the best of Hopkins, an unwillingness to release his mind from the physical contact of words, which are conceived not only as the means but also and very strongly as the materials of expression, and used with the undiluted stroke of some modern painters who wish to let color or *touche* speak for itself. Rhythm, sound, and sight involve for Hopkins a sense of the body, the total and individual body, and his poems and notes are full of pride and despair at the inseparable sensuous character of his vision ("my taste was me; / Bones built in me, flesh filled, blood brimmed the curse"). The drama of Hopkins is played out between his senses and the thing observed, and perception becomes act in the full sense of the word. But though perception is sensuous and distinctively individual, neither the act of sight nor the true medium are found to change the nature of the thing perceived. In the poem comparing the Blessed Virgin to the air we breathe, Hopkins addresses the reader. How the air is azured, he cries; lift your hand skyward and the rich blue sky will lap round and between the fingers:

> Yet such a sapphire-shot,
> Charged, steepèd sky will not
> Stain light. Yea, mark you this:
> It does no prejudice.
> The glass-blue days are those
> When every colour glows,
> Each shape and shadow shows.

So in his poem on spring the blue is described as all in a rush with richness; air diversifies, reveals, intensifies the intrinsic character of leaf, blossom and timber. There is no blending or blurring between object and object, object and air, object and observer, such as is often found in impressionist painters who are just as sensitive to the "act" of sight as Hopkins; nor is echo (as for example in Shelley) the disembodiment of sound, its spiritual form, but each reverberation in Hopkins is a singular, incisive beat which "strikes like lightnings."

Hopkins' poetry is first an expression of sense experience and wants at first to be taken as such. *The act of sight has become a moral responsibility,* and whereas Milton or Wordsworth might talk about a chastity of the mind, Hopkins would talk about a chastity of the sense. A poet who can write "The Windhover" or "Harry Ploughman" shares the great religious subject of the century of Marvel and Milton—the dialogue between the resolved soul and created pleasure—but in a special way. He works in the belief that "Man's spirit will be flesh-bound when found at best" and claims for his theme the dialogue between the created senses and created beauty. We will not understand "The Windhover" unless we first understand this dialogue. Hopkins once avowed that "God's Grandeur" was written to accommodate its fine first images, which would not mean that the poet does not think, or thinks by spurts, but that he renders his thoughts in terms of natural perception. Moral and religious meaning do not belatedly disclose themselves to reason, judgment or rationalization, they are given in the very act of perception, and when Hopkins catches sight of the windhover, he sees it first in its individual and brute beauty.

II

"The Windhover" bears a religious dedication: *To Christ our Lord,* and yet contains no explicit element of traditional religious symbolism except, possibly, the falcon. Its imagery is one of natural perception and its one simile, comparing the motion of the bird to a skate heel's turn on a bow-bend, expresses only ease and balance, physical grace. Hopkins, at times, even tries what has rarely been done before him in a sonnet: to introduce technical terms and observations. Thus "rung" may be a word adopted from falconry to suggest the spiral ascent of the windhover. (The suggestion of R. V. Schoder, "What does the Windhover mean?" in *Immortal Diamond: Studies in Gerard Manley Hopkins*, ed. Norman Weyand (New York: Sheed and Ward, 1949), chap. 9. There is, however, no reason to think that "rung" refers only to the falcon's spiral ascent. We point out, with respect to "buckle," that Hopkins uses words to indicate physical actions or their effect, and the word may be used to suggest more than one thing: (1) the stress exerted on a bell, and its ringing out, (2) the stress on the rein of a horse to control and direct it, creating perhaps a whiplike snaking in the rein parallel to that in the "wimpling wing," (3) the spiral of flight. Hopkins might have said that all three actions have the same "inscape" or "instress.") But more significant is the mention of "blue-bleak embers," for Hopkins has noticed the bluish tinge of coals when in full heat but not yet burst or died; and instead of using "blue" absolutely in order to indicate Mary's color and the color of the sky, like the more conventional religious poet, he will use it only in context of a technical observation on the physical world, and may see the presence, or here the absence, of Mary in a piece of coal. The religious dedication is quite genuine, even required. As in other poems that start with some kind of invocation ("Glory be to God for dappled things"), end with a benediction ("Praise Him"), but in between offer a series of fiercely sensuous and quite untraditional symbols, it indicates that dedication to God is also possible by means of natural perceptions which are, as it were, the first fruits of the senses.

Although religious and natural perception fall together in Hopkins, this is not without its difficulty. The poems after "The Windhover" echo with a plaint on the "skeined stained veined variety" of life. Our present purpose is to find by what means and with what success Hopkins reconciles the sensuous and the religious imperatives, how he passes from a vivid and immediate sensing to religious insight without rejecting or modifying the former. It should first be said, however, that Hopkins is in no way a mystic, except perhaps in one of his late sonnets, "Carrion Comfort," where the combat with God is conceived as a personal one. Even here the concern is merely that of all his poems in its extremity: in my actions, in my perceptions, is it God I feel and credit, or myself? "O which one? is it each one?"

The mystic, seeing the windhover, might be snatched away by it, divinely raped like Ganymede by Zeus the Eagle. Hopkins describes the particular bird, his individual pattern in the air. This, if it cannot suggest the mystic, might make of Hopkins a divine analogist, who sees or seeks in the windhover resemblance to godly action, and such a view is implicit or explicit in most studies on the poet. But Hopkins sets no store by a system of correspondences, perhaps because he acknowledges just one correspondent, Christ—"the Master, / Ipse, the only one, Christ, King, Head"—and so the image of the windhover must give way in the poem's second part to the figure of Christ. Yet this Christ, as in the first part, is not symbolized through the traditional symbols or in the original story of the New Testament. He is found rather in clay and coal. The real and increased question before us is how Christ can be considered not only the component of natural perception but also the component of a material or physical world.

What catches the eye of the poet is the windhover's mastery of the wind, the control of a proud rider over his tumultuous horse, the strong stress and balance. The simile on the skate heel's smooth turn is also based on a feeling for stress, and whatever image we choose in Hopkins, perhaps "When weeds, in wheels, shoot long and lovely and lush" or "With the gnarls of the nails in thee, niche of the lance," or "For rosemoles all in stipple upon trout that swim," the odds are that there will be found in it a sensitivity if not to actual stress then to touch, muscular action, and pressure. *The sense of pressure or stress is the sixth and radical sense in the experience of Hopkins.* It is evident to the tongue on reading his poetry. Even words like "rung" (upon the rein) and "rolling," which seem to take their effect from a simultaneity of sight and sound, stem from this deeper sense. There is also a construction in Hopkins which does not often seem to have been remarked, about which one is not absolutely sure, but which may be exemplified in our poem by "plough down sillion." It gives a figure of thought rather than of speech, and is an attempt to describe muscular action: the strip of land is there to have a plow pushed through, a thing is conceived in terms of the physical action prompted by it. So thing and perceiver, thing and actor, tend in the sight of Hopkins to be joined to each other as if by electrical charge; they are connected like windhover and wind in terms of stress given and received.

Action under stress or by stress is not only a particular condition in Hopkins' universe, but the one condition showing forth the *resilience* of things, their inexhaustible individuality. Whether we consider the relation of eye to object, of creature to creature, or of any of these to the medium—air, water, earth—in which they live, we find that Hopkins has rendered this relation in terms of resilience. There is, for example, the pressure of eye against object and answering pressure of object against eye, each intensifying the "deep-down-thing" freshness of the other. The water in which the trout moves, the movement itself, does not disturb but increases the poet's sensuous apprehension. The blue sapphire-light of the sky which the leaves and blooms of the pear tree are said to brush does not with its strong monotone draw out other shapes and colors but adds to their resistant individuality. The fact is further pointed up in the poem "Spring" by describing the pear tree as "glassy." Even when, as in a snowfall, it seems least possible to remark the individual forms of things, Hopkins still manages to do so:

> It tufted and toed the firs and yews and went to load them till they were taxed beyond their spring. The limes, elms, and Turkey-oaks it crisped beautifully as with young leaf. Looking at the elms from underneath you saw every wave in every twig . . . and to the hangers and flying sprays it restored, to the eye, the inscapes they had lost.

His concern is evidently with the spring of the trees, their resilience; and we meet the word "inscape" which together with "instress" is the poet's technical term describing the individual form of resilience as the quality or effect of a particular thing. The above is also noteworthy in point of style, for by the double indirect object ("to the hangers," "to the eye") Hopkins indicates the compulsion exercised by object on eye.

The act of hard perception, then, where the naked eye becomes an instrument of analysis, does not decrease a thing's individuality, but affirms it. The stronger the pressure of sight or sense, the greater the sensuous yield, but also the resilience, of what is observed. Parallel to God's grandeur, it "gathers to a greatness, like the ooze of oil / Crushed" ("God's Grandeur"). Nowhere is the resilience or "springiness" of the world so directly expressed as in this sonnet, and we realize that there the eternal and unchanged regeneration of the act of sensing and of the world is taken by Hopkins as a mark of the divine. Yet Hopkins' sonnet, however original, is not *sui generis*. It expresses a deep and common religious experience also described in Herbert's "The Flower":

> How fresh, O Lord, how sweet and clean
> Are Thy returns!

But whereas Herbert is witty, homely, almost *ad hominem,* not bothering in the least about oil, foil, and the like to express his delight, citing just a common, unspecified flower, Hopkins cannot speak except with the whole body, with the awareness and justification of all his senses. Hopkins is engaged on a theodicy, and has taken for his province the stubborn senses and the neglected physical world.

But this idea of the world's resilience, however strong in Hopkins and however made clear to the imagination, is an old idea, active in Heraclitus and other pre-Socratic philosophers, incorporate in Aristotle's principle of the eternity of matter, and set forth by the poet himself in the first part of "That Nature is a Heraclitean Fire"— "Squandering ooze to squeezed dough, crust, dust." But to be more in his celebration of oil, clay, and coal than an extreme, modern, industrial pagan, Hopkins must surpass Greek philosophy. And this he does by interpreting the resilience of the world to mind or body, to thought or use, as the source of that individuation of which the culminating point is found in Christ.

For Hopkins leaves aside all speculation on whether the physical universe has or has not a soul and what kind of soul. He is concerned in it with only one thing, its "pitch of self," and he knows that each thing's pitch of self is distinctive and incomparable with any other, and that man's pitch or individuality is the highest. The religious poet before Hopkins often based himself on *Romans* 8:19 (*Etenim res creatae exerto capite observantes expectant revelationem Filiorum Dei*) in order to be permitted to think of the purpose of nature in the divine economy. One of Vaughan's most tragic poems is written under this heading:

> Can they their heads lift, and expect
> and groan too? Why th'elect
> Can do no more.

and Hopkins himself has a poem written on the same theme which addresses the Ribbelsdale landscape simply as "Earth, sweet Earth. . . . That canst but only be, but dost that long." The landscape, then, like the modern poem, does not *mean*, but simply *is*. Its patience of being, its steady *expectatio*, is its meaning. Hopkins has broken with the common belief that nature is the language of God; or, rather, this language is not to be understood in conceptual terms but accepted in its concrete immediacy and resilience to sight. Hopkins does not ask what is nature for, How can man use nature for his spiritual or material welfare: when he catches sight of the windhover, final and mediate cause are out of mind, he is concerned with a description of the bird's individual beauty or mode of action, knowing that whether it has a soul or not, a purpose or not, it has resilience and a "pitch of self," which, if felt and acknowledged, will affirm in man his own greater resilience and "pitch of self": "that taste of myself, of *I* and *me* above and in all things, which is more distinctive than the taste of ale or alum, more distinctive than the smell of walnutleaf or camphor."

We see then that man is more highly pitched than anything else. He is as Hopkins elsewhere says, the "clearest-selved spark" of nature. These two metaphors of pitch and flame are fundamental to Hopkins, first because pitch and flame are the two evident types of resilience, and because in them the action of a thing and its nature are identified. This is clear in "As kingfishers catch fire":

> As kingfishers catch fire, dragonflies draw flame;
> As tumbled over rim in roundy wells
> Stones ring; like each tucked string tells,
>   each hung bell's
> Bow swung finds tongue to fling out broad its name;
> Each mortal thing does one thing and the same:
> Deals out that being indoors each one dwells;
> Selves—goes itself; *myself* it speaks and spells;
> Crying *What I do is me: for that I came.*

"Tucked," "hung," "swung" are not simple, sensory adjectives, but (like, perhaps, "plough down" in "The Windhover") indicate a physical act insepa-rable from the nature of the thing they qualify: the grammatical sign betrays their status: they are not qualities but proleptic forces: they should be joined to the noun, as they sometimes are, by dashes: the craftsman who constructed this bell though he (no doubt) conceived it instantaneously, created on the first day resilience, on the second day its infinite thingness or self out of resilience, and on the third day its capacity for self-revelation.

But supposing this bell to be of the same make as man, since no distinction exists in this poem between inanimate and animate nature, there being mentioned only "Each mortal thing," then the craftsman must have been faced with this problem: everything has durance, thingness, revelation through resilience; as bird is manifest in flame, so bell in pitch, so earth in being plowed; but what is the manifest of man? The poem continues:

> I say more: the just man justices;
> Keeps grace: that keeps all his goings graces;
> Acts in God's eye what in God's eye he is—
> Christ—for Christ plays in ten thousand places,
> Lovely in limbs, and lovely in eyes not his
> To the Father through the features of men's faces.

Christ is for Hopkins the manifest of man, as ringing is of the bell, fire of kingfishers, hurl and gliding of the windhover. We perceive the identity established in the poems of Hopkins, an identity of all things, all mortal things, in resilience, infinite individuality, God. But this identity, close to the central principle of Aristotelian philosophy, and expressed in the first part of "That Nature is a Heraclitean Fire," is then transcended by a further identity, exclusive to man, in resilience, highest pitch of self, Christ, hence— resurrection! To "That Nature is a Heraclitean Fire" is added "and of the comfort of the Resurrection":

> Manshape, that shone
> Sheer off, disseveral, a star, death blots black out; nor mark
>   Is any of him at all so stark
> But vastness blurs and time beats level. Enough! the Resurrection,
> A heart's-clarion!

In this way Hopkins goes from the perception that crushed oil gathers again to "a greatness," to the affirmation of Christ. For if all nature have resurgence, should not man? And how can the resurgence of man be conceived except through Christ's example? Yet Hopkins prefers to take his instances of resilience from the world of coal and clay, from the earth as earth, because resurgence is there more evidently inexhaustible than in the animal creation, and when he sees the windhover he catches sight of him not in isolation but in battle with an element, as if the windhover had not like man quite freed himself, selved, from the earth. This may not satisfy the philosophic mind pointing out that resilience far from being the source of individuation is dependent on the indifferent and undifferentiated character of the earth, and that man's individuality is at the expense of resilience and resurgence. Christ, as he appears in Hopkins, is dangerously near to physical man, while man is still dangerously near to physical beauty, so that Hopkins' work becomes an ode on the eternal nativity of Christ in the world of the senses. In that ode, "The Windhover" is one of the finest stanzas.

III

The poet in the octave marks the "pitch" of the battling windhover, his individual brute beauty, and this is seen deeply in terms of resilience. The poet is in a stage of mere attention, not of analogy; and the hidden heart does not stir for the windhover itself as much as for a bird in general, its balance under extreme stress. Now, a poet is known by his invocations. If Hopkins had felt the windhover to be an immediate symbol for Christ he would have addressed it as spontaneously as he apostrophizes God in *The Wreck of the Deutschland* or "The Loss of the Eurydice"; but when his invocation "O my chevalier" comes in the sestet, the riders have changed, and it is no longer the windhover astride the wind, but Christ's example mastering the poet, which is referred to.

The sestet results from a sudden intrusion of the thought of Christ. For the ideal marked and admired in the windhover by the poet was of elegant balance in the center of stress, and this stress is sought by, not imposed on the falcon who seems to know that a storm center is necessary to display the "achieve" and the "mastery." Yet Christ while also of his own will seeking the center of stress did this not for the sake of elegant balance, but to suffer without mastery the "unshapeable shock night." "Buckle," therefore, addressing the windhover or its accouterments of sensuous magnificence, would be in the nature of an optative and mean more than "buckle on meeting this heart which, thinking of the ascetic Christ, must refuse its admiration"; it suggests, "Let yourself like Christ militant for sacrifice submit to a storm center greater than the power of beauty, valor, or act, and let this example grapple with, become a buckler for, dent my heart." (In a discussion of what the word is, generically speaking, Hopkins concludes that it is properly neither the thing referred to nor the response called up in the reader but "the expression, *uttering* of the idea in the mind. That idea itself has its two terms, the image (of sight or sound or *scapes* of the other senses), which is in fact physical and a refined energy accenting the nerves, a word to oneself, an inchoate word, and secondly the conception" (*Journals and Papers*). This precept dispenses with certain exclusive hypotheses concerning the "meaning" of "buckle." There is, in Hopkins, an audacious attempt to conceive words generically, as beings in their own right and not merely as carriers of an idea. In some later poems there is a method of rhythmic stuttering, as it were, that would make the word a point, the strongest non-referential intention of speech (see, e.g., "I cast for comfort I can no more get," *Poems*). The final tendency is toward purely vocative speech, what Hopkins might call the inscape of speech. And "buckle," therefore, is in the nature of a pure speech movement, an "explosive.")

Thus the flame breaking from windhover or the Christ-assaulted heart indicates self-sacrifice in the maximum of stress. But why should the AND be in capitals and the resulting flame be described as a billion times lovelier (aesthetically seductive) and more dangerous (morally seductive) than the windhover's previous image? The AND expresses the poet's surprise that the splendor of self-sacrifice should surpass the splendor of equilibrium: the image of the flaming windhover or of the crucified Christ becomes a greater spiritual temptation than could ever have been exerted by the former image of elegant equilibrium. Then Hopkins, in the final tercet, adds "No wonder of it," for he finds that even the humblest things bear the mark and splendor of sacrifice imprinted on them like a physical law, even the lowliest thing galls itself and flames, so that the poet feels ("ah, my dear") fear? regret? resignation? perceiving Christ's Passion as a universal and haunting phenomenon. He has not escaped brute beauty: the very means which caused him to reject the windhover have revealed to him a different beauty, less elegant indeed, but just as brutally evident, lovely and dangerous.

The poet, then, sees the sacrifice of Christ imprinted like a physical law in even the lowliest corner of nature. He thought Christ superinduced on the windhover to be unique, but finds the call to sacrificial action also in coal. This law, which holds for all nature, is simple and contains three things: maximum stress, the disintegration that follows maximum stress, the flame that follows or is the visible sign of disintegration. In such processes Hopkins comes to see an imitation of Christ's Passion, Crucifixion, and Resurrection; and this fact haunts him, that what should be written large in matter has not become organic to man.

If we regard the images of the sestet, we find them all kinaesthetic in nature, determined by the sense of stress or muscle. Even syntax helps toward this: the grammatical status of "Buckle" cannot be fixed with absolute precision, Hopkins often using words to describe more than qualities, things, relations: "Buckle" mimics a muscular movement, a physical act. "Buckle" is not meant to suggest simply the actual object or the act of buckling, but the process whereby when two stresses clash one has to give way, to buckle or be buckled, and this would catch the senses by a displacement of, for example, light flashing from an uneven breastplate— "AND the fire that breaks from thee then." For whereas a lesser poet than Hopkins might have used "fire" in a purely figurative sense, in Hopkins the figurative sense is always derived from physical phenomena. The same thing can be shown of the other images in the poem which are also conceived as emitting light: the coal obviously, but also the "shine" of "plough down sillion": it is neither the shining plow nor the new earth but the kinaesthetic effect of plow-breaking-through-earth. Thus our three images are seen to express contacts and disintegrations that have caused a surprising outward burst of splendor greater than the original splendor of equilibrium.

Stress, disintegration, and flame are caught as one process and almost rendered as such in Hopkins' poetry. But we may go somewhat further to determine how Christ enters this purely physical observation. Here is a skyscape recorded by the poet:

below the sun it was like clear oil but just as full of colour, shaken
over with slanted flashing "travellers," all in flight, stepping one
behind the other, their edges tossed with bright ravelling, as if
white napkins were thrown up in the sun but not quite at the same
moment so that they were all in a scale down the air falling one
after the other to the ground.

Though in tenor entirely descriptive, the passage reflects a kind of instinctive
epistemology on Hopkins' part: the brilliance of the particular depends on
individuation, but individuation also, because group intensity is lacking,
tends to destroy brilliance; therefore the moment of greatest brilliance in the
particular is in its just-emergence from the group, when a measure of off-
balance catches the sun—in the moment of disintegration.

Another passage should be given in support, this time in description of a
thunderstorm:

I noticed two kinds of flash but I am not sure that sometimes there
were not the two together from different points of the same cloud
or starting from the same point different ways—one a straight
stroke, broad like a stroke with chalk and liquid, as if the blade of
an oar just stripped open a ribbon scar in smooth water and it
caught the light; the other narrow and wire-like, like the splitting
of a rock and danced down-along in a thousand jags.

The two flashes are compared to the splitting of a rock, and the ribbon scar
caused by the stroke of an oar on smooth water. Both images, kinaesthetic,
repeat that the greatest brilliance of the particular is in the moment of
disintegration or off-balance from the group to which it belongs, and both
remind us of the images in "The Windhover." If we now recall that Christ for
Hopkins is the highest pitch of self, the summit of human individuation, we
also perceive the identity inevitably made between the highest pitch of self,
Christ, and the greatest brilliance of the particular, disintegration. Thus the
antinomy of self and self-sacrifice would be resolved: the oil has to be crushed
before it may gather to greatness. This identity shows the temptation under-
gone by Hopkins to equate Passion and Salvation. It is not absent from "The
Windhover."

In this poem the balance of the bird in the storm wind is rejected for the
buckle that flames up when struck or made uneven, the furrowing act of the
plow that catches light like the furrow made by the stroke of an oar on smooth
water, for the dull embers that suddenly flare forth in falling apart like

volcanic rock or jagged lightning or like the grandeur of God which "will flame out, like shining from shook foil" or like the body of the crucified Christ who galled himself and gashed gold-vermilion. The brilliance, brutality, stress and necessity of individuation are connected and apperceptively fused with the sacrifice of Christ and turned by him into a figure for resurrection. The windhover, chevalier in perfect mastery of his winged horse, fitted out with all the accouterments of an elegant-brute-beauty, suddenly falls, buckles, flames, and Christ appears, chevalier of true-brute-beauty, and valor and act.

ELISABETH W. SCHNEIDER

The Dragon in the Gate

For a long time the luxuriance of baroque imagery so conspicuous in even the earliest poetry of Hopkins has tended to obscure one of its fundamental characteristics. His is a poetry of statement, intellectually formulated even when at emotional white heat, and scarcely at all, in any usual sense, a poetry of suggestion or atmosphere. He could not have permitted himself to write otherwise even if he had wished, and he did not wish. Though obviously the poetry does not lie in the statement—he himself was explicit about this—still, when he found that even Robert Bridges had continual difficulty in making out his literal meaning, he resolved, he said, "to prefix short prose *arguments*" to some of his work. "These too," he added, "will expose me to carping, but I do not mind."

His writing was contemporary with that of the French Symbolists (he was born in the same year as Verlaine), and after his earliest years both he and they were bringing something fresh to the language and rhythms of poetry. But there is no evidence that he was aware of their work, or of French Impressionist painting either, for all his lively interest in the art of his day; and in method he and they were as far apart as can be imagined. His aim was nearly opposite to that implied in Mallarmé's dictum, "nommer un objet c'est supprimer les trois quarts de la jouissance du poème . . . le suggérer voilà le rêve"; his effort was to name, to pin down with the utmost precision, the individual thing of which there could be no duplicate, the distinctive pattern and design that made the living individual or the natural scene unique; and his roots were all native. The precepts of Ruskin's *Modern Painters* had recently opened the eyes of many

From *The Dragon in the Gate: Studies in the Poetry of G. M. Hopkins.* © 1968 by The Regents of the University of California. University of California Press, 1968.

Englishmen, and Hopkins's drawings, both of architectural subjects and of nature, were avowedly "Ruskinese." The spirit of Ruskin's chapters on "truth of clouds," "truth of water," "truth of foliage" and branch and twig is present everywhere in the detailed observations of nature recorded in his journals and poetry, as well as in the attention to both detail and design in his drawings. In no sense did he write symbolist poetry or the verbal equivalent of "mood music," though in their passionate exactitude his language and imagery are often supralogical, addressing themselves directly to the sensual imagination. His structure, however, is always logically conceived; its rigid severity suggests mediaeval Aristotelian thought more nearly than poetic imagination.

Like the temperament from which it sprang, however, his is a poetry of extremes, distinguished on the one hand, as was already becoming apparent in his youthful writing, by passionate sensuousness reminiscent of Keats—a love of the richest colors, tastes, physical beauty, sensation of all kinds—and on the other by an equally urgent desire for law, rigid control—by asceticism in fact. Willfulness, then, and an impulse toward extreme license are set against the bent towards self-denial and utter subjection of the will. In his life the extremes were perhaps rarely at peace; in his poetry at its best they are reconciled, and much of the individuality of his work derives from the tension so created. Something resembling this kind of opposition naturally underlies any poetic organization and not Hopkins's only, being in fact present wherever form is imposed. In such a writer as Keats, however, the control is felt to be no more than the normal human love of order at work in creating aesthetic form; there is no tinge of asceticism in it. Hopkins, in whom the ascetic was so strong, as a poet transformed this into a positive power over form, but his form carries the marks of its particularly intense origin. Both form and language are therefore paradoxically on the one hand severe and on the other wayward, extravagant, sometimes outlandish. A single descriptive epithet may be both willfully odd and determinedly subjected to literal fact, his grammar and idiom eccentric and yet precisely explicable by rule or precedent, the thought of a poem eccentrically conceived but developed on a rigidly logical plan. In both its successes and its sometimes embarrassing failures, Hopkins's poetry owes much of its peculiarly explosive character to these oppositions inherent in the detail as well as the whole design of nearly every work.

Under this light, in spite of a number of valuable studies that have appeared in recent years in consequence of which it has ceased to be quite the fearsome "dragon folded in the gate to forbid all entrance" that Bridges once thought it, there remain certain things to be said about Hopkins's longest poem, the first significant work of his maturity. *The Wreck of the Deutschland* is beginning to take its place in the company of the great English odes and elegies. It is not a flawless poem, but we are coming to see it as unmistakably a great one. It is also something of a miracle, for its success is won against every probability. Given all that it attempts and given the intractable, unmastered emotion that went into it, it should have been doomed from the start to failure. The whole undertaking presents itself as a piece of reckless daring, and the poem lays a teasing claim upon our interest, therefore, as an almost unheard-of kind of success.

However much its remarkable language may obscure the fact and however complex its final effect may be, the *Wreck*, like every other completed poem of Hopkins, is extremely simple, not to say also rigid, diagrammatic, in its primary structure. The naked skeleton is not particularly beautiful and its character is likely to be uncongenial to many modern readers, but the skeleton alone gives coherence to the parts, and it alone makes intelligible the shape and proportions of the whole. It therefore needs to be set forth as clearly as possible.

Stated baldly, the poem is an ode on conversion, conversion to the Catholic Church. As Hopkins reminded Bridges, it is an ode, not a narrative; the wreck of the German liner which provides the title is the occasion, not the theme. The poem is in two parts, a mode of thought that in Hopkins seems to have deep roots if one recalls its almost constant appearance in his subsequent work. The main theme of Part the First is his own conversion; that of Part the Second, the hoped-for conversion of all England, for which certain events connected with the shipwreck are conceived as the spark and the signal. Within the limits of its bare thematic frame, however, Hopkins explicitly or by implication crowded nearly everything in life about which he felt deeply. Reading the poem, one has the feeling that, his poetic pen licensed after that decade of largely self-imposed silence, he was writing as if he might never again be free to write and must set down in this one work all that remained to him of value and hope on earth. It is not a promising prospect, for the control of so much intensely felt and apparently disparate material would seem to pose insuperable difficulties.

Among Hopkins's most abiding hopes and deepest longings was the wish that England might become Catholic, not in some remote future time, but soon, or now. To a degree this was natural, especially for a convert; and for a young man whose last experience of secular life had been the Oxford of the fifties or sixties with conversions and rumors of conversion still a matter of high excitement, the possibility need not have seemed altogether absurd. Hopkins would not have forgotten what he had written to Newman while still at Oxford, when four friends had taken the step almost simultaneously, "All our minds you see were ready to go at a touch and it cannot but be that the same is the case with many here." The hope did not die easily: as late as 1881, knowing well how hostile Bridges would be to the thought, Hopkins was nevertheless impelled to write to him of the approaching three-hundredth anniversary of the martyrdom of Edmund Campion, "from which I expect of heaven some, I cannot guess what, great conversion or other blessing to the Church in England." On this occasion too he was undertaking to write an ode, in a vein "something between the *Deutschland* and *Alexander's Feast.*"

The basis of Hopkins's longing for others' conversion, however, was personal as well as religious, and the intensity of the personal feeling undoubtedly affected his rational judgment. He had been one of a close and congenial family, and the shock of his conversion and dedication to the priesthood brought grief to all, himself not least; though superficial friendliness was preserved by an effort on both sides, the old intimacy was broken for good. A similar barrier had fallen between himself and certain of his dearest friends. Sensitive and dependent on affection, the happiness of sharing his love of natural beauty, poetry, painting, and high thoughts with family and friends suddenly gone, Hopkins was a lonely, sometimes desperately lonely, man. No new human ties took the place of the old ones, for he did not transfer affections easily and the companions of his new life shared few of his intellectual interests or tastes. As he was fully committed to his adopted religion, nothing short of a general movement of conversion in England could reunite him to those he loved; nothing less could heal the breach within himself that remained a source of the pain described in a sonnet of the next decade:

> To seem the stranger lies my lot, my life
> Among strangers. Father and mother dear,
> Brothers and sisters are in Christ not near
> And he my peace / my parting, sword and strife.

His letters show an almost pathetic effort to grasp at whatever common interests could still be shared without stirring bitter depths. The stanzas of the *Wreck* having to do directly with the conversion of England are marked by a personal intensity over and above the natural desire of even an ardent Christian for the salvation of his fellowmen; and the forced significance which he read into one event of the wreck is accountable, biographically if not historically or aesthetically, on the same ground.

A lifelong interest in shipwrecks remained one thing that he could still share with his family. Wrecks, it will be remembered, were a main part of the business of his father, who as head of a firm of marine average adjusters not only wrote technical works on marine insurance but, only a short time before the *Deutschland's* disaster, had published *The Port of Refuge, or Advice and Instructions to the Master-Mariner in Situations of Doubt, Difficulty, and Danger*

(1873), a book practical in purpose but adorned, beyond its alliterative title, with quotations from *The Ancient Mariner* and the occasional purple phrases of a man who would have liked to be a poet (and who in fact did produce some verse that may be described as well meant). The whole family seems to have been a company of horrified amateurs of maritime disaster, too high-minded to rejoice in others' misfortune but vividly interested. Hopkins's brother Arthur exhibited at the Royal Academy paintings inspired by shipwrecks; and, for a landsman's, Gerard's own poetry is surprisingly full of images and symbols—nearly always highly charged with feeling—derived from wrecks, often in the most unlikely contexts. It is not by accident that in his earliest known poem religious martyrdom and imagery of shipwreck are brought together in one of the passages so strongly tinged by masochistic feeling: the "poor collapsing frame" of the saint—whose "crack'd flesh lay hissing on the grate"—"hung like a wreck that flames not billows beat." Nor is it by chance that in the late "Heraclitean" sonnet the second turn is marked by the words "Across my foundering deck shone / A beacon, an eternal beam"; and in between these are very many other images of shipwreck, some explicit, some half submerged. When the liner *Deutschland* was lost, Gerard's mother sent him newspaper clippings describing the event, which, he told her, had made a deeper impression on him than "any other wreck or accident" he had ever read of. It was a disaster that for personal reasons, therefore, touched him more closely than it did most Englishmen.

It stirred the rest of England too, however, with an uncommon shock of guilt, for the liner had run aground near the mouth of the Thames not far from shore, its distress signals had been seen, yet no attempt at rescue had been made for some thirty crucial hours; and subsequently the vessel was looted by the owners of local fishing smacks who, it was said, even tore rings from the fingers of dead bodies aboard. This was an ugly record for the English with their national pride in maritime competence and in certain kinds of human decency. The inquest and a local inquiry were followed by a full-dress admiralty investigation, and the sense of national guilt was voiced in more than one *Times* editorial concerned with the "painful surprise" and "shame" with which the nation learned "that a wreck could be stranded off the English coast, appealing to English sailors for aid, and for thirty hours should be left without that aid." "It is shameful," the same editorial said further, "that where men were found in considerable numbers thus bold enough to defy the law [i.e., the pillaging smacksmen] there were none found daring enough to risk anything for the sake of saving life." The disaster was thus felt by others besides Hopkins as something of a public moral crisis, and it might therefore without overstraining be looked upon as an event of spiritual significance, though few would have read into it all that Hopkins did.

As the cause of the wreck itself, however, lay not in man but in nature, the blinding winter storm that drove the vessel off course, there was implicit in the event the question of cosmic justice, the old crucial problem for the Christian of explaining the suffering of the innocent and particularly such suffering as appears to be caused by nature, not by fallen man himself. This relation of the natural to the moral world was an issue sharpened in Hopkins's day by the impact of the Darwinian doctrine of the struggle for existence, with "nature red in tooth and claw." For Hopkins personally, nature presented another problem of deep concern, that of reconciling his strong emotional attachment to the physical beauty of the world with the claims of the spirit, a problem that reduced itself to the simple question of whether he might not be guilty of loving material nature too passionately and too much for the sake of beauty itself (on several occasions, once for a period of six months, he renounced the sight of nature as a penance, refraining from looking about when out of doors). On a theological plane both these problems had recently been resolved for him by a doctrine he had found in the writings of Duns Scotus. All this, including the doctrine itself, went into *The Wreck of the Deutschland*.

Then there was the matter of miracles. Hopkins was not among the Victorian Christians who found those a stumbling block in the way of belief. On the contrary, not only did biblical and the early saints' miracles move him deeply, but he also eagerly sought reasons to believe any accounts of contemporary miraculous healing or other supernatural signs of grace, and these appear often to have been associated in his mind with the conversion of England. Miracles enter prominently into the *Deutschland*, and the whole poem really turns on the hint of a miraculous presence through which the wreck and the conversion of England are brought within a single focus.

This is a great deal for a man to dare combine in one ode, particularly when it is all felt with somewhat abnormal personal intensity: the central spiritual event of his own life, his hope for "rare-dear" England, the shipwreck with both its public and its personal significance, the suggestion of a new miracle, the Scotist doctrine of the Incarnation, the reconciliation of evil and suffering in the world with the Christian belief in an all-powerful, all-wise, all-good God. And then there was the final daring of the form. In the *Wreck* Hopkins experimented for the first time with his new "sprung rhythm" and, to increase the difficulty immeasurable, invented for it a new stanza, one of the most complicated ever employed in English verse. No one, it would seem, in his right mind would experiment with such form on such material; few would attempt to cope with the material even in a simple or established form. All this is what I meant by saying earlier that the poem succeeds—supposing that it does so—against all probability. Almost phenomenal technical skill was required and extraordinary control over the refractory and too intense emotional material. Both skill and control, particularly the latter, break down occasionally; the absence of distancing and failure of judgment are felt here and there, somewhat as they are in *Adonais* and for not altogether dissimilar reasons.

To return, however, to the skeleton of thought, which has yet to be traced at its literal level. The two divisions of the poems are unequal, the autobiographical first part being appropriately shorter but still parallel, serving as microcosm, prelude, and, in a sense, pattern to Part the Second, with the implication that what has happened in one soul may happen in all.

The poem opens with a solemn stanza addressed to God Omnipotent, lord of all living and dead, of land and sea, of the speaker himself—God omnipotent to create and destroy:

> Thou mastering me
> God! giver of breath and bread;
> World's strand, sway of the sea;
> Lord of living and dead;
> Thou has bound bones and veins in me, fastened me
> flesh,
> And after it almost unmade, what with dread,
> Thy doing: and dost thou touch me afresh?
> Over again I feel thy finger and find thee.

The imagery is universal and would be appropriate to any poetic acknowledgment of the power of God; at the same time it is deliberately bent toward the particular circumstances so as to sum up much of the poem, living and dead, land and sea foreshadowing the shipwreck on a sandbank as well as embracing all the earth and mankind, and the personal "mastering me" in the first line, which I take to be a deliberate alteration of "masterful" or "all-mastering," signaling at the outset the personal direction of Part I. The last line, with its anthropomorphic image and apparent but not real tautology, is a specific theological statement illumined by Hopkins's own commentary on the *Spiritual Exercises* of St. Ignatius, where the "finger" of God is explained as symbolizing God's power exerted on the external world of matter—here, of course, the wreck—as distinguished from "thee," the very self of God, God as love.

As the oracular tone changes to a more personal one in what follows, the rhythm falls into conventional and soon predominantly anapestic meter with

only an occasional sprung foot. In this rhythm the account proceeds of the
poet's conversion, or at least of a crucial moment connected with it, a decisive
night of violent spiritual terror and suffering that ended with the free choice of
his heart, responding to God's grace. The moment of choice is summed up in
the somewhat mannered "To flash from the flame [of hell] to the flame [of
Christ or the Holy Spirit] then, tower from the grace to the grace," a line that
illustrates Hopkins's not always happy efforts to render theology in poetic
terms. Poetically there is probably no value in our knowing precisely what the
two kinds of grace are; it is, however, well to know that they are doctrinal and
definite, not vague or mystical; they are explicitly distinguished in his prose
meditations. The resolution of this crisis is succeeded by a spiritual serenity
which is the subject of the beautiful "hourglass and well" stanza:

> I am soft sift
> In an hourglass—at the wall
> Fast, but mined with a motion, a drift,
>   And it crowds and it combs to the fall;
> I steady as a water in a well, to a poise, to a pane,
> But roped with, always, all the way down from the
>   tall
>   Fells or flanks of the voel, a vein
> Of the gospel proffer, a pressure, a principle, Christ's
>   gift.

This is the serenity of Dante's "Our peace in His will" or of that prayed for in
Ash Wednesday, "Teach us to care and not to care," here symbolized in images
that reconcile stillness and motion—stillness in the willing renunciation of
individual will, and motion, readiness to act in willing response to God's
will—with the profound peace of this reconciliation. So the "soft sift" of the
quiescent soul is motionless at the wall of the hourglass but at the center
"crowds" and "combs" (like an inbound comber on the shore) in the willing
motion to fulfill its destined function, the telling of time. And the spirit is
confidently quiet like the water in a clear well, yet not stagnant but marked by
motion from the inflow of mountain springs, "Christ's gift," that perpetually
feed it. (The well is not named in the poem, but the image is of a particular
sacred well, that of St. Winefred at Holywell, the scene of a series of reputed
miraculous cures including a recent one that had particularly interested
Hopkins.) Though parallel and similar in drift, the two images of the stanza
are not redundant, for though both represent the will as at once active and
passive, motion in the hourglass image implies the spending of self, that in the
well renewal. The essence of the whole passage, however, is the serenity of a

dedication that has followed upon the agonizing choice of the preceding stanzas.

The doctrinal substance of that serenity is the subject of the next several stanzas. First it is given in emotional terms: the poet accepts and indeed welcomes not only the stars of the world but the storms, the beauty and the terror. The first comes naturally, "I kiss my hand to the stars," from which the spirit of Christ is easily felt to be wafted; the other is achieved through acceptance by faith of the Christian mystery (by "mystery," Hopkins once explained to Bridges, a Catholic does not mean "an interesting uncertainty" but "an incomprehensible certainty"). The great mystery significant for the circumstances of the poem is not Christ's relation to stars (beauty)—that the devout man feels without effort—but his relation to storms, to the suffering attributable in naturalistic terms not to man's sin but to the constitution of the external world.

> I kiss my hand
> To the stars, lovely-asunder
> Starlight, wafting him out of it; and
> Glow, glory in thunder;
> Kiss my hand to the dappled-with-damson west:
> Since, tho' he is under the world's splendour and
> wonder,
> His mystery must be instressed, stressed;
> For I greet him the days I meet him, and bless when
> I understand.
>
> (stanza 5)

Another extremely mannered line here, the seventh, I take to mean simply what has been said above: though Christ is (i.e., is naturally felt to be) under the world's splendor (the stars), His mystery also (the storms) must be instressed (scored in upon ourselves, dwelt upon inwardly) *when stressed* (by storm) in the natural world. *Stressed* in this reading is simply the equivalent of an elliptical clause, a common enough construction, which elsewhere as well as here Hopkins employed in eccentric ways.

In the stanzas that follow, the intellectual foundation of the poet's serenity is presented through a cryptic summary of the Scotist doctrine of the Incarnation, which provided the reconciliation of "stars and storms," "lightning and love," that met Hopkins's personal need. He seems to suggest that Scotus's heart, like his own, must have been "at bay," needing this particular truth so desperately that the very need generated its intuitive discovery. Briefly and somewhat crudely summed up, the doctrine held that the Incarnation was not a consequence of the Fall and so not primarily a sacrifice to redeem man, but that in some sense it preexisted, that it is in fact coeval with time itself and hence with material creation, In this sense the Incarnation rides the whole course of time "like riding a river"; it is not confined to the historical life of Jesus however central that may be to Christianity, is not a moment in the stream of time but rides that current from beginning to end. As Hopkins rephrased the doctrine in his meditations, the "first intention" of God outside Himself, the "first outstress" of His power, was Christ, who went forth from God "not only in the eternal and intrinsic procession of the Trinity but also by an extrinsic and less than eternal, let us say aeonian one." He added, significantly, "It is as if the blissful agony or stress of selving in God had forced out drops of sweat or blood, which drops were the world." The created world, therefore (I oversimplify, omitting discussion of Lucifer's place in all this), by virtue of its origin "is marked everywhere with the confusion, clashing, and wreck which took place in the higher one." What this comes to—a commonplace, but not of orthodox theology—is that storms as well as stars are part of the essential constitution of matter, antecedent not only to the Fall but even to the creation of man, and further, that they are intimately bound up with the sacrificial Incarnation from the beginning. This view of creation is very different from the usual Thomist one, and it is the doctrine expressly but elliptically asserted in the sixth and seventh stanzas of the poem. "Few know this," the poet says parenthetically, for the Scotist doctrine was not generally accepted though it had never been declared heretical and so was not forbidden to a Catholic: concerning it, therefore, "the faithful waver" (i.e., remain undecided, differ among themselves), while the faithless "fable and miss" altogether. The truth comes home to all sometime; and when it does so, it penetrates the whole being like the physical shudder produced by a sudden sour-sweet taste (stanza 8).

This Scotist doctrine, with its potentially masochistic implications, had found immediate response in the temperament of Hopkins. To conceive Christ's sacrificial Incarnation, as well as the concomitant "storms" of nature, not as solely redemptive of man and therefore not as spiritually practical or functional for man's good, but rather as free supernatural sacrifice for its own sake, is to conceive both sacrifice and storms as exquisite, to be rejoiced in for themselves (not simply endured for the good they may be thought to produce), the pleasure-in-pain sour-sweet of the sloe raised to the highest pitch of emotional and spiritual intensity (the extremely sensuous image of the sloe's taste is exact, though it has been criticized, and I think readers must often find it somewhat repellent). This doctrine, then, in conjunction with the related Scotist theory of the constitution of matter, which, in addition to accounting

most satisfactorily for "storms," gave to nature an altogether higher place than
it holds in Thomist thought and which thus might afford a fuller spiritual
sanction to the peculiar intensity of Hopkins's love of nature, underlay the
serenity and peace of the sifting sand in the hourglass and of the water in the
sacred well, for it answered to several needs and brought them into harmony:
sensuous love of nature, ecstatic asceticism, and the need for an orderly logical
framework.

The progression of thought, then, if not the thought itself, in these
central stanzas of Part I is rational and simple: first there is the spiritual crisis,
then the choice, the serenity following the choice, and the main emotional,
followed by the doctrinal, basis of that serenity. Part the First then closes the
chapter of spiritual autobiography with two stanzas addressed, like the
opening of the poem, to God, but with the stars and storms now reconciled;
the poet prays that all men may be brought to God, whether by violence as in
the conversion of Paul—and of himself as he has been describing it—or gently
as with St. Augustine.

Part the Second prefaces the narrative of the wreck with perhaps the most
beautiful passage in the poem, a stanza on the worn theme of the inevitability
of death:

> "Some find me a sword; some
> The flange and the rail; flame,
> Fang, or flood" goes Death on drum,
> And storms bugle his fame.
> But wé dream we are rooted in earth—Dust!
> Flesh falls within sight of us, we, though our flower
> the same.
> Wave with the meadow, forget that there must
> The sour scythe cringe, and blear share come.

Death speaks in images that blend the traditional—sword, flame, fang,
flood—with the (in 1875) still modern railroad train; and it must be the quiet
unmannered precision of the words, as well as their absorption into the
remarkably elaborate though unostentatious alliterative and assonantal pattern, that permits this surprising yet, as written, scarcely noticeable colloca-
tion. The meeting of flange and rail is the cutting edge of death to the victim
in its path, and the image of the railroad train, divested of all else, here
becomes one with sword and scythe. "The sour scythe cringe" too is one of
those incredibly exact flashes of physical, almost visceral imagination that
sometimes distinguish Hopkins's lines. Here it imparts life to the ancient
rhetorical device of the transferred epithet. It is the victim, not the scythe, that

cringes, but the shape of a scythe is the shape of a cringe. Reading Hopkins's words, one feels the tightening ventral curve with almost the physical immediacy of the prodded caterpillar. The language of this whole stanza deserves (but does not need) an essay to itself.

The story of the wreck follows in a finely controlled, flexible but conventional anapestic meter (or in that logaoedic iambic-anapestic which constitutes nearly all successful verse that goes by the name of anapest). The "sprung" effects that in the earlier stanzas mingle with this standard rhythm and that will reappear later are almost wholly absent here. The narrative is straightforward, literally exact, sometimes following word for word the published testimony of survivors, till Hopkins reaches the subject of the chief of five nuns who perished and the cry she was said to have uttered. Here the factual narrative ends and the poet begins to prepare for his climactic half-statement; and here it is necessary to pause for an explanation of what appears to be the only viable reading of the fourteen stanzas that follow. These seem to me clearly to embody the suggestion that a miracle had occurred, that during the night of terror at sea Christ had appeared to the nun, not in a subjective or imagined vision but as a real miraculous presence and that this event, once acknowledged and published to the world, might become the needed signal, the turning point for the conversion of English Christians.

This reading requires defense. To turn, therefore, first to the external facts with which Hopkins was dealing—for he invented no explicit additions to them. Newspaper reports had detailed the events: the vessel, driven off course in the winter storm, struck a sandbar (the Kentish Knock); its propeller broke; distress signals brought no aid. As the tide rose without setting the vessel afloat, many attempted to take refuge in the rigging; hope dwindled as the water rose; women and children wailed; one heroic sailor died trying to save the more helpless. These events all became part of Hopkins's narrative. Five nuns, emigrating from Germany to America in consequence of Bismarck's repressive measures against the Catholic Church, were among the many who perished; the *Times's* account of the wreck contained two brief reports of them. One of these said that the women had "clasped hands and were drowned together, the chief sister, a gaunt woman 6 ft. high, calling out loudly and often, 'O Christ, come quickly!' till the end came." The report of their funeral two days later contained a slightly different version: "One [nun], noted for her extreme tallness, is the lady who, at midnight on Monday, by standing on a table in the saloon, was able to thrust her body through the skylight, and kept exclaiming, in a voice heard by those in the rigging above the roar of the storm, 'My God, my God, make haste, make haste.'" Nothing at all beyond this was reported of their actions, no strikingly heroic act, and

Hopkins added nothing; yet he made of the leading nun's cry and its meaning (not, it should be noted, of their death, which many Catholics regarded as martyrdom) the central event of the poem. To do so, at such length, would seem to make sense under one contruction only.

The chief nun appears first at the end of the seventeenth stanza—"a lioness arose . . . a *prophetess* towered . . . a *virginal tongue told*"—and the thought of her call moves his heart to speak out, moves him to tears too, but tears of joy. Before her call is actually quoted, Hopkins interposes five stanzas in which the history of the nuns is interrupted by a recurrence to the Scotist reconciliation of stars and storms through their coupled origin in time—"from life's dawn" they have been joined: St. Gertrude, "lily," and her fellow townsman Luther, "beast of the waste wood," Abel and Cain, "storm flakes" and flowers. Foreshadowing the final hoped-for reconciliation of the specific storm that wrecked the *Deutschland*, these allusions are further interlaced with a rhapsody on the sacred symbolism, associated with miracles, of the number five: the wounds of Christ and their miraculous appearance in the stigmata of St. Francis. There were five nuns and they belonged to a Franciscan order.

At last the chief nun's call is quoted, "O Christ, Christ, come quickly" (stanza 24). To most readers such a cry wrung in such circumstances from anyone reared in Christian faith would seem the most natural of utterances. The poet, however, exclaiming, "The majesty! what did she mean?" and asking the Holy Spirit to answer his question ("Breathe, arch and original Breath," stanza 25), devotes some four stanzas (out of a total of thirty-five for the whole poem) to an exploration of her possible meaning, eliminating at last all explanations but one. Was it eagerness to sacrifice her life in imitation of Christ? Not even his disciples were of that mind, the poet says, and recalls the biblical account of Jesus miraculously calming the waters of the Lake of Genesareth when his disciples were frightened and the other miracle so often associated with it, his walking through the storm over the waters to his disciples and again calming wind and wave. Or was the nun longing for heaven because of the acuteness of her present suffering? Both meanings are dismissed at length on naturalistic, rather penetrating psychological grounds. Yet the whole discussion is far-fetched, gratuitous in fact, except as it is seen leading to the supernatural meaning in the crucial stanza (stanza 28), which implies without quite saying what the nun did mean:

> But how shall I . . . make me room there:
> Reach me a . . . Fancy, come faster—
> Strike you the sight of it? look at it loom there,
>   Thing that she . . . There then! the Master,

Ipse, the only one, Christ, King, Head:
He was to cure the extremity where he had cast her;
Do, deal, lord it with living and dead;
Let him ride, her pride, in his triumph, despatch and
have done with his doom there.

Poetically this does not quite work, but the intention is surely evident.
What he has to say, what the nun's cry really meant, is beyond the power
of speech except for breathless, fragmentary exclamation, "look at it loom
there, / . . . There then! the Master, / *Ipse* . . ."—*his very self*. Hopkins did
not ordinarily introduce foreign words into his English poems, but our language has no intensive to match for emphasis and condensation the Latin *ipse*,
with its utter concentration of selfhood. For Hopkins, moreover, the word
would have carried a further, very particular, association because of its prominence in the Mass, at the minor elevation. The drift of this stanza, then, clearly
is that the nun saw Christ's very self; and it seems to me equally clear that what
is implied is a supernatural event, not an ambiguous "vision" or a hallucina-
tion. If it were either of these, the preceding stanzas would be an absurd
building up to an anticlimax and much that follows would be pointless and
very nearly meaningless. For the nun is now identified with Simon Peter (to
whom in particular Jesus was said to have appeared miraculously walking over
the waters) and then, fulfilling an earlier foreshadowing (the "virginal tongue
told" of stanza 17), becomes an analogue of the Virgin Mary, to whom also, as
the poem goes on to say, the Word, Christ, came—through the Annunciation—and from whom the Word issued: Mary *"uttered* thee ["Jesu"] outright"
(stanza 30). The connection between the two stanzas embodying these parallels is cemented formally by a repetition of the three words of the major
rhyme, in inverted order, the thymes *right, night, light* of stanza 29 becoming *light, night, outright* in stanza 30.

There is a preliminary hint of the miraculous event earlier: the nun is said
to have "one fetch in her," an odd expression, by some critics interpreted to
mean that she has one resource available, her faith. I think it means more than
this. In Ireland, Scotland, and much of the north and west of England, *fetch* is a
name for an apparition, wraith, ghost, or spirit, sometimes of the living,
sometimes of the dead. Scott uses it ("His . . . fetch or wraith or double-
ganger"), and so does Yeats. More important, so does Hopkins himself, and
with reference to a *miraculous event which he was taking pains to distinguish from a
subjective vision*, a context, that is, identical with that of the poem: "At any rate
I suppose the vision of the pregnant woman to have been *no mere vision but the
real fetching, presentment, or 'adduction' of the persons, Christ and Mary, themselves."*

Adduction, according to Father Devlin, is "the technical term used by Scotus . . . where he proves that *it is strictly possible for the same body to be in more than one place at the same time.*

In Hopkins's circumstances, and for more than one reason, it would not have been proper for him to proclaim a miraculous event explicitly, but there was nothing to prevent his suggesting it as he did, clearly though not quite explicitly, in a poem that he would publish, if at all, only with the approval and under the auspices of his order. When the *Wreck* was rejected by *The Month*, Hopkins gave up the thought of publication. Probably his quite exceptional statement to Bridges—"granted that it needs study and is obscure, *for indeed I was not over-desirous that the meaning of all should be quite clear, at least unmistakable*" (my italics)—had reference to this particular meaning, for invariably on other occasions Hopkins was more than eager to have his literal sense understood, and I can think of nothing else in this poem that he might have wished to leave half veiled.

It seems likely that many readers have been aware of these implications in the central stanza; one or two critics have referred somewhat neutrally to the nun's "vision." Most have avoided the subject, perhaps because the meaning is distasteful or because it opens Hopkins to the charge of credulity (though extreme and eager credulity in such matters is inescapable in his letters and journals), or because it was desired to save the poem from controversy or skeptical contempt. To ignore the literal meaning of the central stanza would be my own preference if it were not for the fact that this is the pivot upon which the main thought of the poem turns. Without it the structure of the whole falls apart: lines and stanzas of an otherwise inexplicably feverish intensity float loose from either rational or poetic moorings. Much of what is said about the nun before and after this stanza can be justified, as to what is said and at what length, only if a miracle is pointed to. The overall proportions of the poem require it, for we have to reckon with the fact, already referred to, that, though the nuns undoubtedly died bravely, no other specific acts of heroism were attributed to them either in the newspapers or by Hopkins and that essentially all of the fourteen stanzas about them (out of a total of thirty-five in the poem) hinge upon the *cry*, not the martyrdom, or the courage or deeds, of the chief nun. This cry may "startle the poor sheep back," the poet says. But more than those sufferers of the particular disaster are meant as the statement is broadened into a question, "Is the shipwreck then a harvest, does tempest carry the grain for thee?" where the themes of conversion and reconciliation of suffering are explicity brought together.

The climactic *ipse* stanza brings a return to sprung rhythm, which has been largely in abeyance after the opening lines of Part II, but which from this point on is dominant, becoming more and more irregular, the meter now for the first time stretched to its limits as Hopkins later defined them. The effect is of an increasingly broad, orchestral movement as the theme itself broadens toward its conclusion.

The four closing stanzas begin with a recapitulation of the opening acknowledgment to God the wielder of all power, framed in sea and shore imagery now of even greater magnitude than at first and in language that harks back to the appalling declaration of omnipotence in the book of Job, when the Lord speaks out of the whirlwind. But what in the first stanza was a bare acknowledgment of Power, "Lord of living and dead," and afterward in the climactic stanza was intensified to "Do, deal, lord it with living and dead" (the verbs are indicative, not hortatory), now becomes affirmation as well: "I admire thee," the poet says, and the word *admire* carries both its ancient or Miltonic and its modern sense. This celebration of Power is balanced by a succeeding stanza on divine Mercy and Compassion, and the two stanzas are again bound together within a common rhyme and into a single sentence as well:

> I admire thee, master of the tides,
>   Of the Yore-flood, of the year's fall;
> The recurb and the recovery of the gulf's sides,
>   The girth of it and the wharf of it and the wall;
> Stanching, quenching ocean of a motionable mind;
> Ground of being, and granite of it: past all
>   Grasp God, throned behind
> Death with a sovereignty that heeds but hides, bodes
>   but abides;
>
>   With a mercy that outrides
>   The all of water, an ark
> For the listener; for the lingerer with a love glides
>   Lower than death and the dark;
> A vein for the visiting of the past-prayer, pent in
>   prison,
> The-last-breath penitent spirits—the uttermost
>   mark
>   Our passion-plungèd giant risen,
> The Christ of the Father compassionate, fetched in
>   the storm of his strides.
>
>   (stanzas 32–33)

The recapitulatory character of this passage is underscored by the reappearance of a great many key words, several of them used earlier in strange or striking ways, and by recapitulatory images as well: "Thou mastering me / God! . . . sway of the sea," from the opening stanza, is now "I admire thee, master of the tides"; "world's strand" is now intensified into "the recurb . . . of the gulf's sides . . . ground of being and granite of it"; *fall, wall,* and *past all* repeat rhyme words of the hourglass stanza *(wall, fall, tall); the uttermost mark,* an unusual phrase, echoes the earlier, mannered line, "Mark [verb], the mark is of man's make" (stanza 22); and *"fetched* in the storm of his *strides"* repeats both the allusion to Christ's walking on the waters and the strange "fetch" of stanza 19, which had prefaced the appearance of the "Master."

The cryptic statement of the second of these stanzas has been variously read but seems to me to be this, continuing from the preceding, addressed to God: "past all grasp God, throned behind death with a sovereignty . . . ; with a mercy . . . an ark for the listener [i.e., for him who already listens to God]; [and] for the lingerer [the laggard in faith] with a love [that] glides lower than death and the dark; a vein [parallel with ark] for the visting." The sentence breaks in the sixth line with the dash, and *uttermost* is a summarizing and emphatic substantive, the *very uttermost,* of whom he has been speaking. The word is used both in its sense of extremes (i.e., those in extremity) and in the archaic sense so powerful in Milton, whose *utter* is *outer* as well as extreme darkness, or as in the still current phrase, the "uttermost parts of the earth"; those in extremity, those at the outermost fringes, farthest from God, "mark [a verb] our . . . giant risen, Christ, fetched [a participle: brought to the scene, materialized, like the "fetching" of Christ and Mary described in his prose devotional writing] in the storm of his *strides"* as He had once walked upon the stormy waves of Galilee. The passage is thus part of the recapitulation, paralleling an earlier passage toward the end of Part I: "Hither then, last or first, / To hero of Calvary, Christ,'s feet— / Never ask if meaning it, wanting it, warned of it—men go" (stanza 8).

Finally, in the last two stanzas the poet calls upon Christ as he had called upon God at the end of Part I, praying that He may return upon England not with the destruction of doomsday and not humbly unknown as at his birth but, "royally reclaiming his own" strayed sheep, may return as "a released shower, let flash" to the shires of England, not as a "lightning of fire hardhurled." And the nun is asked to intercede in heaven to this end, that "our King" may return to "English souls," that the sun may rise again upon "rare-dear Britain."

The fact that it is especially English conversion that Hopkins prays for at the close is signified not only by the specific naming of English souls and shires and Britain itself, but also by the metrical stresses,

> Dáme, at oúr dóor
> Drówned, and among oúr shóals,

in which the second *our*, if not the first, wrenches the natural reading of the line badly, for the sake, evidently, of this special emphasis.

The prayer ends with a series of epithets of Christ, evidently meant to bring the whole to a prophetically triumphant, all-inclusive close like the great resolution of a large-scale organ fugue:

> Pride, rose, prince, hero of us, high-priest,
> Our hearts' charity's hearth's fire, our thoughts'
>   chivalry's throng's Lord.

Poetically, these last two lines seem to me to fail; they are simply too mannered to produce the tremendous, all-stops-opened effect at which they evidently aim. The final line is symmetrically constructed and locked together in the hook-and-eye grip of the possessive case that seems meant to create the closest unity of all human values in Christ; but the effect, upon this reader at least, is of eccentricity rather than power: what should be a satisfying resolution I find myself preferring to forget. It is one of those passages in which Hopkins's art is betrayed by his schematic ingenuity. In a sense, the possessive case may be regarded as the closest of grammatical relationships, most nearly making one thing out of two by force of grammatical law. This, at any rate, seems to me the rationale of the line, but the result is more ingenious than beautiful or moving. Schematic logic seems to have clouded Hopkins's poetic judgment here, and not only in the syntactical linkage. The sound pattern is most elaborate, but its stresses can be made out with confidence only through manuscript authority, which places a stress on the monosyllables: "hearts' . . . hearth's fire; thoughts' . . . throng's Lord," leaving the trisyllabic *charity's* and *chivalry's* arbitrarily without any metrical stress. Alliteration, assonance, and stress (and even singulars and plurals) are thus distributed symmetrically with reference to the monosyllabic and the trisyllabic words. The symmetry increases the more one looks at it, but the effect is arbitrary and labored; one has no sense of the inevitable in the succession of epithets.

No poem of Hopkins shows a more carefully wrought structure than the *Wreck*. The "design, pattern or what I am in the habit of calling 'inscape'" meant to him finding, for an experience that was to become a poem, its individual form, with the particular kind of formal balance it required, the organic symmetry of a living form (though, as we have just seen, overingenious logic now and then betrayed him into a mechanical symmetry instead). In these terms the parts and their proportions in *The Wreck of the Deutschland* are conceived, and the clarity of the design is a remarkable achievement in view of the recalcitrant material. As I suggested to begin with, the primary outline is simple but the detail of the design complex. There is, for example, the framing of the poem by the measured, sonorous apostrophes at the opening and the close: the prayer of submission to the God of power in the first stanza reappearing magnified, altered, and enlarged so as to draw all the strands into the recapitulation. Part I, as the individual rehearsal of the more universal theme, has its own smaller but matching conclusion, Part II its not quite matching opening, in which the note struck is again a universal but a different universal (the human one of death), defeating a too exact symmetry while sharpening its relevance as a preface to the narrative of shipwreck.

The inclination of Hopkins toward two-part forms led him to some extravagant pseudo-rational theorizing about the sonnet, of which the two-part Italian form was for him the only one that counted. On the proportions of the parts he was for a while quite doctrinaire, having got it all down into a mathematical formula of which he found close counterparts in St. Augustine's discussion of the placing of certain caesuras in *De Musica* and in the relation between pentachord and tetrachord in the major and minor diatonic scales and the earlier modes of plainsong in music. Equal proportions alone are too symmetrical and too simple, and so also, he said, is a mere 2:1 proportion. As he did not specifically discuss the proportions of the *Deutschland* in this way, one is not obliged to suppose that a special virtue inhered in its mathematical proportions of 2:5 (10:25 stanzas), though he would be capable of arguing even this. The form is distantly comparable in his terms—or he may have thought of it so—to the plagal mode in music, in which he noted the reversal of the more common order by the tetrachord's being placed first, a form not unlike that of an upside-down sonnet. It is tempting to see in Hopkins's preoccupation with two-part poetic structure, at any rate, in preference to the more common and more easily unified single and three-part forms, a symbolic reflection of the unresolved dualism in his own temperament.

A further element complicates the primary design of the *Deutschland*. The narrative and descriptive account of the wreck itself differs in conspicuous ways from the rest of the poem. Its objective physical literalness causes it to stand out prominently, like the foreground in a landscape, in contrast with the subjective and spiritual matter that precedes and follows it; the narrative stanzas, moreover, move more swiftly in thought, and their verse, almost all smoothly anapestic, moves with corresponding speed. As these objective stanzas occupy the middle place in the poem, they tend to create an effect, structurally, of a three-part form superimposed upon the primary two-part one. So strongly marked is this secondary division that some critics have noticed it alone and, interpreting the poem, have ignored the more fundamental, explicitly numbered two-part form and its correspondent meaning altogether. Other complexities arise out of the knotty texture of the thought in certain passages; and, of course, throughout the whole runs the intricate texture of the language, the several related themes, the recurrent imagery, and the changing music and meter, of which the reader becomes more and more aware as his familiarity with the poem increases. The final effect, obviously, is of a complex, nor a simple poetic organization, and also of a tightly knit one, though the shipshape tightness becomes apparent only when the thought structure has been more or less fully made out.

There are two criteria—or it may be they are fetishes—that have particularly marked today's criticism and poetry, and it is interesting to see where Hopkins's poem stands with reference to them. Modern readers have become accustomed to the employment of imagery for structural purposes, and modern criticism has made us so aware of this element in poetry of the past as well as the present that we have come to see it almost everywhere. Actually, however, its use by older writers was sporadic, usually unsystematic, and when present often quite slight. In particular, it is not a notable feature of the Romantic and early Victorian poetry from which that of Hopkins emerged. Its prominence in his work is one of the least noticed aspects of his modern appeal, along with this link to the seventeenth century. No doubt Herbert, whose work he knew and loved, influenced him, though his use of imagery for formal design must be mainly owing to his care for "inscape" in painting and nature and to the precepts of *Modern Painters*.

The other modern principle in the light of which it is interesting to consider *The Wreck* is that now commonly referred to as the need for a "persona." By this criterion the poem, like nearly all the mature work of Hopkins, will be found most unmodern and most "Romantic." When he told Bridges, justifying the poem in the face of his friend's dislike, "I may add for your greater interest and edification that what refers to myself in the poem is all strictly and literally true and did all occur; nothing is added for poetical padding," the contemptuous word *padding* makes it evident that he recognized no aesthetic or theoretical need for a separation between himself, Gerard Hopkins, and the speaker of the poem. Where is the irony, where is the mask, where is even the thin screen of the impersonal that can lend aesthetic distance to make this a poem and not simply an unmodulated, moving perhaps but embarrassing, personal cry of longing and faith? As Eliot long ago pointed out, in somewhat different terms, this is a major weakness in all but the greatest Romantic poetry: as a poet you automatically take a stand slightly elsewhere than where you are, but often, if you are a Romantic poet, you fail to stay there. This results in the uncertainty, the unreliability of tone that so often breaks the charm of that poetry. More recently, the argument has been advanced that even the Romantic poet's "I" is not his real self, and such writers as Byron, Whitman, and later Wilde have been particularly instanced (but what of Wordsworth, Keats, and Shelley?). It may be true that wherever there is aesthetic distancing there is in some sense a "persona," yet I think this rather extends the meaning of a cult word beyond the point of usefulness. I am not sure that I can put my finger precisely on the means by which Hopkins transcends the difficulty of the too personal; and in fact, as I have indicated in other terms earlier, in certain passages he obviously fails to do so. But at his best he does transcend it, and his success must be due mainly to his remarkable mastery over a distinguished form—after all, form is a kind of persona or serves the same purpose—and to the elevation of style, which lifts the speaker above the level of the human Gerard Hopkins to that of a universalized poet-prophet speaking as if out of a vision even when he speaks in personal terms.

Considering *The Wreck of the Deutschland* purely as a poem, then, what do we have? Some passages, as I have said, seem to me to fail through loss of the established tone or through eccentricity of taste or feeling, sometimes deriving from the frigidity of scholastic logic insufficiently transformed. One finds oneself put off here and there also by words, phrases, and images that seem out of key. After his undergraduate days were over, the aesthetic side of Hopkins's life had to develop almost entirely in isolation with the partial exception of the friendship of Bridges. . . and as even from youth his temperament bordered on the eccentric, it was probably inevitable that his thought, feeling, and expression should have become sometimes queer. He knew this. Freer contact with the cultivated lay world might have toned it down, or might not. More pervasive in the *Wreck* is another difficulty, the fact that not all the emotional intensities of the poem are felt to be adequately accounted for within the poem. If the theme is fully understood, however—if the implication of a miracle with profound consequences to come is recognized as the central event—and if the reader is capable of suspending his disbelief for the moment (possibly a large *if*), the discrepancy between heightened emotion and its represented cause disappears except in isolated lines such as that describing the "glee" in his heart as he weeps (stanza 18), where the requisite dignity of tone is wrecked by, I think, unacceptably abnormal emotion.

The *Deutschland* is a poem, then, of unequal but indisputable greatness, to be ranked among the great odes of the English language. Structurally it impresses the reader with the sense of magnitude and order; and as to the detail, in passage after passage a thought, emotion, or sensation seems inevitably married to its language and to the sound of that language. A blizzard at sea is epitomized for all time in the two lines, bound together by their *w* and long and short *i* sounds and moving with the abrupt fall from quintessential concrete sensation in one line to the depths of abstraction in the next:

> Wiry and white-fiery and whirlwind-swivellèd
>   snow
> Spins to the widow-making unchilding unfathering
>   deeps.

Even the worn abstraction of sea into *deeps* here regains a century's lost impressiveness, following as it does after the concrete distinctive epithets of the snow and after the abysmal negative abstractions. Nor do I know any passage in English poetry in which alliteration, assonance, and other kinds of sound pattern are more expressive, and more fully under disciplined control than in the great stanza on death. Perhaps the poem will continue to be valued most frequently as a mine of fine poetical phrases and images, but it is far more than this; and the phrases themselves are finer when they are known as part of an intelligible whole.

Finally, there is the remarkable rhythmic beauty and sweep of the poem and of many individual stanzas, with the changing movement so subtly responsive to the shifting mood. It is a new music that we hear, and stanza after stanza haunts the memory because of it—a new, flexible, and expressive rhythm the beauty of which is due at least as much to Hopkins's subtle and sensitive handling of the dangerously facile English anapest as to his newly invented sprung rhythm but also—and most of all—to the refinement with which the two rhythms are combined and to the structural relation which they bear to the meaning and design of the whole.

PAUL L. MARIANI

The Dark Night of the Soul

Even if we could determine the chronological development of the six sonnets of desolation with certainty—which we cannot—Hopkins himself has given us a series working from deepening desolation toward consolation. (St. Ignatius defines desolation in the "Rules for the Discernment of Spirits," the appendix to his *Spiritual Exercises,* in the following manner: "I call desolation all that is contrary to the third rule [spiritual consolation], as darkness of the soul, turmoil of the mind, inclination to low and earthly things, restlessness resulting from many disturbances and temptations which lead to loss of faith, loss of hope, and loss of love. It is also desolation when a soul finds itself completely apathetic, tepid, sad, and separated as it were, from its Creator and Lord.") In analyzing the sonnets, then, I will use the order which Jean-Georges Ritz gives as the logical order of the poems, without suggesting that this is the order of their composition. *To seem the stranger, I wake and feel the fell of dark,* and *No worst, there is none:* each descends deeper into the emptiness within. Then there is the beginning of the upswing in *Carrion Comfort,* which continues in *Patience, hard thing,* and *My own heart.* Of course the sonnets can be read in and for themselves, but the series provides an added dimension which follows too closely the classical descent and ascent of the Ignatian Exercises to be fortu-itous. Thus, while the following analysis will concentrate on the sonnets as individual and self-sufficient creations, their interrelationships will also be examined. In fact, the very order of explication will help explain the larger conception inherent in the sonnets.

From *A Commentary on the Complete Poems of Gerard Manley Hopkins.* © 1970 by Paul Mariani. Cornell University Press, 1970. Originally entitled "The Dark Night of the Soul: 1885"; and "'Summertime Joys' and 'Winter World': 1886–1889."

To seem the stranger is a cry from Hopkins' deepest self at a "third / Remove" in Ireland. It is a triple lament for an ever deepening isolation from those objects which were so dear to him. The first line and a half announce the theme of the sonnet: "To seem the stranger lies my lot, my life / Among strangers." The key word, "stranger[s]," appears near the beginning and is repeated at the critical close of the statement. Hopkins seems a stranger to those around him and those around him are strangers to him. Although it is the expected portion of the missionary priest, the separation is nevertheless difficult and even bitter. In the first quatrain Hopkins echoes the stern words of Christ, that in following him he would be expected to separate himself from his family:

> Do not imagine that I have come to bring peace to the earth; I have
> come to bring a sword, not peace. I have come to set a man at
> variance with his father, and the daughter with her mother, and
> the daughter-in-law with the mother-in-law; a man's enemies will
> be the people of his own house.
>
> (Matthew 10:34–36)

(None of Hopkins' large family followed him into the Church, and his most important interest was a closed matter between him and his family. "Religion, you know," he told Baillie once, "enters very deep; in reality it is the deepest impression I have in speaking to people, that they are or that they are not of my religion.")

Hopkins always had a profound love for his native England; by his own admission he was a very great patriot who earnestly desired to forward the honor of his country whenever and in whatever way he could. He firmly believed, as did Carlyle and Ruskin especially, that there was a definite cause-and-effect relationship between the strength of a nation and the moral fiber of its people. But for Hopkins, this also meant the conversion of England back to traditional Catholicism. This wish had been made strongly in both *The Wreck of the Deutschland* and in *The Loss of the Eurydice*, and the wish is there in *In the Valley of the Elwy* and in *Duns Scotus's Oxford*. And now Hopkins, estranged from England by his religion and by his very vocation, loving England as a "wife" but disappointed in her, laments;

> England, whose honour O all my heart woos, wife
> To my creating thought, would neither hear
> Me, were I pleading, plead nor do I: I wear-
> y of idle a being but by where wars are rife.

Victorian Hopkins refuses to "plead" with his wife, although he loves her dearly, for in a very real sense his poems and songs are the offspring of this love.

The middle-aged idealist sadly realizes that England will not listen, that she is too set in her ways to change, and that pleading would be useless. He is weary, most obviously, of the constant and seemingly fruitless struggles of the British Empire, specifically in Ireland, to keep its possessions intact. On the theological level, he is weary of the incessant struggle to make England listen to the "word / Wisest," to Christ, the Logos, to whom he was giving his very life. For as the Empire grew, Hopkins was learning, it was also becoming more and more unchristian.

Both the political and theological themes interact in the second quatrain, and there is an illuminating passage in a letter to Patmore which sheds light on Hopkins' Christocentric vision of Empire:

> I remark that those Englishmen who wish prosperity to the Empire (which is not all Englishmen or Britons, strange to say) speak of the Empire's mission to extend freedom and civilisation in India and elsewhere. The greater the scale of politics the weightier the influence of a great name and a high ideal. It is a terrible element of weakness that now we are not well provided with the name and ideal which would recommend and justify our Empire. . . . Then there is [the Empire's gift of] civilisation. It shd. have been Catholic truth. That is the end of Empires before God, to be Catholic and draw nations into their Catholicism. But our Empire is less and less Christian as it grows. . . . It is good to be in Ireland to hear how enemies, and those rhetoricians, can treat the things that are unquestioned at home.

But at least Hopkins had been in England, at Roehampton, in Wales, in London, at Stonyhurst; even in the industrial midlands near Manchester or in the North, at Liverpool and Glasgow, he was on his native soil. Then, in January 1884, he was elected to a fellowship at the Royal University of Ireland in Dublin; his duties were to examine students from all over Ireland in the classics for the B.A. degree. Simultaneously he was placed on the faculty of University College, Dublin, to teach Latin and Greek. And this separation from his homeland, which meant intimate contact with a growingly nationalistic and anti-British people, added a new loneliness to the limbo of his existence. "I am in Ireland now; now I am at a third / Remove."

"We have enemies here—indeed what is Ireland but an open or secret war of fierce enmities of every sort?—and our College is really struggling for existence with difficulties within and without," he complains to his mother. And a little over three months later he sighs that "the grief of mind I go through over politics, over what I read and hear and see in Ireland and about England, is such that I can neither express it nor bear to speak of it. . . . They are crying

some bad news in the streets. All news is bad." What particularly galled
Hopkins was that in his position there was nothing he could do, for many of his
coreligionists and his students were Irish nationalists. All that was left for him
was to pray for Ireland and for himself as a professor of classics in Dublin. "Ask
his help," he writes in his meditation notes for March 17, 1885, the Feast of
St. Patrick. "Ask his help for Ireland in all its needs and for yourself in your
position." (Hopkins' sense of honesty and justice eventually made him realize
that if Ireland was a state of smoldering rebellion, England's arrogant aloofness
was largely to blame . . . . Hopkins more and more came to believe in home
rule for Ireland as the only realistic solution to the growing clamor by the
nationalists for freedom. But for Hopkins it was a solution based on a weariness
with an intolerable solution.)

   In line ten the delayed *volta* appears: "Not but in all removes I can / Kind
love both give and get." Hopkins is never whining; he can, in the deepest
gloom, keep his judgment clear. There are always those of his "kind" who will
give him "kind" love. And the one who really matters, Christ, is with him no
matter where he goes. The ability to get and receive love is not what troubles
Hopkins so much. The source of his own inner life is felt here in this sonnet.
The trouble is without, in his relations to those around him:

> Only what word
> Wisest my heart breeds dark heaven's baffling ban
> Bars or hell's spell thwarts. This to hoard unheard,
> Heard unheeded, leaves me a lonely began.

   This is the cry of a priest whose life seems outwardly to have been spent in
vain. There may be a reference here to his poetry or to his many "beginnings of
things, ever so many, which it seems to me might well have been done, ruins,
and wrecks." But the "word / Wisest" is the Word of God, the Christian
message. He has tried to give freely and without stint to others what had been
the transforming experience of his life, the "word / Wisest." Christ—who, one
would have thought, would benefit by the spread of his Kingdom—has apparently checked the priest. And the frustration is not so much that *he* has
been checked as that Christ's work does not go forward. His own family, for
whom he must have prayed constantly, did not hear his "word," nor did his
friends Bridges or Dixon or Baillie or, years earlier, Urquhart. In fact, there is
no hard evidence that Hopkins ever felt he had been the triggering action for
even one convert. Yet conversions are what he wished for all his life.

   Hopkins sees himself as one "hoarding" up treasures which he would
gladly share with others, but he remains unheard. And when he is heard his

words go unheeded, for men are turned to their own self-bent. "My Liverpool and Glasgow experience laid upon my mind a conviction . . . of the degradation even of our race, of the hollowness of this century's civilisation: it made even life a burden to me to have daily thrust upon me the things I saw." In the last line Hopkins does not, as Bridges suggests, mean "leaves me a lonely [one who only] began." Hopkins has not omitted a relative pronoun. He is here making "began" a substantive and thus inscaping his whole sacerdotal life as one who *is* a "lonely began." He is not simply a beginner; the curve of his action is relegated to the past, to what had seemed such a brilliant prologue in his years in Wales. But the intermittent years of service in the field, as he himself deepened in his understanding and love of Christ, do not seem to have resulted in any spiritual fruit in those he had been sent to work with. He is caught in a self-imprisoned past action ("a lonely began"), like a cob of ripe corn imprisoned in its own husk, unable to spread its own seeds and steadily losing its own vitality.

The stark, bare, straightforward style of this poem, together with the delayed *volta* in the tenth line, shows the influence of Milton and, according to Hopkins himself, of Dryden. "My style tends always more towards Dryden," he tells Bridges in late 1887. "What is there in Dryden? Much, but above all this: he is the most masculine of our poets; his style and his rhythms lay the strongest stress of all our literature on the naked thew and sinew of the English language." There are few poetic experiments in this and the following sonnets. Besides the verbal substantive of line fourteen, there is the break of "wear- / y" in lines 7 and 8, which acts to draw out the word and to imitate the speaker's weariness in getting the word out. What helps make the word-break successful, however, is that Hopkins duplicates the chime of "hear / Me" in "wear- / y," carrying the rhyme into the following line and thus making a double rhyme. "I am sure I have gone far enough in oddities and running rhymes (as even in some late sonnets you have not seen) into the next line," he tells Bridges in February 1887. But it is an oddity only in relation to the starkness of the sonnet as a whole.

The style fits the stark, somber colloquy between Hopkins and Christ. Christ is not once mentioned in the poem, but the very tone of the entire sonnet group becomes increasingly personal: it is the voice of one speaking to a very dear, close, and sympathetic listener. The sonnet in fact becomes more and more a prayer form, a personal talk between the priest and his God.

In *I wake and feel the fell of dark*, the shadows have deepened and the loneliness of the speaker has intensified to exclude Christ, who "lives alas! away." The rhythm of *To seem the stranger* is counterpointed, but here the rhythm is freer and sprung in places. There is a greater sense of anxiety and

even that sense of fear experienced by a lost child. The speaker awakens from
his broken sleep with a start to feel the palpable presence of darkness on him:
"I wake and feel the fell of dark, not day." Several meanings of "fell" are
operative here. First, it is the past tense of fall used substantively. Night has
already fallen; the process is complete. That night of the soul which Hopkins
accepted but feared in *Spelt from Sibyl's Leaves,* that night which "whélms,
whélms, ánd will end us" has come. Second, night is seen as a fell, or desolate
moor, similar to Dante's *selva oscura* in the opening of the *Inferno.* Again, night
smothers him like the skin of some animal. And finally, the adjectival
meaning of "fell" as fierce, cruel, or deadly, used substantively here, is probably also implied and certainly fits. It is that "intense darkness which one
can feel" (Exodus 10:21) which was the ninth visitation of God's wrath upon
the Egyptians.

The speaker addresses his inmost self, his heart:

> What hours, O what black hoürs we have spent
> This night! what sights you, heart, saw; ways you went!
> And more must, in yet longer light's delay.

The blackness and terror of the seemingly unending night have revealed to the
speaker a new and nameless night within. And the worst is not yet over, for
although the speaker knows that light *must* come, that light seems purposely
to linger. The images here are fundamental and basic: light and darkness, day
and night. They represent God's disappearance and the terror of the soul that
realizes its complete dependence upon Him. But they also represent God's
eventual return in His own good time.

"There are three principal reasons why we are in desolation," St. Ignatius
writes:

> The first is because we are tepid, slothful, or negligent in our
> Spiritual Exercises, and so through our own fault spiritual consola-
> tion is withdrawn from us. The second is that God may try us to
> test our worth, and the progress that we have made in His service
> and praise when we are without such generous rewards of consola-
> tion and special graces. The third is that He may wish to give us a
> true knowledge and understanding, so that we may truly perceive
> that it is not within our power to acquire or retain great devotion,
> ardent love, tears, or any other spiritual consolation, but that all of
> this is a gift and grace of God our Lord. Nor does God wish us to
> claim as our own what belongs to another, allowing our intellect to
> rise up in a spirit of pride or vainglory, attributing to ourselves the
> devotion or other aspects of spiritual consolation.

It is this last point which most concerns Hopkins because it deals with his essential self and his growing realization that apart from God he was nothing, a mere "Jackself," a "scaffold of score brittle bones," as he wrote in his powerful sonnet *The shepherd's brow* only two months before he died.

Hopkins insists, as he had in *The Wreck of the Deutschland,* that what he is saying is autobiographical and absolutely true: "With witness I speak this." But what happened on one particular night happened, with varying degrees of intensity, over a much longer period. On the other hand, that one night seemed to last for years. Time itself becomes warped and plastic here; the subjective stress on the speaker and not the external regularity of any chronometer counts for the experience of time.

> But where I say
> Hours I mean years, mean life. And my lament
> Is cries countless, cries like dead letters sent
> To dearest him that lives alas! away.

The image of "dead letters" is a nightmarish simile which is unsettlingly modern; the speaker pictures himself as a lover sending love letters to his beloved who has left no forwarding address. The lines of communication are cut, and the countless letters pile up unread to gather dust in some dead-letter bin. It is up to "dearest him" to send the speaker news of his whereabouts; in the meantime all the speaker can do is wait. This sense of frustration in being totally unable to act leads logically to the *volta* at the beginning of line 9. Metaphor replaces simile, as the speaker *becomes* what he is conscious of feeling within him; he is a bitter taste, a burning.

> I am gall, I am heartburn. God's most deep decree
> Bitter would have me taste: my taste was me;
> Bones built in me, flesh filled, blood brimmed the curse.
>
> Selfyeast of spirit a dull dough sours. I see
> The lost are like this, and their scourge to be
> As I am mine, their sweating selves; but worse.

God's seeming withdrawal has left the speaker with himself, his innermost being. The paeans which Hopkins had so often sung to the selves of a sprawling, diverse creation dwindle into stark, groaning pains when he looks at his own poor self apart from the sustaining force of God.

"Searching nature," he writes during his retreat in late August 1880, "I taste self but at one tankard, that of my own being." That awareness of oneself, of "my selfbeing, my consciousness and feeling of myself, that taste of myself, of I and me above and in all things, . . . is more distinctive than the taste of

ale or alum, more distinctive than the smell of walnutleaf or camphor, and is
incommunicable by any means to another man." And a few pages later in his
retreat notes he stresses the bitterness of his self-taste: "I have and every other
has, as said above, my own knowledge and powers, pleasures, pains, merit,
guilt, shame, dangers, fortunes, fates: we are not chargeable for one another.
But these things and above all my shame, my guilt, my fate are the very things
in feeling, in tasting, which . . . nothing in the world can match."

Hopkins had first written "my self-stuff" for "Selfyeast of spirit." The
new phrase is more felicitous, but the earlier also tells. Yeast pressed into
kneaded dough raises the whole loaf, making it lighter and tastier. But
selfyeast only puffs up and sours. The image of preparing bread is used several
times in both the Gospels and in the Pauline Epistles. For example, there is
this from I Corinthians 5:7 − 8, used in the Epistle for Easter Day: "Purge out
the old leaven, that you may be a new paste, as you are unleavened. For Christ
our pasch is sacrificed. Therefore let us feast, not with the old leaven, nor with
the leaven of malice and wickedness, but with the unleavened bread of
sincerity and truth." St. Paul bids us to become the unleavened bread, the
matzo of the Feast of Passover, made without yeast, and to purge ourselves of
our self-yeast which sours the whole being. But Hopkins can do nothing by
himself except realize the curse of self-loathing which brims up within.

This self-imprisonment, Hopkins says, is what hell must be like, for hell
is only incidentally, as he explains in *Spelt from Sibyl's Leaves,* the stress of fire.
Hell is essentially a living with what one has really chosen in place of one's
Creator, to live chained for all time to one's self. As the choice of Dante's Paolo
and Francesca for one another over God ends in their being intertwined
forever, so the fate of the lost for Hopkins is to have to taste at one tankard
forever their sweating selves. "Sweating" is Hopkins' inscape for the self
deprived of God. There is the acute, pungent odor of living with one's own
sweat, generated by one's own uncomfortable heat. God is He whom Hopkins
asks in *Thou art indeed just, Lord* to "send my roots rain," and He is, in *The Wreck
of the Deutschland,* "A released shower." And when God is removed, the only
waters which the self can of itself produce are the stinking, salt-bitter drops of
sweat.

Hopkins is intensely aware of the hell of isolation within. But he is also
intensely honest; as bad as he feels his condition to be, it is limited by what a
man can suffer before his very body short-circuits itself. But the bodiless souls
of the lost do not admit this limitation; their suffering is forever. The
theological dimension of this melancholy desolation was better understood by
the forty-year-old Jesuit, but the attacks of melancholy themselves were a

habitual recurrence. "I had a nightmare that night . . . ," the twenty-nine-year-old Hopkins wrote in his journal.

> The feeling is terrible: the body no longer swayed as a piece by the nervous and muscular instress seems to fall in and hang like a dead weight on the chest. . . . It made me think that this was how the souls in hell would be imprisoned in their bodies as in prisons and of what St. Theresa says of the 'little press in the wall' where she felt herself to be in her vision.

Earlier in that same month, completely depressed and fagged, he complained that "nature in all her parcels and faculties gaped and fell apart, *fatiscebat*, like a clod cleaving and holding only by strings of root. But," he noted with resignation, "this must often be."

And again, in the notes Hopkins kept of his eight-day retreat in January 1889, there is the following echo of the sestet of the sonnet: "Jan. 2—This morning I made the meditation on the Three Sins, with nothing to enter but loathing of my life and a barren submission to God's will. The body cannot rest when it is in pain nor the mind be at peace as long as something bitter distills in it and it aches. This may be at any time and is at many."

The lowest pit of desolation and inner torment is touched in *No worst, there is none*. Here there is no relief, no escape except to wish for escape in death or in the temporary truce afforded by sleep. Here Hopkins, with the awareness of his own unworthiness before God and tortured beyond his endurance, comes closest to accepting the comfort of despair. He wishes for a cessation to his torments, although not, I think, for annihilation. God here seems to have forsaken Hopkins and Hopkins can do nothing but cling to the walls of the steep cliff. The poem is intensely honest and intensely painful. And while Bridges thought that *Carrion Comfort* was probably the sonnet Hopkins told him in May was "written in blood," *No worst, there is none* was probably meant. For in this sonnet alone there is no hope, no underlying comfort for the speaker in knowing that he is suffering with a purpose, as he realizes in *Carrion Comfort*. The poem is all darkness.

The poet startles us with the intensity of his unnamed experience: "No worst, there is none." Hopkins employs the superlative "worst" rather than the comparative. He has touched bottom: "Pitched past pitch of grief, / More pangs will, schooled at forepangs, wilder wring." Hopkins, like a violin string, is strung tighter to play at the higher, more piercing and metallic tone of grief. "Pitch" for Hopkins is the distinctive self, and in man this pitch is the most distinctive, most highly strung or stressed of everything in the world.

"Nothing else in nature comes near this unspeakable stress of pitch, distinctiveness, and selving, this self-being of my own." The pitching of the speaker, then, racks the whole being, hurling him even beyond grief.

But what grief? The grief itself is unstated, and Yvor Winters sees this outpouring of intense emotion over the nameless as a major flaw in the poem. Not that the grief need be stated, for the pain has the unmistakable ring of authenticity. Nevertheless, the affliction is "a chief- / Woe, world-sorrow"; it is Hopkins' terrifying realization that man, rebellious creature, is unworthy of God's concern. In strict justice, the spiritual syphilis passed on from generation to generation, the "world-sorrow" of sin in both the first parents and in Hopkins, is enough to separate him forever from God. The "cliffs of fall / Frightful" may also refer to man's original Fall and severance from God.

There is no comfort or relief now; the Spirit does not come as a gentle dove, but as the terrible blasting Pentecostal wind which cleanses away the dross of the soul. In two sprung lines the speaker almost admonishes the Blessed Virgin and the Comforter, who is Christ as well as the Holy Spirit, for not coming to his aid:

> Comforter, where, where is your comforting?
> Mary, mother of us, where is your relief?
>
> My cries heave, herds-long; huddle in a main, a chief-
> woe, world-sorrow; on an age-old anvil wince and sing—
> Then lull, then leave off. Fury had shrieked "No ling-
> ering! Let me be fell: force I must be brief."

All of Hopkins' anguished and "countless" cries coalesce around "a chief- / woe" like frightened sheep gathering closer together, so that their individual cries blend into one general confused woe. His cries are like the shrill metallic ring of searing metal being molded on an anvil, only the heated metal is the speaker himself instressed with the transforming fire of God, whose hammer pounds the kinks from the twisted shape. "With an anvil-ding / And with fire in him forge thy will," Hopkins had asked of God almost ten years before in *The Wreck of the Deutschland*. Now the reality of that metaphor comes home to the poet.

The pain has its duration, and the curve of pain drops away sharply, leaving a dull, throbbing sensation. Fury realizes that its attacks must be swift and intense. And the curve of its attack and withdrawal is wonderfully caught in the hyphenation of "ling- / ering." The sharpness of the first syllable catches up the reserve of pain associated with the other chime words, "wring" and "sing." In "ling- / ering" itself, the chime of the third syllable echoes the pain of the first, but the lack of a stress on the last syllable gives the impression of a dying away. "Fell" in line 8 has, of course, the same complexity of meanings which that word had in *I wake and feel the fell of dark*. But in its verbal connotations it seems to join with the preceding "be" to become "Let me befell." Fury does not say "Let me befall," for as soon as we are aware that the pain has come, its intensity has already passed by. The terrible thing, however, is that Fury's drive is recurrent and insistent. "And worse I may be yet," Edgar says in *King Lear;* "the worst is not / So long as we can say 'This is the worst' " (IV, i, 27−28).

In the sestet there is no turn in the argument. Rather, the speaker meditates on the bitter fruit of his ordeal: no man has plumbed the depths and heights of his own interior world. Those who have never experienced the terror within will dismiss this anguish as histrionics; those who have experienced the anguish need no explanation:

> O the mind, mind has mountains; cliffs of fall
> Frightful, sheer, no-man-fathomed. Hold them cheap
> May who ne'er hung there. Nor does long our small
> Durance deal with that steep or deep.

The self is likened to a mountain climber clinging desperately to a steep mountainside, unable to see either to the top above or to the bottom below. He is powerless to move while the strong "whirlwind" threatens to unhinge him. Hopkins is left with only the barren submission of his will to God's will, with the will to keep on clinging, for to let go would be despair.

He can only take whatever small comfort is available and despise his weakness for doing so:

> Here! creep,
> Wretch, under a comfort serves in a whirlwind: all
> Life death does end and each day dies with sleep.

Like the terrified mountain climber who crawls into a mountain crevice as the winds blast against him, Hopkins can only crawl under his bedsheets and hope for a dreamless sleep and temporary cessation from pain. The only comfort lies in the realization that all life comes to an end in death, and so must his. And every day "dies with sleep." The "all" of line 13 seems ambiguous, and yet it is crucial to a correct understanding of the sestet. Since it receives a stress, it seems to mean that with death there is total annihilation:

$$\overset{/}{\text{all}_{/}}$$
$$\overset{/}{\text{Life}} \text{ death does end.}$$

But while an argument might be made for such an interpretation, it does not square with what we know of Hopkins. The line more likely means that since death is a part of every life, then the speaker cannot suffer forever. Hopkins became increasingly weary of life, even at times to wishing for death, but he never seems to have surrendered himself to despairing of God's mercy, as the speaker does not let go and fall into despair here. "I do not feel then that outwardly I do much good," Hopkins admitted near the end of his life, "much that I care to do or can much wish to prosper; and this is a mournful life to lead. In thought I can of course divide the good from the evil and live for the one, not the other: this justifies me but it does not alter the facts. . . . I wish then for death."

The whirlwind or tempest is a rich symbol for the activity of God upon man. Suffering Job answers Baldad the Sueite's taunting about why he, Job, remains patient before God:

> If I appealed to him and he answered my call,
> I could not believe that he would hearken to my words;
> With a tempest he might overwhelm me, and multiply my
>   wounds without cause
>
> (Job 9:16−18)

But it is also the whirlwind (*spiritus*, spirit, wind) which preceded the tongues of fire that rested besides the disciples of Christ, the fire of the Comforter at Pentecost: "And suddenly there came a sound from heaven, as of a violent wind [*spiritus*] blowing, and it filled the whole house where they were sitting" (Acts 2:2−3). And while God is One and his powers complementary, the speaker is aware of only the first manifestation of God's power, the terrifying whirlwind. The speaker manifests only incomprehensibility and terror at the Holy Spirit's intimate workings on him. The terrible irony, of course, is that the speaker tries to hide from his Comforter and to seek out a more cowardly comfort, but one, at least, which his animal fear can understand.

The sonnet implies a cyclical repetition of Fury's assault. The first quatrain describes the impending attack of Fury and the absence of any spiritual relief. The second quatrain presents the last attack of Fury so vividly that something of its pain is recreated. Finally, in the sestet, in place of any spiritual relief, which must come from without as a gift of God, the speaker ("Wretch") settles for the comforting thought that even these pangs cannot last forever, as he tries to hide from the "Fury" of God. Nevertheless, there is the hypertensive expectation of still another onslaught of the storm.

Carrion Comfort shows Hopkins' pertinacity in willing at least not to despair and to weld his free will to the will of God. Here, finally, light begins to shine through, and God's handling of the speaker at last becomes more readily discernible both to the speaker and to us, as the age-old pattern of desolation followed by consolation and illumination crystallizes. The speaker has maintained his desire to do God's will; however weak and sterile that fiat might seem, it is all he has managed to salvage from "the war within."

Defying the "carrion comfort" of despair which has been proffered him, the speaker resists the powerful temptation to go slack, to fall apart, and to cease to care any longer. The emphatic downbeat on the first syllable and the three repetitions of this "not" in the first eleven words stress the will's refusal to capitulate to the enemy. The roping imagery of "untwist," "slack," and "strands" makes it quite possible that there is a pun on "not." This is quite striking when the poem is read aloud, as Hopkins' poetry should be. He will not untwist; he will *knot* the strands which keep him a man, no matter how tired he is. "Can," which occurs three times, is here the effective reversal of "not," and the quatrain ends with an emphatic yet humble double negative which stresses the final negation of "not":

> Not, I'll not, carrion comfort, Despair, not feast on thee;
> Not untwist—slack they may be—these last strands of man
> In me ór, most weary, cry *I can no more.* I can;
> Can something, hope, wish day come, not choose not to be.

The rhyme words of the first quatrain are particularly important, for "thee" (despair) is essentially the choice of "not to be"; and what assures the continuation of the speaker as a "man" is his ability as a free agent and his choice of continuing to say he "can."

As one critic has pointed out recently, Hopkins' first quatrain may be consciously repudiating Newman's *The Dream of Gerontius*. Gerontius, the "old man," is in his death agony, lying in bed and surrounded by those praying for his soul. As the tide of death overwhelms him, Gerontius can only gasp,

> I can no more; for now it comes again,
> That sense of ruin, which is worse than pain,
> That masterful negation and collapse
> Of all that makes me man; as though I bent
> Over the dizzy brink
> Of some sheer infinite descent.
> (ll. 107−112)

Hopkins refuses to untwist "these last strands," for as long as he is man he can at least refuse to give his consent to annihilation; Newman's position seems to suggest a more passive state in which the soul dissolves with a whimper before the oncoming flood of darkness. But Hopkins' will is more stubborn. The responsibility to "not choose not to be" cannot be surrendered; death is the surrender of the body only, not of the self.

The second quatrain opens with the speaker abruptly directing a string of four questions to a second addressee who is called only "terrible" and who combines the power and terror of the lion and the tempest. The questions at once show the anger of someone deeply frightened, something of the erotic admiration for a champion (especially in the triple sighs), and a pervading tone of respectful awe. God is a herculean contender who rudely rocks the speaker, a contender powerful enough to wring the entire universe and keep it under his sway. Like a victorious lion over its prey, he seems to rock his still-living victim contemptuously back and forth with his foot. There is no rebellion now, no movement that would bring the foot crashing down. The verbal action of rocking back and forth is continued in the sifting action of fanning the wheat, as the hot summer wind burns through the speaker who lies now completely passive to the Winnower.

"I will reign over you with a strong hand," Yahweh tells his people, "and with a stretched out arm, and with fury poured out. . . . And I will bring you into the wilderness of people, and there will I plead with you face to face" (Ezechiel 20:33, 35). But it is God's foot which rolls the supine wrestler back and forth in that ring-world ("wring-world") of the wrestlers. The "darksome devouring eyes" of God have the qualities of a terrible, awesome power, but they are also the eyes of a passionate lover. For God's single love manifests itself to man as man can best cope with it. Hopkins admits his terror in feeling God's searing love; rebel and coward that he is, he would "avoid thee and flee."

The *volta* comes in line 9 with the one-syllable question so simply asked yet so profoundly answered: "Why? That my chaff might fly; my grain lie, sheer and clear." Using one of the metaphors which Christ himself frequently employed, Hopkins realizes that his ordeal has been fraught with meaning, a meaning that is glimpsed only when his will has submitted to that ordeal. Hopkins' nonessential concerns have been burned away and the essential self remains purged, "sheer and clear"; the *arbitrium,* the will of the self, is coiled more intimately with the self of God.

Speaking of Christ under the figure of the Winnower, Hopkins wrote in his last retreat in January 1889 that Christ

> baptises with breath and fire, as wheat is winnowed in the wind
> and sun [tempest and fire], and uses . . . a fan that thoroughly
> and forever parts the wheat from the chaff. . . . The grain is either
> scooped into this or thrown in by another, then tossed out against

the wind, and this vehement action St. John compares to his own repeated 'dousing' or affusion [in his baptism of water]. The separation it makes is very visible too: the grain lies heaped on one side, the chaff blows away the other, between them the winnower stands; after that nothing is more combustible than the chaff, and yet the fire he [Christ] calls unquenchable.

But Almighty God is seen as other figures: besides the lion and the wind, he is the wrestler, the hero, the giant; he is a python, strength-giving water, the rod, and the hand of a master which Hopkins, like a thankful servant, kisses. The ambivalence of the speaker's feeling, oscillating between terror and fawning, is admirably caught in the nervous, staccato alternating exclamations and questionings. Both the Adversary and the mortal speaker dissolve and crystallize into protean shapes on the wrestling-threshing floor; this metamorphosis approximates the speaker's attempt to present the dynamic, blurred violence within:

> Nay in all that toil, that coil, since (seems) I kissed the rod,
> Hand rather, my heart lo! lapped strength, stole joy, would laugh, chéer.
> Cheer whom though? The hero whose heaven-handling flung me, fóot tród
> Me? or me that fought him? O which one? is it each one? That night, that year
> Of now done darkness I wretch lay wrestling with (my God!) my God.

It is the paradoxical nature of the religious struggle that the speaker, in spite of (and yet because of) his sound thumping, has also been victorious, for in finally bending to God's will he has found himself. In kissing the rod—a sign of capitulation—he realizes that his freedom is to be found in becoming God's servant. As he kisses the hand, his heart drinks in strength and joy and would "laugh, cheer" for the match in which both God and he are winners.

As the sonnet rounds to an end, the syntax and the rhythms become surer and more regular, although the metrical outrides gives a sense of astonishment and breathlessness. Furthermore, as the meaning of the struggle assumes its final shape in the last line, the real nature of the two contenders becomes clear and fixed: Hopkins, the "wretch," has been fighting with God, who is only now named.

In his illumination of whom he has been fighting in "That night, that year / Of now done darkness," he sees that his has been the privilege of being crucified with Christ, and he echoes the agonized words of the dying Christ in his "(my God!) my God." But there is also something of a startled, shrill whisper as he realizes Who was wrestling in the darkness with him. With the second "my God" there is a sense of resolution, of fulfillment in submission. "Our hearts will not rest, O God, until they rest in thee" is the prayer of Hopkins as well as of St. Augustine.

"One who is in desolation," St. Ignatius tells us in the eighth of his "Rules for the Discernment of Spirits," "must strive to perserve in patience, which is contrary to the vexations that have come upon him. He should consider, also, that consolation will soon return, and strive diligently against the desolation." Patience is the virtue which the hypersensitive and fastidious Hopkins had constantly to work hard for. His will, he knew, was imperfectly aligned to God's will. Nearly six years earlier, he had lamented the loss of peace in his curtal sonnet *Peace*. In its place his Lord had left behind "Patience exquisite." But Hopkins had struggled too hard with himself in the interim to use any such delicate epithet now. Patience is now in the terrible sonnet that "hard thing"; in place of the cooing of the wood dove, we now "hear our hearts grate on themselves."

Hopkins realizes wearily what it means even to pray for patience, and in the threefold use of the word in the opening two lines of *Patience, hard thing* there is the sense of endearment, but also the gritty ache as if he were biting on a cinder:

> Patience, hard thing! the hard thing but to pray,
> But bid for, Patience is! Patience who asks
> Wants war, wants wounds; weary his times, his tasks;
> To do without, take tosses, and obey.

Not only is patience a difficult acquisition, but it is extremely difficult even to ask for it. Those who ask are asking for a bitter conflict and suffering within. They are asking for weariness and drudgery for Christ's sake, as Hopkins was constantly harried in having to "examine a nation." One must learn self-abnegation, be buffeted about, and, what seems to become increasingly more difficult, one must learn to give perfect obedience. No wonder, then, that the virtue of patience is not widely understood, is rarely sought, and even more rarely attained.

But unless one has actively sought patience (for it is the paradox of patience that is a virtue not for the weak but for the heroic and iron-willed) in these things, it cannot be bought. This is the currency with which patience is "bid for" and purchased. In the second quatrain, we see the fruit of patience:

> Rare patience roots in these, and, these away,
> Nowhere. Natural heart's ivy, Patience masks
> Our ruins of wrecked past purpose. There she basks
> Purple eyes and seas of liquid leaves all day.

The difference in tone between the first and second quatrains is distinctive and is meant to be so. One notices in the first quatrain the frequent harsh dentals and full stops, the exclamations, monosyllables, end-stop punctuation, and the sprung lines. These are countered in the second quatrain by the many liquid *l*'s and *r*'s, frequent sibilants, more frequent polysyllables, the relative scarcity of punctuation, and the approximation of a stately prose rhythm reminiscent of Newman.

Patience, like ivy, grows slowly, but it covers over the ruins of our past plans and projects which we had hoped to see realized. Patience, writes Boyle commenting on these lines, "is rooted in pain and endurance; it stays with the suffering heart, wrecked so often in its past high endeavors, and masks the scars." While all one's past lies like a ruined edifice, the lowly ivy dresses up the ruins and imparts to them a serenity and hallowedness. The picture of the purple berries surrounded by the multishaded green ivy, which from a distance look like a rippling sea, is almost Virgilian in its bucolic evocativeness. Hopkins also suggests here the sea change which patience can effect in the tempest-tossed shipwreck of the self.

The two themes of the severity and serenity of patience, so admirably caught in the rhythms of the octet, are repeated in the sestet. The tone of harshness and severity in the first tercet catches the emotional strain the speaker feels in learning that hard thing, patience. But the tone of the final tercet is muted and serene. The argument of the sonnet is starkly clear; each word is a mark of acceptance etched on the speaker's heart. In *Spelt from Sibyl's Leaves* the speaker, painfully confronted with the moral value of his every action, laments that the self-stress working against God's stress creates a terrible friction so that his "thóughts agaínst thoughts ín groans grínd." Here, too, the desire to go against his own natural bent is to hear his very heart grate against itself. To continue the siege upon his heart is to bruise himself more seriously. Yet even so, we do "bid" God to straighten the heart's ways. Hopkins, continuing the auctioneering diction of the opening lines, will bid the dear price necessary to buy patience.

In the final tercet Hopkins uses another bucolic image. The speaker likens the patient man to the prepared crisp honeycombs which the bee, Patience, slowly fills with the honey of "Delicious kindness." This is the increased kindness of God bestowed on the patient man, as well as the growing kindness of the patient man toward others. But unless the walls of the combs are securely firm, "crisp," the honeybee Patience will not fill them. And the way to make them crisp, Hopkins sighs, with a possible pun on "combs" as a verb, "comes those ways we know." Those ways have been mentioned in the first quatrain. There is no other way to gain patience (*patiens* = suffering, and also the Passion of Christ) but by bending (crisp = *crispus* = *curvus* = curved) the stubborn, grotesquely twisted heart to God. Patience, like every other grace, is a gift from God. And written in his Dublin Notebook as a meditation note for the Feast of the Annunciation, March 25, 1885, Hopkins speaks of grace in terms metaphorically similar to those of the final lines of the sonnet. The Blessed Virgin, he notes, "was full of grace, that is / she had received and stored up in her every grace offered and now overflowed in the Son / Christ. So the preparation for grace is grace corresponded with." For Hopkins this last sentence, like the sonnet on patience, was more than an imaginative exercise in thought. It was a means for transforming himself into the likeness of his Lord.

My own heart let me more have pity on is the last of Hopkins' desolate sonnets of 1885 and it signals Hopkins' awareness that he has been too hard upon his "poor Jackself." The opening quatrain is in the form of a triple imperative to his will to lift the siege on his all-too-human heart. The "let me" formula is repeated and then implied in the third elliptical clause:

> My own heart let me more have pity on; let
> Me live to my sad self hereafter kind,
> Charitable; not live this tormented mind
> With this tormented mind tormenting yet.

The "me" of line 1 is used to signify Hopkins' *arbitrium*, his free will, aspiring at whatever cost toward complete harmony with God. "My own heart," on the other hand, is the natural bent of the self into its own curve of interests. Still, there are not two selves but one with two contrary stresses, and that self which would force itself beyond its endurance ends by simply being a "sad self."

Among the insights of the final lines of the previous sonnet was the realization that kindness would come to the man who was patient. In this sonnet Hopkins literally takes this insight to heart; he is to be more patient with himself, more kind and charitable to himself, and to pity himself for his past sins and imperfections.

"Pray not to be tormented," Hopkins writes in a meditation on the demoniac in St. Matthew. The note is contemporary with his composing of *Spelt from Sibyl's Leaves*. By summer, when Hopkins wrote *My own heart,* the fury of the attack had at last temporarily subsided. But the speaker recalls here that so all-pervasive is his torment that he not only possesses a tormented mind, he lives it. The mind begets torments which yet beget further torments in a cyclical frenzy caught in the triple verbal repetition: "tormented," "tormented," "tormenting."

In the second quatrain the speaker realizes that he is utterly incapable of being the author of his own comfort:

> I cast for comfort I can no more get
> By groping round my comfortless, than blind
> Eyes in their dark can day or thirst can find
> Thirst's all-in-all in all a world of wet.

"Cast" is a key word here; it has the meaning of directing one's eyes in search of something. But it also means that the speaker sends out his thoughts like a pack of hunting dogs in search of a trail. To look within oneself for comfort is an empty task, for the speaker himself is "comfortless," and the epithet has a substantival force. His thoughts can only feel about blindly as they stumble in the interior darkness.

The search is as fruitless, the speaker laments, as blind eyes groping around in the darkness within for the day which is without. Or the search is as impossible as thirst's ever being satisfied, although there is a whole world of water which remains exterior to it. There is a pronounced sense of panic in the metaphors Hopkins has chosen to present the futility of the self to comfort oneself. Only the comfort of the Comforter, who is directly addressed in *No worst, there is none*, can bring the speaker what he casts for. For God is as pervasive as the daylight, although the blind man cannot see it. He is as omnipresent as the waters themselves, although thirst can be present in the midst of plenty.

The tone of the hortatory sestet is remarkably tender and kindly cajoling; the speaker addresses his "Jackself," much as St. Francis affectionately referred to his body as his jackass. He "advises" himself to stop probing the darker recesses of his soul and to stop tormenting himself. He has let his thoughts, like a pack of vicious hunting dogs, snipe too long at his poor Jackself, tormenting the poor beast to near madness. There may be here an intentional sardonic parallel between Actaeon turned into a hart and torn apart by his own hunting dogs and the poor, jaded Jackself of Hopkins being internally torn apart by his own tormenting thoughts.

Unless the thoughts which dog the speaker are called off, comfort or consolation will never be able to take hold within. Like the slow, steady growth of patience imaged in the fledgling and the ivy, comfort will not take root unless the soul prepares itself for its reception. "Consolation should be our normal state and . . . when God withdraws it he wishes us to strive to recover it/. Cf. 'da nobis in eodem Spiritu recta sapere et *de ejus semper consolatione gaudere*' " (Grant us through the same Spirit a right judgment and help us to rejoice always in his consolation), Hopkins wrote during his tertianship. (Ignatius defines spiritual consolation as follows: "I call it consolation when the soul is aroused by an interior movement which causes it to be inflamed with love of its Creator and Lord, and consequently can love no created thing on the face of the earth for its own sake, but only in the creator of all things. It is likewise consolation when one sheds tears inspired by love of the Lord, whether it be sorrow for sins or because of the Passion of Christ our Lord, or for any other reason that is directly connected to His service and praise. Finally, I call consolation any increase of faith, hope, and charity and any interior joy that calls and attracts to heavenly things, and to the salvation of one's soul, inspiring it with peace and quiet in Christ our Lord.") The priest must prepare himself for the graces of consolation, which will come from without in God's own time and in God's own place and meted out with God's own measure ("size"). The colloquial phrasing emphasizing the intimacy between the speaker and his self, which almost touches on good-natured swearing in "God knows what."

The consolation ("smile") of God is likened to the sudden appearance of the pied, dappled skies breaking through the overcast heavens between two mountains like a pie wedge, lighting up a "lovely mile" on the pilgrim's journey. The largeness and bountifulness of God's consolation are reflected in the macrocosmic terms of the simile—"skies," "mountains," "mile"—and are contrasted with the smallness, darkness, and thirst of the self. The wedge of light between the mountains also suggests God's enormous smile, which, when it comes, is completely disproportionate to what was reasonably expected. "[We] want a light shed on our way and a happiness spread over our life," Hopkins wrote near the beginning of his last retreat. And that light, which is the consolation of God, when it breaks through the gloom, shines without stinting:

> Even natural "consolation" or good spirits come and go without any discoverable reason and certainly God *could* make us most happy without our knowing what we were happy about, though of course the mind would then turn with pleasure to any, the first pious thought that came, as its object. . . . But the greater the disproportion [between what is expected and what is given] the greater the likelihood of the consolation being from God.

Significantly, to find in Hopkins' sonnets a cousin to this sacramental image of God's smile flashing between the mountains in the valley of the shadows, we must go back almost eight years to *Hurrahing in Harvest* of September 1877, with its vision of God's shoulder wedged between the hills, upholding his world. For while some of the sonnets of 1879 and 1880 inscape the distinctive selves of places and men, the vision of God in nature belongs uniquely to the sonnets written in the springtime world of Wales, just as much as the terrible sonnets are a product of the "winter-world" of Dublin. And even the image of light breaking through the mountains recalls "dark Maenefa the mountain" of northern Wales rather than the terrain of Dublin.

The sonnets of desolation, conceived and written in an appropriate secretive darkness, are the literary remains of a time of intense mental anguish which most of us can only imagine, in which there are few lights and even the lettering on the road signs is in a different language. Road maps usually make poor literature because their purposes are utilitarian rather than aesthetic. But the seven sonnets of desolation, [the six "terrible" sonnets and "Spelt from Sibyl's Leaves"] admired by so many readers for so many different reasons, are most clearly read by following the map of St. Ignatius' *Spiritual Exercises*. With this guide for the way, it is clear that Hopkins, like Dante before him, was going down profound depths only to go upward toward God. . . .

Structurally *That Nature is a Heraclitean Fire* is a further experiment in the caudated sonnet form. It has twenty-four lines eked out by three codas and a final refrain or echo line, and has the following rhyme scheme (the first line of each tercet and the last line are half-lines): abba abba cdcdcd dee eff fgg g. The final burden line of *That Nature is a Heraclitean Fire* links this sonnet with *Harry Ploughman*, which ends with a similarly short line. But it is clear from a comparison of the pattern of the rhyme scheme of Milton's caudated sonnet with *That Nature is a Heraclitean Fire* that Hopkins has firmly grounded his sonnet on Milton's and has gone on his own road from there. Another extension of the caudated sonnet form is Hopkins' employment of an Alexandrine sprung line with a heavy medial pause which creates a marked percussive tempo—in fact, a vigorous chant. The rhythms mirror the widely modulated activities presented in the poem, from the nuances of subtle, rapid change to a grave, heavy flatness, and finally to the stark, emphatic monosyllabic beat of the closing lines.

That Nature is a Heraclitean Fire opens with a vivid composition of place. The speaker is out walking, apparently alone with his thoughts, observing the storm scape of still-turbulent clouds ("yestertempest") racing over the countryside. Sensitive to and perceptive of his surroundings, his imagination catches fire and responds joyfully and playfully to the protean cloud formations. The storm clouds are unsubstantial, and their shapes change as rapidly as they move. The speaker watches the light through the trees and observes the kaleidoscopic effect of light, altering between "roughcast" and "dazzling whitewash," fleck and change as the clouds pass behind the elm branches. Light and shadows shift patterns constantly.

Turning his eyes earthward, he sees how the strong warm wind seems, like a giant, to wrestle the earth and dry up all the standing pools from the recent storm. He checks off the steps by which the sun and wind transform watery mud into dust, literally pulverizing the soft footprints of the men who preceded him down the dirt road:

> Delightfully the bright wind boisterous | ropes, wrestles, beats
>   earth bare
> Of yestertempest's creases; | in pool and rutpeel parches
> Squandering ooze to squeezed | dough, crust, dust; stanches,
>   starches
> Squadroned masks and manmarks | treadmire toil there
> Footfretted in it.

The mood of the speaker, who humanizes the activity of the clouds and the wind, becomes more sober as he is made more aware that nature itself is indifferent to the cyclic processes that it generates, and that the process is always toward change and annihilation of the scape of a particular object. The carefree wind and heat obliterate all traces of the storm. But they obliterate too all signs of man's signature in the earth, here scaped in the lowly image of footprints—those "Squadroned masks and manmarks"—"Footfretted" in the soft mud, which crumble away to dust. In fact, the beauty of nature is kinetic; it depends upon a continuing process of destruction and generation; the old is peeled away to reveal the new. And this process of the new springing from the funeral pyre of the old continues, seemingly, for its own sake: "million-fuelèd, nature's bonfire burns on." The clouds moving across the heavens now assume an uncanny resemblance to the smoke from a huge conflagration, the bonfire of the whole world.

The speaker's reflection continues to spiral downward and inward, toward the inevitable chaos and strife at the center of a materialistic and atomistic universe: the dark cold waters at one pole of the Heraclitean flux. At this point the eternal process simply reverses itself and all is caught up in an equally indifferent fire, but Hopkins dwells on the nadir, since the Heraclitean upswing offers no comfort to man. For even man, nature's "bonniest, dearest to her, her clearest-selvèd spark," is part of nature's vast bonfire and is eventually "quench[ed]" in the black waters of personal extinction. And what is more, even the most individuating marks of collective humanity—the fame of man's greatest exploits ("firedint"), as well as the genius of man's ideas ("mark on mind"), to say nothing of the vast, anonymous majority of mankind—all are soon erased from the fluctuating and unsteady consciousness of the mind. From the long-range viewpoint, the flux ultimately "beats level" man and all his works:

But quench her bonniest, dearest | to her, her clearest-selvèd spark
Man, how fast his firedint, | his mark on mind, is gone!
Both are in an unfathomable, all is in an enormous dark
Drowned.

The speaker has plumbed as far into chaos as the mind can go. Following this desolate meditation to its inexorable conclusion, he has come to a modernistic vision of man's utter insignificance and impermanence. Despite his apparent worth, in a world thus conceived (and Heraclitus speaks for many) man seems to have no more intrinsic or lasting value than the four elements—air, earth, fire and water—of which he is composed. Nature's bonfire scoffs at man's claims to any special dignity or permanence:

O pity and indig | nation! Manshape, that shone
Sheer off, disseveral, a star, | death blots black out; nor mark
Is any of him at all so stark
But vastness blurs and time | beats level.

The speaker's mood has shifted from gaiety and playfulness in the opening lines to a growing depression from line 10 to the middle of line 16. Now the second *volta* in the speaker's meditation occurs. And it occurs immediately:

Enough! the Resurrection,
A heart's-clarion! Away grief's gasping, | joyless days, dejection.

This is a summons to the heart, a clear, shrill, unmistakable trumpet blast. The dark waters of chaos and despair which had threatened to swamp the poor wreck who is the speaker are suddenly dispersed. The strong, steady, eternal beacon of the risen Christ beckons. It has always been there had the speaker but looked upward; it was there for the nuns in the terrible night on the deck of the wrecked "Deutschland," and it is there for the fagged and harried wreck of a priest. There is a significant poetic yield in declaiming the preposition "Across" slowly so that what is suggested is "a cross" shining in the dark to the speaker: "Across my foundering deck shone / A beacon, an eternal beam."

Having received this assurance of the theandric nature of man—and therefore a guarantee of the intrinsic worth of all that he does, however trivial or apparently meaningless—the speaker can afford to flaunt death with an outrageous impunity. Let the body "fade" out like a light waning, he orders:

> Flesh fade, and mortal trash
> Fall to the residuary worm; | world's wildfire, leave but ash.

The "residuary" worm, the inheritor of man's physical estate, will receive the "mortal trash," what Hopkins had elsewhere called his "bone-house, mean house." The "world's wildfire," which is seemingly eternal flux of nature, will burn up all substances (wildfire was an inflammable mixture used by the Greeks which would burn on any material). But in the Christian revelation, too, the bonfire will end in the final consummation of the world and will leave but ash. The classical Greek world view is thereby imaginatively reduced from a self-perpetuating alpha and omega to a mere instrument of God.

Hopkins blends several biblical images of man's sudden metamorphosis into a unified visual and auditory image. (See II Peter 3:10, I Corinthians 15:52−54, and Matthew 24:29−32.) We are given a superb catalogue of worthless fragments which have in common their accidental being. But the catalogue ends with a substance—a self—which is as permanent and immutable as any we know. There is no doubt that man changes constantly, but the essential self abides within the trash:

> In a flash, at a trumpet crash,
> I am all at once what Christ is, | since he was what I am, and
> This Jack, joke, poor potsherd, | patch, matchwood, immortal
> diamond,
> Is immortal diamond.

The final coda is a masterpiece which will repay close study. A "Jack" is a generic and pejorative name for a common fellow, but it also denotes that which is without any specific or definitive self. A "joke" of a man is a laughingstock, but he is also something lacking substance or genuineness. The "poor potsherd" recalls the shard with which poor Job scraped his oozing sores. But it is also a fragmentary object with only accidental being. A "patch" is a ninny or dolt (from the Italian *paccio*), but it is also a scrap or odd leftover used to mend something, a superfluity. "Matchwood" is wood splinters which burn away quickly to ash; wood shavings, too, have no more than accidental being. But within this list of insignificant, comical objects, there abides the immortal diamond, which has both an intrinsic as well as a transcendent self. What had always been there is suddenly purified and raised to a new level of being.

Diamond, which of itself is merely a hard, imperishable substance, a fragment of crystallized coal buried in the earth, is suddenly ("In a flash") made a precious, beautiful object by reflecting the light of the beacon (Christ), which gives the diamond its especial value and without which it is merely a cold, hard stone. For it is of the nature of the Incarnation and of its corollary, the Resurrection, that God communicates His divine life to man, and the human vessel reflects this life while maintaining its distinctive self.

It is interesting to note how Hopkins has caught the dynamism of flux and the dynamism of theandric permanence. As the poem rounds to an end, we sense a spatial and temporal contraction in the images and corresponding intensification of emotion. The syntax is forced forward by the catalogue, but the copulative verb "Is" holds the last movement in the permanent moment of self-identity.

The rich flurry of dynamic verbs in the opening section reflects and imitates the continual process of the Heraclitean flux itself: "chevy," "throng," "glitter," "arches," "lace, lance, and pair," "ropes, wrestles, beats," "parches," "stanches, starches," and "burns," The first movement of the sonnet, including the first *volta*, is marked by transitive verbs, shading off in the second part into verbs reflecting processes which are reversible in the Heraclitean flux but which are final in man: "quench," "drowned," and finally "beats" man level.

But in the second turn, the copulative verb, which seems so colorless and thus assiduously to be avoided in poetry, is made at once not only the most affirmative but also the most dynamic verb of the sonnet. It is the perfect verbal equivalent for the supraspatial and supratemporal shift from dynamic flux to transcendent permanence. The transmutation from dust to risen god will happen, Hopkins implies, as swiftly as the poem here turns from dejection to joy.

God's assumption of human nature strikes Hopkins as the strongest argument for the resurrection of man. For if Christ condescended to suffer for man, then the value of men is infinitely more than we may suspect. This is the argument Hopkins hammers home in the pounding monosyllables of

> I am all at once what Christ is, | since he was what I am.

The percussive rhyming of the last two codas also intensifies and clarifies the emotional import of the thought. In the grouping of "trash," "ash," "flash," and "crash," the sharp, shrill rhymes suggest that sudden transformation which will burn away man's trash, revealing the glorified body. Again, the "[wha]t I am, and" is ingeniously rhymed with "diamond" to show the identity between the essential self and its divine spark. And these are rhymed with the second "diamond" to reinforce and make final the identity.

Images of light and sound recur throughout the poem, and these consti-tute one of Hopkins' most subtle effects. The bright lights are reflected off the whitewashed clouds, forever changing in intensity and creating an image of strong but diffused and blurred light. Man is nature's "clearest-selvèd spark," a star shining apart and above; his mark or impression on mind is "firedint." But both man and his works are "quench[ed]," "blur[red]" and blotted "black out" in the primordial chaotic flood, fire's opposite. The images of sound parallel the images of light, and the boisterous and mindless moan of the wind is a correlative of the eternal flux which pervades the first two parts of the sonnet.

But the blurred and muffled quality of the sound and light images, like the involved and congested syntax, gives way to the sharpness and clarity or "flash," "heart's clarion," and "trumpet crash," just as amorphous, ever-changing clouds give way in the poem to the permanence of diamond. Suffocating with the terrible darkness of formless flux without and within, the wreck of the poet suddenly sees the strong, clear, steady beam of the Light shine forth.

That Nature is a Heraclitean Fire is clearly a masterpiece. The amount of sheer intelligence at work in fusing so many elements of sound and sense into an organic experience is both surprising and exciting. And although the conclusion rests on Christian doctrine, it has an integrated and esemplastic harmony with the rest of the poem. Those critics like Claude C. Abbott who suggest that the conclusion of the sonnet jumps out of the pattern like a pious afterthought have not adequately understood what Hopkins is doing.

The three caudated sonnets represent a new direction, a further stretching of the traditionally rigid limits of the Petrarchan sonnet. There is an opulence, a joy in creativity, a new plumbing of the dynamic potentialities of language and melodic rhythm which constitute no less than a chant to the risen Christ. Hopkins had just over ten months to live when he created his optimistic carol to the permanence of man in the Resurrection. His last sonnets, however, cease to be hymns and become more like personal colloquies whispered by Hopkins to his God.

JAMES MILROY

"The Weeds and the Wilderness": Local Dialect and Germanic Purism

It would be difficult to exaggerate the revolution in linguistic interests that took place in England in the middle years of the nineteenth century, or to over-emphasize the progress in knowledge of history and dialects of English that was made during Hopkins's lifetime. Comparative philology, as we have seen, owed its early development to German scholarship in the early years of the century; side by side with this interest in the ancient origins of languages, there developed a vigorous interest in local dialects and in the folklore and customs of country people. For the first time, the mother-tongue, in all its variety, had become an important focus of interest for the linguist. The centre of attention had shifted from Latin to English, and the eighteenth-century concern with standardizing and codifying vernacular tongues (mainly in their "literary" forms) had given way to an emphasis on the variety of non-standard and non-literary forms of languages. Not surprisingly, a kind of linguistic nationalism often accompanied this emphasis: some modern language revival movements, for example those in Norway and Ireland, are outgrowths of it.

Already in late eighteenth-century Germany one can detect the signs of this change of attitude. Herder, as we have seen, admired the strength and "measured pace" of his own mother-tongue. A generation later (1812) we find Jacob Grimm expressing similar views, but with a shift of emphasis. The interest now is in common speech rather than the best literature, in the relics of the medieval past and in popular folklore. Grimm's interests are clearly influenced by the German Romantic movement, by writers such as Tieck (whom Hopkins intended to read in 1864, together with "German medieval-

From *The Language of Gerard Manley Hopkins*. © 1977 by James Milroy. Andre Deutsch, 1977.

ists"). The opposition to the centralized standard and grammatical "correct-
ness" which is implicit in much midcentury English scholarship—and quite
explicitly expounded by some—is already seen in Grimm's preface to his
Deutsche Grammatik (1819). This wholly rejects previous German grammars.
Every German who speaks his language naturally, says Grimm, may call
himself his own grammar and leave the schoolmasters' rules alone. We have
seen that Hopkins's attitude to the "schoolmasters' rules," unlike that of some
of his critics, is similar to Grimm's; already in his undergraduate years,
Hopkins with his observant and inquiring mind knew that the real rules of
language lay deeper than those of the schoolmasters. But in Grimm's attitude
to language, we also see the same kind of reverence as the Romantic poets often
had for wild things in nature. "Each individuality," he wrote, "even in the
world of languages, should be respected as sacred; it is desirable that even the
smallest and most despised dialect should be left only to itself and to its own
nature and in nowise subjected to violence, because it is sure to have some
secret advantages over the greatest and most highly valued language."

In recent years, Hopkins critics have been much concerned with whether
he is best described as "modern," "Victorian" or "Romantic." Clearly there are
senses in which he is each one of these, although his "modernity" has been
exaggerated (sometimes, one feels, because a critic thinks that there is something superior about being "modern," or that all originality is "modern").
Hopkins is clearly a Victorian in many of his social attitudes, in his senti-
ments, in his piety; but—despite affinities with Ruskin and his Pre-Raphaelite
contemporaries—Hopkins's view of nature has much in it that goes back to
early Romanticism, and his attitudes to language partake of the late Romanticism that continued to inspire the philologists well into the 1860s and 1870s.
In other words, if we choose to describe his linguistic interests as "typically
Victorian," we must at the same time acknowledge that Victorian language
scholarship was largely "Romantic" in flavour. A study of the linguistic
scholarship that forms a background to his early diaries and Journal provides a
clear link with the Romantic movement which, in the purely literary sense, he
outgrew in his early verse; and it may therefore help to cast light on aspects of
Hopkins's mature poetry that still appear to us as Romantic.

Each individuality, even in the world of languages, should be respected as sacred.
There is a striking correspondence between Grimm's remark and Hopkins's
reverence for the individuality or selfhood of natural objects and scenes. This is
celebrated in his poetry, joyfully, as when he speaks of each creature sounding
abroad its own name:

> *myself* it speaks and spells,
> Crying, *What I do is me; for that I came.*
>
> (No. 57)

or, regretfully, lamenting the destruction of *inscapes* in nature that cannot be replaced:

> O if we but knew what we do
> When we delve or hew—
> Hack and rack the growing green!
> (No. 43)

Much earlier, in his Journal, he had commented:

> (6 December 1868) At night the most violent gale I ever heard. One of our elms snapped in half. Since then (2 February 1870) a grievous gap has come in that place with falling and felling.

And again (8 April 1873):

> The ashtree growing in the corner of the garden was felled. It was lopped first: I heard the sound and looking out and seeing it maimed there came at that moment a great pang and I wished to die and not to see the inscapes of the world destroyed any more.

His careful observation of the "behaviour" and inscapes of nature is well known. Sometimes he can be observing something as "un-poetic" as an ink-blot (the comment—"Spiculation in a dry blot in a smooth inkstand" is accompanied by a drawing—[*The Journals and Papers of Gerard Manley Hopkins*; all further references to this text will be abbreviated as *JP*]), or frost-patterns on urinal walls. His descriptions of nature are everywhere in the journal; they are very detailed and very observant:

> The next morning a heavy fall of snow. It tufted and toed the firs and yews and went on to load them till they were taxed beyond their spring. The limes, elms, and Turkey-oaks it crisped beautifully as with young leaf. Looking at the elms from underneath you saw every wave in every twig (become by this the wire-like stem to a finger of snow) and to the hangers and flying sprays it restored, to the eye, the inscapes they had lost.
>
> (*JP*)

This is from the journal; in the early diaries the emphasis on natural description is rather less; instead, we encounter, in 1863—long before he became interested in Duns Scotus and long before he had actually coined the word *inscape*, an obsession with the inscape of *words*. A few critics have recognized this. Peters comments that "a word was just as much an individual as any other thing; it had a self as every other object, and consequently just as he strove to catch the inscape of a flower or a tree or a cloud, he similarly did not rest until he knew the word as a self." E. R. August explains that to Hopkins "words are like other creatures: they have inscapes beautiful in themselves . . . the numerous philological notes in the journals record word inscapes." August adds that it is a pity that critics so often overlook the fact that Hopkins "tries to bring into play the whole self of the words he uses." Already at the age of nineteen in his note on *horn* Hopkins was concerned with the inscape of the word and the inscape of its relation to the things it stands for; many of his other philological notes further emphasize relations of sound which exist between words of related meanings (as we have noted), and even suggest the "ring" of the things they stand for. As August remarks: "Hopkins always suspected that the relation between words and things was not arbitrary."

The first recorded use of the word *inscape* is in an essay on Parmenides, written early in 1868:

> this feeling for instress, for the flush and foredrawn, and for inscape
> is most striking and from this one can understand Plato's reverence
> for him as the great father of Realism.

But, as we have seen, he is concerned several years earlier with what is individual and special in words and objects. The earliest appearance of the *idea* of inscape is really in the note on *horn* (1863) in which he tries to catch the individuality of that *word*. Hopkins is clearly concerned with the full semantic suggestiveness of the word, its association with shapes and textures, curves and spirals, and the sensory impressions of touch and sound as well as sight. He is also concerned with its relationships within English and other languages, and he clearly assumes that a relationship of sound may imply relationship in meaning. As we have already seen, Hopkins is aware of the historical perspective and believes that there are certain underlying principles governing linguistic change, notably the principle of figurative change. But we have also noted that the words he discusses in the diaries tend to be monosyllables used in everyday speech, and these monosyllables are usually of Anglo-Saxon (Germanic) origin.

Only very rarely does he interest himself primarily in a long word or a Latinate one. When Hopkins speaks of *current language*, he means the spoken language as opposed to a literary one; but he goes further than most of us would. The essential spoken language is not the educated language of university graduates and the middle classes of large urban centres; it is at its most perfect in the mouths of country people, and, since it is ephemeral and not committed to paper, its interesting features must be jotted down in the diaries just as the inscapes of nature are. Clearly, this *current language* will be largely "Anglo-Saxon" in vocabulary; and this brings a bonus to the poet, since Anglo-Saxon words are on the whole richer in emotional suggestiveness than is the French or Classical vocabulary of English, and may also have wider networks of structural relationship within the language. We have seen that Hopkins was much influenced by the historical and comparatist interests of his day; in his concern with spoken language in the mouths of the ordinary people he is also part of the strong movement concerned with folk-speech and folk-culture, a movement which can also be said to have had its origins in German scholarship. In Germany and England alike the interest in dialect is at this period difficult to separate from the vigorous linguistic and cultural nationalism that we have already noted.

Throughout the century the tone of English philology was one of reverence for the variety and ancient pedigree of humble speech, together with some hostility to centralization and Latinization of English. The signs of what is to come can already be seen in the work of William Cobbett (c. 1818), which displays hostility to the standard classical authorities of grammar. Hazlitt in 1829 is outspoken in his rejection of the classical grammatical tradition, and De Quincey (who is freely referred to in Hopkins's early diaries) calls for more pride in English and its history (1839). In 1864 or 1865 Hopkins thought it worth recording De Quincey's view on Keats: "Upon this mother-tongue, upon this English language, has Keats trampled as with the hooves of a buffalo" (*JP*). Grimm's influence began to be keenly felt in English academic circles from about 1830. His supporter, J. M. Kemble, indulged in lengthy and acrimonious debates in *The Gentleman's Magazine* with those who resisted this influence. Dean Trench's books on the history of words were widely read, and he was closely involved in the early stages of the *Oxford English Dictionary*. Also in the *Gentleman's Magazine* in the early 1830s there appeared several articles by William Barnes, who was to become the most extreme Germanic purist of the century. Hopkins had read Barnes's dialect poems while still at university, and Norman MacKenzie remarks—understating the matter a little—that the importance of this early influence "has probably been considerably underestimated."

MacKenzie is thinking chiefly of Barnes's interest in dialect, but the Germanic purist movement also forms an important background to Hopkins's interests. Its general importance in the period is often underestimated by literary scholars. It can be seen as a reaction against the Latinism of the previous century, and in a relatively mild form it has persisted into the twentieth century. It is discernible in the tenets of the Society for Pure English (founded by Robert Bridges in 1913); it finds its way into language handbooks and the recommendations of composition teachers; and it unquestionably lies behind the views of George Orwell, particularly as he expresses them in his essay "Politics and the English Language." "Never use a foreign phrase . . . "

says Orwell, "if you can think of an everyday English equivalent," and "Never use a long word when a short one will do." In his insistence on *inearnestness*, Hopkins has a great deal in common with Orwell's concern with honesty and decency and his condemnation of those who cover up the truth by using prefabricated phrases. Hopkins's objections to Victorian English have a similar ring and a similar basis in Anglo-Saxonism and simplicity of vocabulary. "It is true that this Victorian English is a bad business," he wrote to Bridges in 1888, "They say 'it goes without saying (and I wish it did) and instead of "There is no such thing" they say a thing is "nonexistent" and *in* for *at* and *altruistic* and a lot more." Years before, he had written: "Disillusion is a bad word; you mean Disenchantment. It is as bad as Or-de-al and Preventative and Standpoint and the other barbarisms" [*The Letters of Gerard Manley Hopkins to Robert Bridges*; all further references to this text will be abbreviated *LB*, 26 October 1880], and then again (5 February 1881), "Disillusion" does exist, as typhus exists and the Protestant religion. The same 'brutes' say 'disillusion' as say 'standpoint' and 'preventative' and 'equally as well' and 'to whomsoever shall ask.' " It is true that these remarks are not in themselves examples of thoroughgoing Germanic purism, but are more obviously condemnations of pretentiousness, of journalese, of bureaucratic and committee English. As Orwell sought clarity and honesty in prose-writing, so Hopkins had to reject "prefabricated" language both in poetry and prose. However, in Victorian times, this attitude is in several writers clearly associated with Germanic purism, and Hopkins's delight in local variation of language, which might seem at first sight inconsistent with his rejection of "this Victorian English," is best understood as an outgrowth of his other linguistic attitudes. These are based on a fondness for dialect and Anglo-Saxon words and are clearly associated with a preference for country as against town, for God's works as against man's works, for what is "natural" as against what is regulated by man. We shall return to the relation between Hopkins's attitudes to language and attitudes to nature; let us first consider Victorian Germanic purism and its relation to dialect scholarship.

William Barnes was born in 1801 (or 1800—the date is uncertain), and much of his long life as a country clergyman was devoted to the study of philology, and championship of the cause of Anglo-Saxon purism. His first contribution to the *Gentleman's Magazine* was entitled "Corruptions of the English Language"—a polemic against borrowing words from other languages. Barnes gave several arguments against borrowing, the chief of which were that borrowing is proof of national inferiority and that it is unnecessary anyway since the English language already has rich resources for the creation of compound words or other derivatives as they are needed. Another article in the

Gentleman's Magazine, "Compounds in the English Language," showed in some detail how the resources of English might be used to make new words:

> Lorn, as we have it in lovelorn, is a participle of the old Saxon verb,
> to lose; as verlohren is in German. Hence we may have,
>> Waylorn, having lost one's way
>> Glorylorn, having lost one's glory
>> Reasonlorn, having lost one's reason . . . etc.
> Fare, is from the old verb to go . . . and means a going, or going:
> as fare, a going; thoroughfare, a going through; so that landfaring,
> going by land; airfaring, going in a balloon; are quite as good
> English as seafaring or wayfaring.

Although Barnes could be scathing about the Latinism of the previous century, and regretful that the Saxon potential of our language was neglected ("I am sorry that we have not a language of our own; but that whenever we happen to conceive a thought above that of a plough-boy, or produce anything beyond a pitchfork, we are obliged to borrow a word from others before we can utter it, or give it a name . . . "), his purism in these essays was by no means as extreme as it was to become later.

Hopkins, without doubt, was aware of the vast potential for compounding and derivation that lay unused in English, and he was also capable of extending patterns that are in active use. The adverbial *piecemeal* is the model for Hopkins's *leafmeal* (No. 55); *lovescape* (*Deutschland*, st. 23), *inscape, offscape*, are based on *landscape*; *quickgold* (No. 32) belongs to the same pattern as *quicksilver*; *mealdrift* (No. 38) belongs with *snowdrift*, and suggests it. These simple examples of compounding (and there are many more) closely follow the patterns that Barnes recommended. But Hopkins's poetry is also rich in "complex" or derivative words that extend patterns already existing in the basic grammatical framework of the language. The prefix *a-* (as in *afire, alive, anew*) is extended by Hopkins to *aswarm* (No. 61) and others. The prefix *un-* is extended to nouns like *child, leaf, self, father, Christ* (No. 41) and the resulting forms pressed into service as verbs:

> the widow-making unchilding unfathering deeps
>> (*Deutschland*, st. 13)
> Goldengrove unleaving
>> (No. 55)
> Strokes of havoc unselve
>> (No. 43)

Most of these grammatical operations are performed on the Germanic part of
the vocabulary. . . .

Hopkins refers to Barnes in a letter to Bridges (26 November 1882):

> The Rev. Wm Barnes, good soul, of Dorset-dialect poems . . .
> has published a "Speech-craft of English Speech" = English
> Grammar, written in an unknown tongue, a sort of modern
> Anglosaxon, beyond all that Furnival in his wildest Forewords ever
> dreamed. He does not see the utter hopelessness of the thing. It
> makes one weep to think what English might have been; for in
> spite of all that Shakespere and Milton have done with the
> compound I cannot doubt that no beauty in a language can make
> up for want of purity. In fact, I am learning Anglo-Saxon and it is a
> vastly superior thing to what we have now. But the madness of an
> almost unknown man trying to do what the three estates of the
> realm together could never accomplish! He calls degrees of com-
> parison pitches of suchness; we *ought* to call them so, but alas!

Barnes's *Outline of English Speech-Craft* (mis-named by Hopkins) was published
in 1878, and its language is remarkable. The technical terms of grammar
(*noun, verb, transitive* and so on) are replaced by Germanic words.

"Sundriness of Sex, Kindred, Youngness and Smallness," says Barnes,
are "marked by sundry names or mark-words or mark-endings." Grammatical
genders become "the *carl* sex, the *quean* sex . . . *unsexly* things, as a stone."
Suchnesses, as we have seen, are adjectives, and may be of *sundry pitches* (different
degrees). Transitive verbs are *outreaching time-words*, and intransitive verbs are
unoutreaching.

However eccentric Barnes may appear, his *Speech-Craft* is merely the most
extreme product of a movement which was vigorous at the time, related as we
have seen to the growth of the new philology and much more outspoken in
condemnation of Latinism or foreign borrowing than we would think reason-
able today. Signs of this linguistic nationalism are seen, for example, in
contributions to the publications of the *Philological Society* and in the work of
dialect scholars and medievalists, culminating (1899) in a rather strong
Germanic nationalism in the pronouncements of Henry Sweet, probably the
greatest British linguist of the century. Sweet was not at all sure that it was
necessary to teach the Classical languages to schoolchildren, but the Classics
should in any event come later than German and Anglo-Saxon, which should
be taught to every schoolchild. The Balliol scholar, T. Kington Oliphant, in a
historical work entitled *The Sources of Standard English* (1873) calls his chapter
on French influence "Inroad of French words into England." *Inroad into*

England, not "influence on English." A baleful century it was, he says of the thirteenth century

> if we may liken our language to a fine stone building, we shall find that in that wondrous age a seventh part of the good old masonry was thrown down . . . The breach was by slow degrees made good with bricks, meaner ware borrowed from France . . . We may put up with the building as it now stands, but we cannot help sighing when we think what we have lost.

Oliphant is sternly critical of the eighteenth century and the Latinate prose of Gibbon. He commends the "many attempts, like those of Mr Barnes in Dorset, to bring the various dialects of England before the reading public. How many good old words, dropped by our literature since 1500, might be recovered from these sources!" For arousing us from foreign pedantry he gives the credit to Cobbett, and he commends "Mr Tennyson" for helping the revival of pure English. Further strides, however, have been made by Mr Morris, who has shown us, in his "*Sigurd*, how copious, in skilful hands, an almost purely Teutonic diction may be."

It is the work of a less gifted writer such as Oliphant that shows us the true characteristics of this purism—with all its strengths and weaknesses. The sincere concern with clarity and honesty in writing is obviously there, and impressed upon us repeatedly. So too is the conviction that linguistic decline (here identified as foreign borrowing and use of Latinisms by the middle class) is somehow bound up with moral or social decline. It is the fault of shopkeepers, the aspiring middle class, who send their children to *educational establishments* instead of schools, and the *penny-a-liners* who write barbarous English in the newspapers. Oliphant, like Hopkins, found Victorian English a bad business, and, with Hopkins, thought Anglo-Saxon vastly superior to "what we have now." It is clear from his own writings that Hopkins showed the Anglo-Saxonist's tendency to identify the Germanic element and the "conservative" rural dialects with what is pure and honest in the use of language: "He calls degrees of comparison pitches of suchness; we *ought* to call them so, but alas!"

Hopkins's lifetime coincides with a period of intense activity in English dialect research and interest in the common speech of England. In 1847, J. O. Halliwell produced his *Dictionary of Archaic and Provincial Words,* and this was followed in 1857 by Thomas Wright's *Dictionary of Obsolete and Provincial English*. A. J. Ellis, who is often considered the founder of English dialect research, was active in the 1860s and his *Early English Pronounciation* appeared in four volumes between 1869 and 1874. The English Dialect Society was

founded in 1873 with W. W. Skeat as its secretary. Joseph Wright's monu-
mental *English Dialect Dictionary* did not appear until 1898, but the work was
in progress in Hopkins's lifetime; amongst the names acknowledged as corre-
spondents and contributors of unprinted collections of dialect words is "Hopkins, The Rev. G. M.".

Hopkins's Journal contains many notes on dialect words, expressions and
pronunciations; some words that appear to be of dialect origin find their way
into his prose, and there are many in his poetry. As we have seen, scholars have
considerably underestimated the extent to which dialectal English is woven
into Hopkins's writings from the undergraduate years onwards. As Norman
MacKenzie points out: "Even as good a scholar as Professor W. H. Gardner has
classified most of them [i.e. dialect words] as effective archaisms . . . But
most of the examples which have been quoted by critics as Shakespearian or
Spenserian were in fact used by the common people in Victorian England."
Peters also seems to accept that many "Hopkinsian" words are archaisms:

> Someone might make out a good case against him for employing a
> language as archaic and as obsolete as that ever used by Dixon or
> Bridges . . . "hie" is preferred to "haste," "ghost" to "spirit,"
> "thew" and "brawn" to "muscle," "lade" to "load," "brine" to
> "sea" and so on. "Fettle," "pash," "mammock," "rivel," "rive,"
> "reeve," "wend," "heft," "sillion," "shive," "barrow," "bole,"
> "tuck," "burl" and "buck," are all of them good Saxon words, but
> they can hardly be said to belong any longer to the ordinary
> modern language of Victorian days.

However, many of these words do appear in contemporary dictionaries, such as
Ogilvie or Richardson; others appear in the dialect dictionaries. Peters misses
the point. A great many of these words *do* belong to the ordinary modern
language; they are not part of the vocabulary of standard literary prose, but are
colloquial and dialectal. Others, like *ghost* and *brine*, are certainly part of the
standard language, but Hopkins uses them in *senses* that Peters considers to be
archaic. The words themselves are plainly not archaic. Inspired by the philologists of his age, Hopkins's notion of *current language* (or "ordinary modern
language") is much broader than that of his critics, embracing the forms of
casual speech (as against formal English), country speech and the vocabulary of
rural crafts and trades. All of us, without realizing it, are much influenced in
our attitudes by the standardization of language. Although critics do not
intend it this way, there is actually something slightly presumptuous about
dismissing forms as "archaic" when they do not happen to conform to the
usage of standard literary prose or poetry. If they are still labelled "archaic" or

"obsolete" even when they are known to occur in dialect speech, that is in a sense even worse; there is nothing truly archaic about words and expressions that are part of the everyday usage of fully competent native speakers of English even if they do happen to live a long way from the metropolis. To call such forms archaic is to assign an unwarranted and unscientific superiority to the standard language which is implicitly taken as the norm. It smacks of patronage, and an assumption that "provincial" language is necessarily quaint, backward, inferior and so on. It is even more unfortunate that those who are not curious about language are thereby enabled to put on their blinkers and to seem justified in so doing. The immense variability of English in the usage of even one person and in the dialects of different areas can with impunity be ignored or underestimated. While Hopkins may often be innovative in the way he uses a dialect word, there is very little in Hopkins's poetry that cannot be directly related to modern speech. Indeed it must be said that Hopkins did not venture into dialect nearly as far as he might have done. There are many dialect forms (seemingly archaic if compared with the standard) that he either did not know or did not wish to use.

The extent of variability in English usage is little appreciated, but the work of dialect scholars and linguists during the past century has made a great deal of the information available, and in recent years students of urban speech have done much to show how variable usage may be even within the same urban community. The *Survey of English Dialects* (1962 *et seq.*) and the archives of the Linguistic Survey of Scotland bulge with information about the sounds, grammar and vocabulary of "provincial" speech. In Ireland, the background, phonology and vocabulary of Ulster speech have been investigated by such scholars as John Braidwood and G.B. Adams, who have shown in some detail the conservative nature of much local speech. In sound-pattern, for instance, there is no doubt that the "Elizabethan" distinction between *beat* and *beet, peak*, and *peek* and so on is very consistently preserved in much Ulster vernacular speech. In syntax, the Middle English *for to* construction (as in "he came for to see me") is preserved in most Scottish and Ulster vernacular. Even so, it came to me as a surprise to hear a shepherd in a remote part of Donegal referring to his jacket as a *frock* (from frock-coat), and it is commonplace in Donegal to hear small rocky fields referred to as *parks* and one or two cottages in their surrounding wilderness spoken of as *towns* (from townlands).

In Hopkins's day, the great popularizer of English word-lore was Richard Chenevix Trench. *On the Study of Words*, which was first published in 1851, reached its twentieth edition in 1888. In Trench's influential work we find reverence for the treasures of humble speech closely associated with that love of the countryside that is so much a characteristic of Victorian England. Indeed,

there is a very close, sometimes an uncanny, resemblance between Trench and
Hopkins in their association of language and the countryside.

Poetry, says Trench, is enshrined in the words of a language just as much
as in an *Iliad*; indeed a language is itself far greater and richer than the great
works composed in it. The poetry inherent in language can be seen in the
names of flowers, beasts, birds and fishes: *lady's finger, love-in-idleness, larkspur,
rosemary, ladybird, kingfisher* and many others including, notably, *windhover*:

> Any one who has watched the kestral [*sic*] hanging poised in the
> air, before it swoops upon its prey, will acknowledge the felicity of
> the name "windhover," or sometimes "windfanner," which it popu-
> larly bears.

Trench was by no means an Anglo-Saxon purist, and he calls attention to the
fossilized poetry embedded in Latin and Greek borrowings, but it is plain that
his richest stores of living metaphor were found in country speech in which the
Anglo-Saxon element is, naturally, strong. Significantly, the reference to the
windhover occurs in a list of dialect usages: "in our country dialects there is a
wide poetical nomenclature which is well worthy of recognition." Hopkins
thought so too and often noted such usages in his journals: in Lancashire, "the
mossy cankers on rose-bushes" are called "*Virgin's Brier* (they say breer)" (22
August 1872); cormorants, in the Isle of Man, are *Black Divers* (7 August
1872). It is to be expected that Hopkins would prefer the term *windhover* to
kestrel when he came to write his famous poem: not only is it an Anglo-Saxon
type of compound, it is also a country word obviously expressive of the bird's
movement. It is noteworthy too that some of the words that occur in Hopkins's
poems and notebooks are those that Trench uses as exemplification: *minion*, for
example, is used to show degeneration of meaning. *Shire*, says Trench "is
connected with 'shear,' 'share,' and is properly a portion 'shered' or 'shorn'
off." This is very reminiscent of Hopkins's note on *shear* and other words
(1863) in which he too subscribes to the incorrect derivation of *shire* from *shear*.
But it is the tone of celebration—of glorying in the associations of words—
that is most striking in Trench's book, and this book could well have con-
tributed to the young Hopkins's enthusiasm for language.

Trench is also notable for his clearly expressed preference for what is
"natural" in language and his hostility to prescription, correction and
standardization:

> There have been found from time to time those who have so little
> understood what a language is, and what are the laws which it
> obeys, that they have sought by arbitrary decrees of their own to

arrest its growth, have pronounced that it has reached the limits of
its growth, and must not henceforth presume to develop itself
further . . . But a language has a life, as truly as a man or as a
tree . . . As a forest tree, it will defy any feeble bands which
should attempt to control its expansion, so long as the principle of
growth is in it; as a tree too it will continually, while it casts off
some leaves, be putting forth others.

Müller, a few years later, is equally plain in stating that the life of language is
in its dialects and that standard languages are artificial:

What we are accustomed to call languages, the literary idioms of
Greece, and Rome, and India, of Italy, France, and Spain, must be
considered as artificial, rather than as natural forms of speech. The
real and natural life of language is in its dialects.

And it is in the dialects that Müller finds the twin principles of "phonetic
decay" and "dialectal regeneration" that are the pillars of his theory of linguistics
as a physical science, to be studied in a manner similar to the study of biology.
No longer was it lower class language that was to be "suffered to perish with
other things unworthy of preservation" (Dr Johnson).

The early publications of the Philological Society, which was founded in
1842, demonstrate very clearly the linguistic interests of the period, showing
how far they had moved from traditional classical preoccupations. In the
volume for 1860−61 there are several articles on English etymologies, observations on plans for the New English Dictionary, collections of obscure
English dialect forms, editions of little-known medieval texts in English and
Cornish (by Whitley Stokes), articles on exotic languages and language-
groups (such as Chinese), proposed emendations of Shakespeare and a rather
notable article on "Metrical Time, or the Rhythm of Verse, ancient and
modern" by T.F. Barham, expressing views on rhythm not dissimilar to those
of Hopkins. The following quotation from a paper by Ernest Adams, "On the
Names of the Wood-Louse," captures much of the flavour of Victorian
word-collecting:

I am informed, on the authority of a Kentish coastguardman, that
the inhabitants of his district uniformly call the creature a *Monkey-
Pee*. The explanation of this mysterious word I obtained last
summer, on exhibiting a specimen of the animal to an urchin who
was tending pigs in a rural part of Kent. He unhesitatingly
pronounced it to be a *Molti-pee*, and was supported by a young

companion who was invited to give his opinion. This is of course
the Kentish form of the Latin *multipes*. I confess I was somewhat
surprised at the time, because from that class of English boys, in a
thoroughly rural district, I had expected a lawful Saxon word
rather than a miserable specimen of corrupt Latin. It was the ghost
of Aristotle's πολυπους [polypous] troubling these shores.

This passage demonstrates the typical attitudes quite plainly. Rural speech, it
was felt, was somehow purer, more "natural," and would preserve older forms
unsullied by standardization, bookishness and artificiality. "Natural" language had an implicit association with the countryside and the soil, and the
biological metaphor of growth and decay, which was so commonly used of
language, encouraged this association. It went hand in hand with an interest in
folklore and country crafts, with Anglo-Saxon purism and with the movement
to preserve the countryside from unwanted improvements. In Hopkins's
sonnets of 1877–8, the joy and lushness of the countryside is contrasted with
the dirt and meanness of towns:

> And all is seared with trade; bleared, smeared with toil;
> And wears man's smudge and shares man's smell: the soil
> Is bare now, nor can foot feel, being shod.

Of the sea and the skylark and the town of Rhyl, he says:

> How these two shame this shallow and frail town!
> How ring right out our sordid turbid time, being pure!

. . . Hopkins in his notebooks and in his poems regretted the destruction of
the inscapes of nature. His objection to "this Victorian language" was an
objection to official and bureaucratic styles that necessarily rise up in urban
and centralized civilizations; it was part of his objection to the mean and
squalid character of industrial cities generally and his corresponding preference for the country. In this last point of view Hopkins was not unusual among
the intellectuals of his day; it was merely that he extended his views to the
sphere of language and, with typical consistency and dedication, pushed the
point as far as he could. In the country—in the weeds and the wilderness—
one can find not only beautiful words, but also that which is pure and innocent
in speech as well as in natural phenomena:

> What is all this juice and all this joy?
> A strain of earth's sweet being in the beginning

In Eden garden. — Have, get, before it cloy. . .
Innocent mind and Mayday in girl and boy,
(No. 33)

These lines, like so many others by Hopkins, can apply to language as well as
to their more obvious topic, and the corruption and degeneracy of city life and
speech are, by implication, condemned.

Of course it can be argued that Hopkins, together with the purists and the
country-worshippers, went too far. His view of the country was an idealization
and it did not take into account the harsh and poor conditions in which many
country people lived. He was a townsman, born in what was then the largest
city in the world, and his knowledge of the country was that of a privileged
outsider. But it is all the more striking for that. Few countrymen would be
likely to observe so closely and record their observations so carefully. The
bluebells and the horned violets they would take for granted, and they would
fell the aspens with never a thought, for it would be part of their daily work.
Hopkins comes to the country scenes with the fresh eye of one who does not
take them for granted, and who is moreover gifted with remarkable powers of
observation and concentration. His interest in dialect, together with the
general movement towards dialect scholarship, can be seen as part of the
Victorian town-dweller's flight to the country. The typical interest in flowers,
birds and insects, in collection of rock specimens, and in oral folk-tale is all
part of this.

It is not merely that Hopkins was *influenced* by this movement; he was
part of it. We do not know when his interest in country dialect began, but it
was probably in his schooldays. In a letter to Bridges in 1882, Hopkins
indicated that he had read Barnes's dialect poetry while he was still an
undergraduate. In his early diaries, most of the linguistic notes are on
etymology, but there are some entries on regional speech. While some of this
information may have come from personal observation, it is likely at this stage
that some of it came from reading. It is after September 1864 that the etymological notes really give way to notes on the poet's personal observation of
country usage, and there are many such notes in the later Journal. Often it
was a dialect word or phrase that took his fancy, but sometimes he was more
interested in pronunciation, and occasionally in grammar. If it was a word or
phrase that he recorded, it might be its figurative value that interested him
(e.g. *Virgin's Brier* and *Black Divers*), or it might be the sound or its
etymological associations, or just the fact that it existed. But he was interested
too in country folklore (he records stories of ghosts, fairies and mystical
experiences) and in the vocabulary of certain trades and professions.

The Journal is best known for its descriptions of natural phenomena, but it is significant that in the midst of this careful description Hopkins should have thought it worth remembering small points of regional usage—often for a few days at a time—to record in his notebooks. On 1 September 1867 several notes on speech are interspersed with description of nature:

> One tree—a beech, I think—I saw on which the ground cast up white reflection like glass or water and so far as I could see this could only come from spots of sunlight amidst the shade.
> Back to Benediction; then to Bovey by Gappath (which they pronounce Gappa).
> When I got to the middle of the common they call Knighton Heathfields (for heaths they call heathfields here) I saw the wholeness of the sky and the sun like its ace; the colours of Dartmoor were pale but else the common was edged with a frieze of trees of the brightest green and crispest shadow.
> Mr. Cleave says they call a wooden bridge over the river a *clamp*.

"I am three and twenty" wrote Hopkins, on a warm summer day in the same year. Already, long before he had developed the complex poetic style in which he sought to capture what was special and unique about natural scenes and events, we find him treasuring humble forms of speech alongside the inscapes of nature. As Grimm had urged, Hopkins was holding sacred the individualities of language.

The true language enthusiast is fascinated by the wonder of language, which in its apparently endless variety yet seems to be governed by orderly "laws." We have seen this enthusiasm in Müller and Trench, and the implications of the linguists' notions of "law" in language are as relevant to Hopkins as are the strikingly similar views of Ruskin on the "laws" of natural beauty, reflected for example in Hopkins's undergraduate essay in which the orderly regularity of leaf patterns is discussed. In 1866, Hopkins defines *law* as "finding order anywhere" and speaks of the definite *structure* of the wood-lark's song (*JP*). In the same year (*JP*) he remarks that the "organization" of the oak-tree is "difficult," and later exclaims (*JP*) that he has now found the "*law*" of the oak-leaves. Language in its rich variation is also orderly, not through an artificial order imposed from outside (as in prescriptive rules of grammar), but because of its own inner nature.

This is a simple point, but an important one. Already in the diaries Hopkins's etymological speculations are based on the perception of orderliness in the rich variety of language history. In the Journals, orderly "laws" of phonology and syntax are assumed to exist in regional speech. After 30 April

1869, he presents what amounts to a phonological analysis of the speech of
several of his colleagues. After some remarks about the Latin pronunciation of
a Sicilian priest (Hopkins finds this "instructive"), he goes on to record that
"Fr Goldie gives long *e* like short *e* merely lengthened or even opener (the
broad vowel between broad *a* and our closed *a*, the substitute for *e*, *i*, or *u*
followed by *r*)." This appears to mean that Fr Goldie pronounces the Latin
long *e* in *Deus* with a vowel similar to the Southern English vowel in *bird, hurt*,
and not with a diphthong (ei) as in Southern English *gate, train*. Hopkins goes
on to describe the pronunciation of his superior, Fr Morris (it is plainly North
Country) and . . . he describes lengthening of vowels in certain kinds of open
syllables that is still characteristic of Northern English. Hopkins noted these
regional features (and examples of "interference" from other languages) not as
mere curiosities or deviations from a more "correct" standard, but as features
which are themselves governed by regularities within the speech concerned.

Indeed, it would be hard to find a poet more acutely conscious than
Hopkins of the orderliness and pattern of language. It is implicit in his
etymological and philological notes which, as we have seen, assume a certain
orderliness in the processes of language change and even an orderliness in the
relation of sounds to the things they stand for. The same attitude is implicit in
his dialect notes, not only at the level of sound (phonology), but also at the
grammatical level.

He is a collector of words that end in the suffix *-le*. In 1869 he notes Br
Wells's *grindlestone* for 'grindstone' and in March 1872 he notes that *stickles* are
"Devonshire for the foamy tongues of water below falls." As early as 1864 we
find "wade: waddle—stride: straddle—swathe: swaddle—ming (mix):
mingle." Hopkins's later notes extended these sound-meaning relationships
to dialect words in which the same kind of pattern (*stick: stickle*; *grind: grindle*)
is exhibited and he is aware of a "vowel-change" relationship obtaining in some
of the pairs. He exploits these *-le* words most obviously in *"Pied Beauty"*
(No. 37), where he uses *dappled, couple, stipple, tackle, fickle, freckled, adazzle*
(one might also count *original*, the suffix of which has the same pronunciation).
In the second line he prefers *brinded* to *brindled*, which must be counted as a
deliberate variation in the sound-pattern of the poem; it also reminds one of
the *grind-grindle* relation of Hopkins's note on Br Wells.

It is clear that Hopkins sees the characteristics of dialectal *syntax* as
regular meaningful alternations rather than random and degenerate deviations
from a more "correct" norm. This is illustrated by his remarks on what he takes
to be the omission of the definite article in Northern English: "The omission of
the is I think an extension of the way in which we say 'Father,' 'government,'
etc: they use it when there is a relative in order to define." Hopkins appears to

mean that the North-country usage extends the "standard" omission of the
article with proper nouns, mass nouns (*milk*, *water*, etc.) and abstracts, but for
once his basic observation is wrong. The definite article is seldom actually
omitted in Northern speech, but is usually present in reduced form (often a
"glottal stop"). Later, in 1872, Hopkins describes a Lancashire youth who
"called felly/*felk* and *nave* short like *have*. *Wind* he pronounced with the *i*
long. When he began to speak quickly or descriptively he dropped or slurred
the article." Whatever Hopkins thought, it is clear that he recognized that
dialectal syntax has its own rules or "laws." Indeed, there seems to be a
connection with Hopkins's observations on the article and his practice in some
of the poetry (my italics):

> and *thrush*
> Through echoing timber does so rinse and wring
> The ear
>
> (No. 33)

> It dates from *day*
> Of his going in Galilee
> (*Deutschland*, st. 7)

> sheer plod makes *plough* down sillion
> Shine
>
> (No. 36)

> Pining, pining, till *time* when reason rambled in it
> (No. 53)

The reasons for this, and the effects it has, are more complex and variable than
has been recognized. But it is clear that in the last example Hopkins, in a poem
about a Lancashire farrier, is trying to suggest North Country language, just
as he does in *all road* (*road* = "way") later in the same poem. Even if this is not
always his purpose, the speculations in the Journal provide an important guide
to his later practice.

It is a compliment to Hopkins's observation of syntax that in current
work by the American linguist William Labov and his associates on the use and
understanding of variable syntax, an allusion made to Wright's *EDD* turns out
to refer to Hopkins's contribution. It is the sole clear example of "positive
anymore" ("anymore" used in a positive rather than in a negative sentence or in
a question): "n. Ir. A servant being instructed how to act will answer 'I will do
it any more' (G. M. H.)." Hopkins was certainly right. Positive *anymore* is
common in colloquial use in many American states ("There's a good movie at

the Regal *anymore*"), but in the British Isles it is restricted to Northern and Western parts. It is elusive and not generally known. As Hopkins observed, it occurs in the Northern part of Ireland. In my own work I have noted it only in Co. Donegal: "I'll be getting six or seven days' holiday *anymore*"; "The nights will be turning [getting longer or shorter] *anymore*." It can also occur with present rather than future reference: "Anymore [i.e. nowadays], you have to do it this way."

Most of the dialect entries in the Journal are concerned with vocabulary or pronunciation rather than syntax, and items of vocabulary are often recorded because they suggest to Hopkins a figure of speech or an analogy, or some underlying rule of language, or sound-symbolism.

In February 1869 he records the dialectal *whisket* for "basket," and in June of the same year he comments that "Br Sidgreaves has heard the high ridges of a field called *folds* and the hollow between the *drip*." These words appeal to Hopkins because they are figurative: *whisket* suggests something that is *whisked* alongside the carrier and is much more suggestive of action than *basket*. It is a "better" word than *basket* in the same way that *windhover* is better than *kestrel*. *Fold* is one of Hopkins's favourite words—both as noun and verb, in prose and poetry—and is often applied to landscape:

> Aug 6—Unusually bright. From Jeffrey Hill on the Longridge fell
> in the ridge opposite with Parlock Pike the folds and gullies with
> shadow in them were as sharp as the pleats in a new napkin (1871)

> Landscape plotted and pieced—fold, fallow and plough
> (No. 37)

> Of a fresh and following folded rank
> (No. 43)

Indeed, Hopkins is particularly fond of words that seem to him descriptive of ridges and the gullies between: *fold, drip, comb* (possibly) *drift, cleave* ("Devon cleave," No. 159, and in the prose) are but a few of them. Figurative interest is further exemplified in Br Wells's remark that the gathering of stones from the meadow was not to be done at random but *in braids* (22 February 1869) and in the earlier note on Devonshire *clamp* for a wooden bridge over a river. "*Braids*" for ordered rows suggests braids of hair, and *clamp* for bridge suggests the firm action of holding together the two banks of a river. It is noticeable too that many of the words we have discussed—and other favourite words that are not especially dialectal—are monosyllabic and ambiguously noun and verb. The basic principles discernible in Hopkins's etymological notes are also discernible here. These simple monosyllables have a rich syntactic as well as figurative potential, and they are often suggestive of clear, firm and decisive *actions*. They are plainly useful to a poet.

Otherwise, Hopkins's dialectal notes are rather varied. In January 1868 he notes that Shropshire people use *nesh* for "unwell, ailing" and records some observations of child language. Later in the same year he notes *"shrimpled up"* (of corn in dry weather) and *wants* for "moles" in Devonshire. Surely *shrimple* appeals to him because it seems to be a *portmanteau* (blend) of *shrink* and *crumple*. In 1869 he has a series of notes on vocabulary, grammar and pronunciation (including Br Wells's *grindlestone* and Fr Morris's pronunciation of Latin). He notes the Northern use of *lead* for "carry" (a field of hay, etc.), *geet* as the Northern preterite of *get*, and the expressions *top* and *lop* and *Dead Creepers* for white bryony "because it kills what it entwines." In 1870 he records a list of idiomatic expressions used by Irish priests ("I wouldn't put it past you" and so on) and describes the pronunciation of Br Gordon. In 1871 he records the Lancashire dialect of Br Wells and the vocabulary of haymaking. In March 1872 he notes the Devonshire *stickles, th'hee road* for "the high road" and *steel* for "stile." In August 1872 he comments on the Manx language, the expression *Black Divers* for cormorants, *Virgin's brier* for cankers on rose bushes, and the Lancashire vocabulary of spinning and weaving. On 17 July 1873 he records Mr Vaughan's imitation of "Cornelius the philosopher's servant":

> "—bullockin', ay and a-bullyraggin' teoo," that is bullying, using abusive words; also (as I heard afterwards) how the Queen told the Shah when he wanted one of his courtier's heads struck off for bad horsemanship at Windsor that he had better not coon ahn, that road.

This looks like a forerunner of *all road* in "Felix Randal."

Some of the most interesting entries are those which emphasize Hopkins's untiring curiosity about agricultural and industrial processes and crafts, and the language appropriate to them. He comments on the language of weaving (August 1872) and ploughing (September 1873), and in some detail on haymaking (24 July 1873):

> Robert says the first grass from the scythe is the *swathe*, then comes the *strow* (tedding), then *rowing*, then the footcocks, then breaking, then the *hubrows*, which are gathered into *hubs*, then sometimes another break and *turning*, then *rickles*, the biggest of all the cocks, which are run together into *placks*, the shapeless heaps from which the hay is carted.

The eighteenth century had devoted its efforts to establishing and codifying the huge Latinate vocabulary that English had acquired, and had largely ignored the words of the "laborious and mercantile part of the people." Hopkins, in his delight in country crafts and customs, and the underlying assumption that each activity must have its own special vocabulary with its own rich associations, shows a true nineteenth-century attitude and owes much (directly or indirectly) to the gentleman scholars who trod the country seeking out the names of the wood-louse and so on. He also owes much to the example of men like Trench, Barnes, Max Müller and Jacob Grimm. The vocabulary of the various branches of farming and its associated trades is indeed rich. There are, for instance, words for animals of different ages and sexes, for all the different parts of a plough (or any other tool) and all things associated with the activity of ploughing (or any other activity). Often these industries preserve the literal senses of words which in Standard English are used only figuratively (their "original" senses being forgotten). This is true, for example, of words like *clue* (clew) and *clinch*, which were part of the vocabulary of rope, and are used today in thatching and stack-building. To fail to use the "proper" term is the sign of the outsider, and may cause a raising of eyebrows: the use of the "correct" word in the "correct" circumstances is prescribed. Again, Hopkins the middle-class townsman, might well have been incited to this interest by reading Trench or Müller. Not only are there living dialects of regions, says Müller, but also dialects "of shepherds, of sportsmen, of soldiers or farmers," and he adds:

> I suppose there are few persons here present who could tell the exact meaning of a horse's poll, crest, withers, dock, hamstring, pastern, coronet, arm, jowl, and muzzle.

Müller goes on to quote Grimm:

> "The idiom of nomads," as Grimm says, "contains an abundant wealth of manifold expressions for sword and weapons, and for the different stages in the life of their cattle. In a more highly culti-vated language these expressions become burthensome and super-fluous. But in a peasant's mouth, the bearing, calving, falling and killing of almost every animal has its own peculiar term . . . The eye of these shepherds, who live in the free air, sees further, their ear hears more sharply, — why should their speech not have gained that living truth and variety?"

There are two major points to be made about this. First, just as there is an uncanny resemblance between Hopkins's *inscape* and Grimm's individuality of dialects, so too there is a great deal implicit in this quotation that relates closely to Hopkins's notions of *in-earnestness* in the use of language. The speech of peasants, according to Grimm, has "living truth and variety." Its usage is more *true* and more sincere than the generalized terms of standard speech because it is particularized and accurate. In its natural context, it leaves no room for doubt or vagueness about its meaning. The words used by the blacksmith, the farmer, or the sailor have about them the smell and feel and flavour of their crafts. They cannot lie. Hopkins is interested in these words for their own sake, but also because he feels that, if he can use them aptly, they will help him to capture accurately the inscapes of the world. The second point is that these specialized and dialect usages can be seen as helping to build up a new poetic vocabulary to replace the diction of the standard model that Hopkins rejected. Words like *pash, fettle, mammock* and *sillion* help to give Hopkins's poetry its special flavour: that which marks it out as different from all other poetry. His poetry is *arch-especial* in this sense, as the music of Purcell seemed to be to him. In his language-*inscape* he seems to owe more to nineteenth-century linguistic scholarship than to any other single source.

We are mainly concerned . . . with the diction of Hopkins's mature poetry and the current language that he believed to be its basis. However, while we are discussing the poet's interest in dialect and his concern with using language appropriate to the subject in hand, it is necessary to consider the special style that he developed up to 1875 in the descriptive prose of his Journal. This highly developed prose, carefully adapted to the purpose of detailed description of natural events and phenomena, and clearly intended to communicate feeling, movement, texture, colour, tactile and visual impression, is an important forerunner of the mature poetry. Just as there is a vocabulary appropriate to the crafts of the farmer, the weaver or the blacksmith, so there has to be a vocabulary in which natural phenomena can be described in a way appropriate to one who professes the craft of language, that is, a writer of poetry. This appropriate vocabulary cannot be taken over in full from any established discipline. The terminology of the natural sciences and linguistics will be too abstract, too generalized; it will not communicate the uniqueness of particular events and insights. The vocabulary of literary and art criticism may be slightly more suitable, but it will also be defective in some respects, particularly in the value-judgements that tend to be incorporated in the meanings of many of its terms, which must be inappropriate for pure description. For the enormously difficult art of descriptive prose, Hopkins requires a language that is simple and unaffected and at the same time precise and unambiguous. In a little-known essay written in 1959, Angus McIntosh argued that the English grammatical tradition gave Hopkins considerable problems in his poetry. The idea that words mean "things or relations of things" (*JP*) and the necessity to think of subject and action as distinct, make the notion of *inscape* difficult for us to grasp and for Hopkins to explain. There is no doubt that *inscape* is at least as much concerned with processes as it is with things, and it becomes necessary for Hopkins to develop a very careful and characteristic way of talking in prose about processes. In the very early note on *horn* (1864) he is already beginning to concern himself with movements and processes as properties of the "thing" he is talking about:

> it may be regarded as a projection, a climax, a badge of strength, power or vigour, a tapering body, a spiral . . . something sprouting up, something to thrust or push with . . .

But it is particularly clear that the prose of the later Journal is developed largely for the description of processes, and in the following quotation we can see some of the vocabulary that Hopkins had found it necessary to adapt or invent:

> A beautiful instance of inscape sided on the slide, that is a successive sidings of one inscape is seen in the behaviour of the flag flower from the shut bud to the full blowing: each term you can distinguish is beautiful in itself and of course if the whole "behaviour" were gathered up and so stalled it would have a beauty of all the higher degree.

Hopkins has here devised for himself an "enabling" vocabulary. Without the terms *inscape*, *siding*, *behaviour*, *stalled*, he could not describe this process and effect nearly so precisely. To dispense with the special vocabuary would mean that he would either have to start with the flower itself ("the flag flower is beautiful at every stage of its development . . . ") or use more conventional general terms ("stage" for *siding*; "process" for *behaviour* and so on). If he chose the first alternative, it would be more difficult for him to generalize in the latter part of the passage, and the description would be more verbose and less precise. If he chose the second alternative, his vocabulary would not be *in-earnest*, it would mislead; "if the whole *process* were gathered up and so *fixed*" would be wrong because Hopkins is not thinking of an abstract process that imposes itself on the flower, but of the flower itself as being and *behaving*. It is not a "process," nor is the behaviour gathered up and "fixed." I can think of no word but *stalled* that will say what Hopkins means to say without suggesting further meanings that he does not intend.

Hopkins's eye for fine detail is remarkable, and the descriptions in his Journal are careful and precise. The key words are always *inscape* and *instress*;

he is concerned not with static objects alone, but with relationships, processes and metamorphoses. One of his interests is the formation of vapour from liquids, and there is a remarkable passage (1871) in which he associates the forming of clouds with the bubbling of molten chocolate:

> I have been watching clouds this spring and evaporation, for instance over our Lenten chocolate . . . The throes can be perceived/like the thrills of a candle in the socket: this is precisely to *reech*, whence *reek*. They may by a breath of air be laid again and then shew like grey wisps on the surface . . . They seem to be drawn off the chocolate as you might take up a napkin between your fingers that covered something, not so much from here or there as from the whole surface at one reech . . . The film seems to rise not quite simultaneously but to peel off as if you were tearing cloth; then giving an end forward like the corner of a handkerchief and beginning to coil it makes a long wavy hose you may sometimes look down, as a ribbon or a carpenter's shaving may be made to do. Higher running into frets and silvering in the sun with the endless coiling, the soft bound of the general motion and yet the side lurches sliding into some particular pitch it makes a baffling and charming sight. —Clouds however solid they may look far off are I think wholly made of film in the sheet or in the tuft. The bright woolpacks that pelt before a gale in a clear sky are in the tuft and you can see the wind unravelling them and rending them finer than any sponge till within one easy reach overhead they are morselled to nothing and consumed—it depends of course on their size. Possibly each tuft in forepitch or in origin is quained and a crystal. Rarer and wilder packs have sometimes film in the sheet, which may be caught as it turns on the edge of the cloud like an outlying eyebrow. The one in which I saw this was in a north-east wind, solid but not crisp, white like the white of egg, and bloated-looking.
>
> (*JP*)

Like many of Hopkins's descriptions, this passage is difficult to follow, not least because of the vocabulary. Norman MacKenzie suggests that one reason for this kind of difficulty is that so many of Hopkins's descriptive terms are borrowed from dialect. This is certainly true of *reech*, although Hopkins seems to use it in a sense rather different from the dialectal one of "smoke"; and suggestive of the phonetically similar *retch* (the chocolate is *heaving*). Some of the other usages, however, are not especially "dialectal." They are merely words from the current language that Hopkins has pressed into service and used in rather special senses that deviate from everyday usage. Words like *throes* and *thrills* are used in a literal (rather than the usual metaphorical) sense; *coil*, *fret*, *pitch*, *forepitch*, *quained* are characteristic Hopkinsian words, some of them used in the poetry as well as the prose; *caught* is used as it is in the first line of "The Windhover" (how much weaker the prose would be if "perceived" were used); *in the sheet* and *in the tuft* are Hopkins's expressions for two types of cloud formations, and they are strongly suggestive of the kind of terms that might be used in some craft or industry to refer to metal (or some such thing) in its different states. Certainly, this is prose that could have been written by no one except Hopkins.

Professor MacKenzie has cited many other examples in the Journal in which dialectal influence seems likely, for example, the use of *lodged* and *shock* in the following:

> The bluebells in your hand baffle you with their inscape, made to every sense: if you draw your fingers through them they are lodged and struggle with a shock of wet heads.

It is possible, as MacKenzie suggests, that *lodged* is from the dialectal *lodge* (to lie flat, of corn or grass; to be beaten down by wind or rain: Wright) and *shock* from the Southern and West Country word for a *stook* of corn. But *lodged* may simply mean "stuck fast" and although Hopkins uses *shocks* for "stooks" in his poetry (No. 32) a "shock of hair" is also a familiar expression. MacKenzie also points out the use of *tretted* (from *treat* or *trete*: "the second quality of bran") in "tretted mossy clouds" (*JP*) and "tretted like open sponge or light bread-crumb" (*JP*); and he discusses the remarkable phrase: "a *pash* of soap-sud-coloured gummy *bim-beams*" (*JP*). Here, MacKenzie suggests that *pash* is the dialectal word for a medley, or collection of crushed or broken fragments, and connects *bim-beams* with the Somerset *bimboms* ("originally referring to church bells, but applied to anything dangling down, such as tassels, drops of rain hanging from a rail, or icicles").

It is indeed probable that many of these usages originate in country dialect, but it is also important to note that when Hopkins uses them, or variants of them, he does not necessarily use them as they are used in their original dialect. In prose and poetry alike, his overwhelming desire is to select the word that most perfectly captures the present inscape. Country words will obviously be valuable for this, but Hopkins is always influenced by the belief that sound and sense are related. *Pash* and *bim-beams* are suggestive of sound, colour and texture, and are associated in phonetic pattern with other words in the language (*splash, pom-pom*). Therefore, even when we cannot trace a dialectal origin for such words, we can sense what they mean in context from their sound. In his prose, as in his poetry, Hopkins aims at earnestness, sincerity, honesty. When the prose is purely descriptive, this means in effect using language which is accurate and which correctly and memorably communicates the inscape of the sight or event that gave rise to it. Hopkins's descriptive prose is a special language devised by him for the special purpose of recording precise impressions and, like the poetry, it is largely Anglo-Saxon in character.

ELLEN EVE FRANK

"The Poetry Of Architecture"

THE NOTE-BOOKS: ARCHITECTURE AND ETYMOLOGY

If we leaf through Hopkins's notebooks, any surprise we may have at discovering that architecture has much to do with Hopkins's poetic, should subside: Hopkins's own sketches—of Norman and Gothic windows, stairs, tracery and transoms, arches and columns—lace the pages of his journals, either illustrating his often technical descriptions of buildings, or just oddly afloat between his discussions of word roots, thoughts, or weather observations. In the early Diaries alone there are at least two dozen verbal descriptions and more than a dozen drawings in one brief journal-year. While it is not at all extraordinary that Hopkins took an interest in architecture, especially since at Oxford he was in the midst of clamor and controversy over new college buildings, his interest is not to be explained so simply; and it seems fair to ask what relationship Hopkins's interest in architecture may have to his fascination with words and with nature.

At first it appears that Hopkins's two concerns, with architecture and with words, are discrete, and this seems to be confirmed by the apparent randomness of some journal entries. One such instance is a sequence of three recordings, the first concerning etymology, the second architecture, the third again etymology:

> *Flos, flower, blow, bloom, blossom.* Original meaning to be inflated, to swell as the bud does into the flower. Also φλέω [phléo]

From *Literary Architecture: Essays Toward a Tradition*. © 1979 by The Regents of the University of California. University of California Press, 1979. Originally entitled "'The Poetry of Architecture': Gerard Manley Hopkins."

(*abundo*) and *flaw* (storm), *flare* (English not Latin).

[Drawing of window given]
Note. There is now going on what has no parallel that I know of in history of art. Byzantine or Romanesque Architecture started from ruins of Roman, became itself beautiful style, and died, as Ruskin says, only in giving birth to another more beautiful than itself, Gothic. The Renaissance appears now to be in the process of being succeeded by a spontaneous Byzantinesque style, retaining still some of bad features (such as pilasters, rustic-work etc.) of the Renaissance. These it will throw aside. Its capitals are already, as in Romanesque art, most beautiful. Whether then modern Gothic or this spontaneous style conquer does not so much matter, for it is only natural for latter to lead to a modern spontaneous Gothic, as in middle ages, only that the latter is putting off what we might be or rather are doing now. Or the two may coalesce.

Tāle (galaktos), glagos, *lac* (lactis), *leglin* (pail), *milk*, i.e., *mlik*. [*The Journals and Papers of Gerard Manley Hopkins*; all further references to this text will be abbreviated JP.] (1863)

Hopkins's comment, "There is now going on what has no parallel that I know of in history of art," teases us and distracts us. While Hopkins disclaims a parallel between the arts, he covertly structures one himself: his imagery darts out allusive sparks, the life-death-rebirth cycle of the Phoenix or some combative contest between forces, but the architectural event he nonetheless renders organic, natural, evolutionary; and the artist, for instance the unspecified architect, absents himself from this growth of style as if such growth were *sui generis*, an activity which he could only interfere with, never control. So, too, a paler Hopkins than the one we know unwinds the history of words, as if their growth were also evolutionary. Some word roots, perhaps the phonic *flo, blo, fla*, like certain architectural motifs, notably capitals and pilasters, persist while meaning, even usage, changes; other roots and motifs fade into retirement, outmoded. So Hopkins pursues one concern through twin modes: whether patterned in words or in architecture, what Hopkins looks for and describes is the retention, transition, revival of forms, calling for remarks on the capacity for development or change, or lamenting a regress from the structural to the ornamental.

Does not a Hopkins who documents the etymology of words as he does the history of architectural style also view words as building materials, concrete and visible, of structure-poems? From the ruins of language, does he not superintend the growth of a new style, a gardener-architect so tending vestigial remains that the audience may recover the origin of forms or words, even witness their rebirth or reinvigoration? In this Hopkins is like those writers of the earliest *ars memorativa* treatises who formed images for words from primitive etymological dissection of the word itself, hopeful that readers would remember a more vivid past. In his early Diaries Hopkins jotted down a poetic stanza in which the speaker threatens to topple a poem, to so dislodge the brickish building materials that poem and monument, one and the same, crumble in ruin.

> Let me now
> Jolt
> Shake and unset your morticed metaphors.
> The hand draws off the glove; the acorn-cup
> Drops the fruit out; the duct runs dry or breaks;
> The stranded keel and kelson warp apart;
>
> (JP, 1864)

Concretized, his metaphors also cling to their etymological past: elsewhere in his journals Hopkins had remarked the origin of *keel*.

> *Skill* etc.
> Primary meaning, to divide, cut apart. *Skill*, discernment. To *keel*, to skim. *Keel*, that part of a ship which cuts a way through the water. *Skull*, an oar which skims the water.
>
> (JP, 1864)

A diacritical reading of the poem, demanded by the language itself, recovers primary word meanings so that reading becomes a kind of unbuilding, un-"morticing" of metaphors in order that they release a meaning submerged by time and usage. Hopkins's words and images, in their etymological origins, mime the idea they express: all mean and accomplish, in this journal fragment, an undoing, a dissection; reading becomes and requires analysis of the poem as a built structure. And that analysis is inseparable from remembering.

We might expect Hopkins's word accounts to fill his journals, but such is not the case. What had been incidental, the nature and weather observations, becomes normative; and Hopkins finally declares the journals his "weather record." The takeover does not, however, exhaust architecture. Instead themes, images, descriptions architectural begin to partner nature and weather descriptions. However, the partnership is curiously one-way. The architectural descriptions rarely, if ever, evoke, either mimetically or thematically, the natural. In fact, Hopkins's architectural discussions discover a scientific rigor, a demand for exactitude and precision of description such that

technical terms are required so as to substantiate for us the kind of knowledge
Hopkins possesses. Typical is Hopkins's record of the Cathedral at Exeter:

> Some notes to remember it by—two Norman towers; east of them
> choir, in 7 bays and a little one; nave, in 7, west; nave windows in
> basement story broad, geometrical
>
> (JP, 1874)

or his account of William Butterfield's Babbacombe Church:

> the windows scattered; steeple rather detached . . . with an odd
> openwork diaper of freestone over marble pieces on the tower. . . .
> There is a hood of the same diaper at the east-end gable from the
> spring of the arch of the east window about upward. Tracery all
> simple. Inside chancel-arch much as at St. Alban's, Holborn.
>
> (JP, 1874)

Architectural terminology does not crop up only when Hopkins is
recording throughout the notebooks his experiences of architecture. On the
contrary, that terminology breeds and infiltrates, as if, in his desire for
accurate, precise descriptions of the most minute natural forms or weather
events, it is architectural terms that proffer themselves, irresistibly. Hopkins
perceives nature as, or reconstructs her into, edifices: she has ribs, arches,
traceries, transoms; she frets, copes, cusps, is fluted, moulded, vaulted; her
elements—air, water—form into cloud, dew, then into chips of quarried
building stone; she is seen in patterns of horizontal bands of colored stone as if
on a polychromatic church wall.

Perhaps the architectural vocabulary assumes the burden left over from
abandoned etymological studies; perhaps, too, Hopkins's word curiosity
expresses itself in his search for nature-descriptive terms and Hopkins turns to
architectural language and images to facilitate these descriptions:

> On this day the clouds were lovely. Opposite the sun between 10
> and 11 was the disshevelled cloud [sic] on page opposite. The
> clouds were repeatedly formed in horizontal ribs. At a distance
> their straightness of line was wonderful. In passing overhead they
> were something as in the (now) opposite page, the ribs granulated
> delicately the splits fretted with lacy curves and honeycomb work,
> the laws of which were exquisitely traced.
>
> (JP, 1864)

Always Hopkins is suggesting an inhabitant/structure relationship: in his
nature descriptions, it is nature which moves and shifts, as in the passage

above; in his architectural descriptions, since architecture as completed structure is static, the inhabitant must shift in order to enjoy the optical varieties he
does in a kinetic nature. In "To Oxford" optical illusion depends on the *inventio*
of the speaker:

> Thus, I come underneath this chapel-side,
> So that the mason's levels, courses, all
> The vigorous horizontals, each way fall
> In bows above my head, as falsified
> By visual compulsion, till I hide
> The steep-up roof at last behind the small
> Eclipsing parapet; yet above the wall
> The sumptuous ridge-crest leave to poise and ride
>
> (Poem 12)

But what happens to nature imagery in this poem and others? May we not
read it as description which, evoking the architectural, throws us back to the
poet's perceiving mind, inhabitant of a world which he strangely rebuilds?
Not quite. In "That Nature is a Heraclitean Fire and of the comfort of the
Resurrection," for instance, a transposition of nature into architecture is indeed threatened, but nature does not relinquish her identity for an architectural one:

> Down roughcast, down dazzling whitewash, ' wherever
>   an elm arches,
> Shivelights and shadowtackle in long ' lashes lace,
>   lance, and pair.
>
> (Poem 72)

The conversion of natural matter into architectural rarely, if ever, violates or
abandons the one for the other, nature for architecture or architecture for
nature. Instead the process of conversion discovers, releases, conveys energy,
and that energy is expressed as poetic simile, whether in the poems themselves
or in the descriptions which fill the notebooks. And while the notebook
descriptions remind us of Constable's or Turner's, it is in the unrelenting
search for simile that Hopkins becomes more than scientific naturalist.

While a completed architectural structure is static from the viewer's
stance, as artifact it is dynamic, for its final form depends upon the disposition
of stresses, themselves active. This stressful dynamism of architecture has
much to do with its suitability as analogue for nature. In one passage in his
journals, Hopkins rebuilds a rock-wall into a structure architectural and then

not only remarks the internal stresses of that structure, but suggests as well the function of those stresses when the newly architectural and the natural collide:

> The seawall is picturesque and handsome from below—it is built of white and red and blue blocks and with a brim or lip or cornice or coping curved round to beetle over and throw back the spray without letting it break on the walk above: this shape and colour give it an Egyptian look.—The laps of running foam striking the sea-wall double on themselves and return in nearly the same order and shape in which they came. This is mechanical reflection and is the same as optical: indeed all nature is mechanical, but then it is not seen that mechanics contain that which is beyond mechanics.
>
> (JP, 1874)

If we ignore for the moment the enigmatic, passive construction—"but then it is not seen that mechanics contain that which is beyond mechanics"—we discover what seems a seductively simple progression in Hopkins's thinking. Hopkins begins with an evaluation, the connotative spin-offs of the scene: the seawall is "picturesque and handsome." Yet his explanation is not evaluative but formalistic: the seawall is picturesque and handsome because of its construction. And curiously, its built form reveals and contains motive: its "brim or lip or cornice or coping" mechanically controls the spray, so that what is formalistic is not that alone but is also in some teleological way, mechanical. For Hopkins, nature and architecture are individually and inter-actively each mechanical; but by introducing the words *reflection* and *optical*, Hopkins games with us. While the interaction of wall and water may be a mechanical reflection, *reflection* picks up from *optical* another meaning, not thought rumination but reflection as sighting. Again Hopkins's description begs for an observer, someone to so sight the seawall: something cannot be optical, or by implication, mechanical, without being seen. And it is then that Hopkins, by innuendo, plays with the distinction between visual and religious perception. The seeing of structure, the recognition of mechanics—one's optical perception—is, potentially at least, a divine or religious act such that we suppose Hopkins to be indicting others, not himself, when he remarks "but then it is not seen that mechanics contain that which is beyond mechanics."

At times, as in the seawall passage above, Hopkins's verbs expose and establish for us the dynamic action he seeks to describe; *strike, double, return*, like Hopkins's verbs elsewhere, define the mechanism as one of action and reaction. If the image Hopkins is attracted to is not in the midst of such action at the time of the description, Hopkins often speculatively remakes it or convinces himself, by some slowing down of time, that he can see in a moment the action of years; and in his reconstructions, mechanical action may explain growth and evaluation, and architectural simile may specify the structure and form of that growth. In recording an expedition to North Barrule, Hopkins notes holes in rocks, conceives of them as architectural shapes:

> Round holes are scooped in the rocks smooth and true like turning: they look like the hollow of a vault or a bowl. I saw and sketched as well as in the rain I could one of them that was in the making: a blade of water played on it and shaping to it spun off making a bold big white bow coiling its edge over and splaying into ribs.
>
> (JP, 1873)

Part of Hopkins's expression of interaction depends upon an intricate structuring of analogies or images in which ethereal elements are rendered concrete, here water as "blade," then the entire water spray as a "bow" and finally "ribs." Hopkins's tools are like press moulds, themselves shaped in the same pattern as the final form of the object they in fact help make: the water makes and takes its form from the hole, the bow and ribs of a ribbed vault. Moreover, Hopkins often makes active what is inert. In recalling Denbigh Hill, Hopkins remembers the ruins which lay before him:

> Castle ruins, which crown the hill, were punched out in arches and half arches by bright breaks and eyelets of daylight. We went up to the castle but not in: standing before the gateway I had an instress which only the true old work gives from the strong and noble inscape of the pointedarch [sic].
>
> (JP, 1875)

Background sky becomes mechanically active: it "punches" out, not only silhouetting but shaping, moulding the ruins. Foreground and background vie with each other in what seems an optical equivocation, the background becoming a constructional member of the picture. The interaction of sky and ruin, then, makes a percussive impact upon Hopkins as viewer: "I had an instress," his statement of response, is attributed to the emotional or aesthetic richness of architectural form, the pointed arch. In this context, Hopkins's terms *instress* and *inscape*—involving as they do such obvious distinctions between inner and outer, the accessibility or interpenetrability of forms—are themselves not only mechanical, percussive action and reaction but, in the broadest sense, also architectural.

In order for things to strike, to hit, to punch, Hopkins continually converts the insubstantial into the substantial. Indeed, does not the notion of

poetic stress suggest that words, like objects in nature, also *strike?* that they
have a mechanical, hence optical, hence divine import? Hopkins is explicit
that perception, even of words, is percussive: "The image (of sight or sound or
scapes of the other senses), which is in fact physical and a refined energy
accenting the nerves, a word to oneself, an inchoate word" (JP, 1868). It is no
surprise, then, that a thing may word itself, that nouns, in taking on charges,
become verbs, that things become their mechanical action or architectural
shape. Images gain in density, in weight, in action; and oddly, in assuming
purpose, as the seawall or water blade, they also assume a will and dynamism of
their own. There is also a kind of medieval eye-ing of the object, and an eye-ing
back, by the object, of the viewer. Hopkins remarks that "what you look hard
at seems to look hard at you, hence the true and false instress of nature" (JP,
1871). Hopkins is careful to hedge: "seems to look hard at you." But if this
seeming were simply a projection by Hopkins as observer, Hopkins would be
the initiator of the dynamic interchange and that would be to doubt God's
authority. Likewise, the kinds of percussive reverberations or mechanical
interplay would then lose their physical stress; we must assume Hopkins to be
literal even in his speculation. It seems that the stressful quality of interaction
in fact depends upon its being physical; elements solidify into matter, action
into assertion, making into moulding, and writing or speaking into physical
striking. "Fineness, proportion of feature comes from a moulding force which
succeeds in asserting itself over the resistance of cumbersome or restraining
matter." Intensity of imagery, perhaps the life of Hopkins's poetry, depends
upon the physical injunction of felt things, senses, nature artifacts. Just as
artist may mould, so may soul shape; and just as rocks may be matter, so, too,
it seems, may words and ideas assume density, duration, resistance, resilience;
and the viewer-poet perceives tension, distortion, perspective, always in a
stressed relationship with the things around him.

There is one final relationship Hopkins establishes between architecture
and nature which I have yet to mention. It is the notion of complement: to
construct nature churches, to structure—verbally—proximity between nature
and architecture, to describe the impact architecture and nature each have
on the other in any given scene—all suggest that something is gained in the
way of beauty by the partnership between the man-made and the natural.

> Boughs being prunèd, birds preened, show more fair;
> To grace them spires are shaped with corner squinches;
> Enrichèd posts are chamfer'd; everywhere
>   He heightens worth who guardedly diminishes;
> Diamonds are better cut; who pare, repair;

> Is statuary rated by its inches?
> Thus we shall profit, while gold coinage still
> Is worth and current with a lessen'd mill.
>
> (Poem 96, vii)

While it seems that Hopkins creates a *pas de deux* relationship between architecture as support and nature as prima ballerina, he also argues for refinement, moderation, spareness. And for such an aesthetic value system, an architectural model is once again attractive. Poet-architect must complement, true; but more than that, he must "prune," "shape," "chamfer," "pare" and "repair." It is to Hopkins's poetic theory, then, and to the special richness and suggestiveness of the architectural analogue as he so conceived it, that we shall now turn.

HOPKINS'S POETIC THEORY: ARCHITECTURE'S "FINER EDGE"

Hopkins's remarks on poetic theory are sparse and scattered, confided in letters, preparatory lecture notes, or early Oxford essays. Nevertheless, even in these fugitive writings, we find that architecture is valuable to Hopkins as art analogue. Hopkins's architectural citings, in the context of his poetic theory, appear two ways, either as terminology or as clarifying illustration.

Hopkins's distinction between prose and poetry hinges on architectural concepts: "But what the character of poetry is will be found best by looking at the structure of verse" (JP, 1865). It might help us, for the moment, to recall Hopkins's discussion of the seawall; just as the picturesque character of the wall of rock was explained in formalistic and functional terms, so Hopkins explains poetic character—poetry's moral/ethical nature as well as aesthetic distinctiveness—through a formalistic analysis. Structure determines character. That structure, what Hopkins subsequently refers to as construction, is controllable, man-made; more specifically, it consists of "continuous parallelism" of two sorts, the "marked" or abrupt, and the "gradual," "chromatic," a "chiaroscuro" parallelism. We cannot help but recall Walter Pater's important remarks on literary style:

> The otiose, the facile, surplusage: why are these abhorrent to the true literary artist, except because in literary as in all other art, structure is all-important, felt, or painfully missed, everywhere?—that architectural conception of work, which foresees the end in the beginning and never loses sight of it.

Pater, too, regarded words in a color sense, remarking that "the elementary particles of language will be realized as colour and light and shade through his [the writer's] scholarly living in the full sense of them." What is significant about Hopkins's rendering is that the chiaroscuro of Pater, the soul rather than the mind of style, is also conceived of as structural. In this instance, Hopkins is consistent with contemporary architectural theorists who would also dismiss Paterian chiaroscuro in favor of what is called constructional color or constructional polychromy, color initiative of or contributing to structural organization of a building.

As architectural style and language had shared, for Hopkins, organic life, both evolving in birth, death, rebirth patterns, so architecture in the context of Hopkins's poetic theory distinguishes itself from the organic, and is valued, in part, as structured or constructed artifice:

> The artificial part of poetry, perhaps we shall be right to say all
> artifice, reduces itself to the principle of parallelism. The structure
> of poetry is that of continuous parallelism.
>
> (JP, 1865)

But something curious happens: architecture, although artificial structure, retains for Hopkins its generative capacities; and although architecture remains an art form structurally distinct from that of literature, what is architectural in literature begets wholly literary and expressive offspring. "The more marked parallelism in structure whether of elaboration or emphasis begets more marked parallelism in the words and sense" (JP, 1865). Similarly, "an emphasis of structure stronger than the common construction of sentences gives asks for an emphasis of expression stronger" (JP, 1865). In this way, Hopkins makes causal and fathering what had only been analogous in his theory of language development. In fact, it is structure which draws the reader's attention to syllabic stress and emphasis.

Although Hopkins was not to continue to use the word *structure* to describe the character of verse, he was nonetheless to use an expression also architectural, *construction*. And construction, like structure, assumes an aesthetic and ethical charge: rigorous construction in poetry is an antidote to what is licentious in English verse. While Hopkins means "licentious" literally as verbal excess, like the word *character*, *licentious* is rich with moral suggestiveness. Hopkins's pertinent remarks occur in a letter to Bridges in which Hopkins defends himself against the charge of lawlessness in verse: referring to *The Wreck of the Deutschland*, Hopkins asks Bridges to have a second look.

> If you look again you will see. So that I may say my apparent
> licences are counterbalanced, and more, by my strictness. In fact

all English verse, except Milton's, almost, offends me as "licentious." Remember this.
    [*The Letters of Gerard Manley Hopkins to Robert Bridges*; all further
        references to this text will be abbreviated LB.] (1877)

Rigorous construction is prophylactic, in part because it calls attention to
itself; and therefore what is libertine in verse is thrown into structural relief.
We have the sense that Hopkins's verse structures react against the licentious
as against a form of opulence and ease, poetic mellifluousness which is so
smooth that it may act on a reader without the reader's awareness because it
does not percussively jar him to contend with it. Licentious verse, then, is at
once lawless and seductive, achieving a kind of surface perfection. Hopkins
advocates correction; and verse, the sick patient, must recover in an unusual
way.

>   Perfection is dangerous because it is deceptive. Art slips back while
>   bearing, in its distribution of tone, or harmony, the look of a high
>   civilization towards barbarism. Recovery must be by a breaking
>   up, a violence, such as was the Preraphaelite school.
>
>   (JP, 1864)

Mending itself is abrasive, jarring, sparring. We recall the Hopkins who
"unmortices" metaphors, whose rhythm is abrupt, whose images strike the
reader; and perhaps we begin to conceive a poet who values the imperfect
artifact which testifies to being man-made because it does not tempt us as a
false Una would. One's poetic building involves analytic unbuilding: it is
little wonder that a Hopkins poem demands a diacritical reading. Dissection
as poetic process forces the reader to look at and respect a poem's structure; it
allows him not only to make demands—that the metaphors and images
relinquish or yield up their primary and secondary meanings along with their
past—but to judge a poem's worth on the basis of the result. It is in this
context that Hopkins feared being misunderstood, that is, misread. For this
reason also, it seems, Hopkins worried over prescriptive methods, how to go
about informing the reader of the proper way to read his poems. Again
Hopkins turns to the architectonic as correction, a poem's construction. In
1887 Hopkins wrote of the matter to Bridges,

>   I do myself think, I may say, that it would be an immense advance
>   in notation (so to call it) in writing as the record of speech, to
>   distinguish the subject, verb, object, and in general to express the
>   construction to the eye; as is done already partly in punctuation by
>   everybody, partly in capitals by the Germans, more fully in

accentuation by the Hebrews. And I daresay it will come. But it
would, I think, not do for me: it seems a confession of unin-
telligibility. And yet I don't know. At all events there is a
difference.

(LB, 1887)

Despite his ambivalence, Hopkins presents the appropriate notation to Bridges. It seems that his request, too, for visible construction concedes the possibility of a non-percussive reader-poem relationship, undesirable as it is: words
"are really matter open and indifferent," they may fall without striking the
reader. In calling attention to construction, Hopkins assures himself of
making a percussive impact. Oddly enough, the poem in question is one
whose metaphors mime its theoretic concerns. The first stanza of "Harry
Ploughman" is striking.

> Hard as hurdle arms, with a broth of goldish flue
> Breathed round; the rack of ribs; the scooped flank; lank
> Rope-over thigh; knee-nave; and barrelled shank—
>   Head and foot, shoulder and shank—
> By a grey eye's heed steered well, one crew, fall to;
> Stand at stress. Each limb's barrowy brawn, his thew
> That onewhere curded, onewhere sucked or sank—
>   Soared ór sánk—,
> Though as a beechbole firm, finds his, as at a rollcall, rank
> And features, in flesh, what deed he each must do—
>   His sinew-service where do.
>
> (Poem 71)

Hopkins's poem which expresses "construction to the eye" in terms of poetic
structure also expresses another kind of visible construction, the cathedral
body, the "bone-house" of Harry Ploughman himself. In such an instance,
architecture provides a reservoir of imagery capable of imitating the artistic
intent of the poem. To cathedralize Harry further suggests what we might call
stressed harmony: individual, faith, nature are each in service to the other,
each revered. And in service to them all, what in fact structures their
interrelationship, is the mechanical, either the literal motion of interaction
"that onewhere curded, onewhere sucked or sank—Soared ór sánk" or the
motion of poetic stress and syntax. Is it surprising, then, that a metaphor for a
nature destructive, questioning harmony, physical and religious, among man,
nature, and God, should also be architectural? While cathedralizing Harry in
"sinew-service" to God, Hopkins decathedralizes a God destructive. He does

so, however, only from a human perspective; from a divine one, God still sees
harmony and that harmony expresses itself as a structural, architectural whole:

> Thy unchancelling poising palms were weighing the worth,
>   Thou martyr-master: in thy sight
> Storm flakes were scroll-leaved flowers, lily showers—sweet
>   heaven was astrew in them.
>
> (Poem 28, stanza 21)

While the storm event is not neutral, it appears so because evaluation of it is
relative: to God storm flakes are like Gothic ornamentation; to the nuns at sea
on the *Deutschland* they were something very different. It seems, then, that
to see construction, structural and ornamental, is to perceive harmony and
beauty; not to see it, that is not to see the constructional order in Hopkins's
poetry or in nature, is not to see divinity, harmony, beauty.

While we have been speaking of Hopkins's "visible" construction, we
have yet to look at the elements of that construction, at least in any way other
than a metaphorical one. The elements Hopkins wished to make visible, he in
fact made concrete. In his notes on rhetoric, appropriately titled for our
purpose "Rhythm and other structural parts," Hopkins gives to his building
materials—syllables—architectural characteristics: their presence is physical,
they have weight, strength, density; and they exist in an architecturally
constructed universe which concedes only two spatial alternatives, interiors
and exteriors, what Hopkins simply calls indoor and outdoor:

> [There are] two kinds [of accented syllables]: that of *pitch* (tonic)
> and that *of stress* (emphatic). We may think of words as heavy
> bodies, as indoor or out of door objects of nature or man's art. Now
> every visible palpable body has a centre of gravity round which it is
> in balance and a centre of illumination or *highspot* or *quickspot* up to
> which it is lighted and down to which it is shaded. The centre of
> gravity is like the accent of stress, the highspot like the accent of
> pitch, for pitch is like light and colour, stress like weight.
>
> (JP)

Hopkins's poetic building blocks are substantial; language is not only structurally architectural, it partakes of the same physical characteristics as do the
actual building materials of architecture, having weight, being subject to
gravity, balance, stress, receiving light as accent. We may wonder whether the
analogy is structural in other ways: are the stresses directional, constructional?

To this point, Hopkins remarks that not the "length" but the "strength" of English syllables matters; and he adds:

> But besides the stress or emphasis and pitch or intonation of single syllables one against another, there is a stress or emphasis and a pitch or intonation running through the sentence and setting word against word as stronger or as higher pitched.
>
> (JP)

We have, it seems, a poetic architecture which is mechanically engineered, a system of stresses, of words, syllables pitched, set one against another. The timing of Hopkins's description appropriately recalls the physical action of Harry Ploughman, "By a grey eye's heed steered well, one crew, fall to;/Stand at stress." We remember, too, the density, the direction, the stress and weight of Hopkins's nature descriptions. Throughout, the poetic clash of stresses and syllables one against another suggests the density and compression of architectural structures. In a poem such as "Inversnaid," a poem we would think un-architectural, all these architectonic elements combine; and while the final poem is sonorous and compelling in rhythm, it is built of clashing stresses, of syllables striking against each other, piled on each other, each in a stressful relationship to what precedes and what follows. "Flutes," a word at once musical and architectural, stands at stress, receiving the weight and energy of the motion which builds to it, suspending us, holding us mid-air, before the softer falling home.

> This darksome burn, horseback brown,
> His rollrock highroad roaring down,
> In coop and in comb the fleece of his foam
> Flutes and low to the lake falls home.
> (Poem 56)

As syllables become transformed into matter, so they cease to exist in a neutral relationship to the poet; rather, weighted and occupying space, they seem cumbersome, to be contended with even by the skilled poet, as he tries to construct them into a poetic whole. Poet as architect must be stonemason as well: "Fineness, proportion of feature," Hopkins comments, "comes from a moulding force which succeeds in asserting itself over the resistance of cumbersome or restraining matter" [*Further Letters of Gerard Manley Hopkins including his Correspondence with Coventry Patmore*; 1883]. Hopkins recognizes the battle for poet and for architect; . . .

THE "ACHIEVE" AND "MASTERY": HOPKINS'S POETRY

Duns Scotus's Oxford

Towery city and branchy between towers;
Cuckoo-echoing, bell-swarmèd, lark-charmèd,
    rook-racked, river-rounded;
The dapple-eared lily below thee; that country and
    town did
Once encounter in, here coped and poisèd powers;

Thou hast a base and brickish skirt there, sours
That neighbour-nature thy grey beauty is grounded
Best in; graceless growth, thou hast confounded
Rural rural keeping—folk, flocks, and flowers.

Yet ah! this air I gather and I release
He lived on; these weeds and waters, these walls are
    what
He haunted who of all men most sways my spirits to
    peace;

Of realty the rarest-veinèd unraveller; a not
Rivalled insight, be rival Italy or Greece;
Who fired France for Mary without spot

(Poem 44)

Neither the syntax nor the diction of "Duns Scotus's Oxford" is difficult, and the sense, therefore, of the poem is easily accessible. The poem suspends its mood between celebration and lament. The celebration is for Duns Scotus himself and an Oxford which retains and triggers memory of him, and the lament is for the gracefulness of the past, a past still at the heartfelt center of Oxford. But the lament, nostalgic as it may be, is oddly submerged in the celebration; and when it surfaces, it is transformed into something harsher, not a loss per se but more a criticism of a modern Oxford which defies the harmony between city and country, a harmony of old. The poem then venerates memory, memory whose power and energy render her more immediate than the actual baseness of nineteenth-century Oxford.

The value system is rendered through metaphor—predominantly architectural and natural—through rhyme and rhythm: when nature and architecture are integrated, Oxford is celebrated; when they are at odds, an Oxford of the past is longed for. The opening stanza describes the city, but—as one finds out only in the subsequent stanza—only the city center, what comes to be its essence.

> Towery city and branchy between towers;
> Cuckoo-echoing, bell-swarmèd, lark-charmèd,
>   rook-racked, river-rounded;
> The dapple-eared lily below thee; that country and
>   town did
> Once encounter in, here coped and poisèd powers;

The opening line establishes the condition of harmony, that architecture be natural and nature be architectural. Towers frame the view, opening and closing the verse line and receiving its stresses; "branchy" and "towery" so go together, by virtue of rhyme and placement, that trees and towers seem to share each other's qualities, together a woven or patterned interlacing network. While the first image, "towery city," seems to establish the foreground of our visual field, Hopkins throws the background—"branchy *between* towers"—also to the fore, as if harmony requires and depends on a frontality of forms which are reciprocally architectural and natural ("towery" and "branchy"), equal in importance to each other. The exchangeability, even confusion, of forms is rendered complete in the next line, in which bells and birds occupy the other's roost, take on the other's sound; and we almost have the sense that the "dapple-eared lily" hears them. "Coped" may be architectural and ecclesiastical, "poised" an abstract quality and a mechanical one, too. The contrasting present-day Oxford is the brickish Victorian Oxford whose shapeless suburbs extend into nature and defy harmony: *base* and *brickish* appear the harsher juxtaposed with *towers, powers, flowers*, with *weeds, waters, walls*. The stress we feel, rhymed and constructive, is in the gathering and releasing, in breathing; and harmony almost seems linked to and like that natural process. Mental peace, like architectural harmony, also requires and results from an integration of weeds, waters, and walls; "insight," the special quality which Hopkins selects to distinguish Duns Scotus, constitutes a pun on visual perception, suggesting that the ability to integrate the natural with the man-made, the religious with the organic, Oxford as city with Oxford as country, is a quality rare and worthy. At once visual perception becomes a moral and religious act, one which the poem supports.

While "Duns Scotus's Oxford" seems to build from city to man, from image to action, "Spelt from Sibyl's Leaves" seems to unbuild.

Spelt from Sibyl's Leaves

Earnest, earthless, equal, attuneable, ' vaulty, voluminous,
. . . stupendous
Evening strains to be tíme's vást, ' womb-of-all, home-of-all,
hearse-of-all night.
Her fond yellow hornlight wound to the west, ' her wild
hollow hoarlight hung to the height
Waste; her earliest stars, earlstars, ' stárs principal, overbend
us,
Fíre-féaturing heaven. For earth ' her being has unbound; her
dapple is at an end, as-
tray or aswarm, all throughther, in throngs; ' self ín self
steepèd and páshed—qúite
Disremembering, dísmémbering ' áll now. Heart, you round
me right
With: Óur évening is over us; óur night ' whélms, whélms,
ánd will end us.

Only the beakleaved boughs dragonish ' damask the tool-
smooth bleak light; black,
Ever so black on it. Óur tale, O óur oracle! ' Lét life, wáned,
ah lét life wind
Off hér once skéined stained véined variety ' upon, áll on twó
spools; párt, pen, páck
Now her áll in twó flocks, twó folds—black, white; ' right,
wrong; reckon but, reck but, mind
But thése two; wáre of a wórld where bút these ' twó tell, each
off the óther; of a rack
Where, selfwrung, selfstrung, sheathe- and shelterless, '
thóughts agaínst thoughts ín groans grínd.

(Poem 61)

Unlike "Duns Scotus's Oxford," where evocation of Scotus himself is linked to
city and to air preserved almost hermetically, in "Spelt from Sibyl's Leaves"
there is no such evocation of the past but rather a "disremembering," appropriate, as we will see, to the unbuilding, the "dismembering" in the poem.

For earth ' her being has unbound; her
dapple is at an end, as-
tray or aswarm, all throughther, in throngs; ' self ín self

steepèd and páshed—quite
Disremembering, dísmémbering ' áll now.

Nature does engender: Sibyl's leaves spell and spill, a proliferation verbal, cognition depending upon verbalization; and in a circular way, it is a cognition of that very proliferation. Does wording render idea concrete, accessible? Does nature, not man, spell—that is, word—and make concepts apprehensible?

The first long stanza of "Spelt from Sibyl's Leaves" opens with the struggle for description and definition of something not concrete: space. If Hopkins cannot define it by activating it or filling it—as in "branchy between towers," "branchy" giving substance to "between" in "Duns Scotus's Oxford"—he does so by enclosure: space may be defined as "content" if something else gives it peripheries and appropriate shape; something may be empty if it is enclosed:

> Earnest, earthless, equal, attuneable, ' vaulty, voluminous,
>   . . . stupendous
> Evening strains to be tíme's vást, ' womb-of-all, home-of-all,
>   hearse-of-all night.

The first adjectives seem beyond physical rendering; but "vaulty" gives extension, cathedral shape; "voluminous" gives mass, weight. Similarly, birth, life, and death are rendered in images also of enclosure, images again suggesting contents and outside limits; definition, verbally sought, of what is abstract and conceptual is in fact accomplished by physical delineation which is implicitly architectural, having spatial dimension, weight, and size. So, too, the movement of the poem seems to involve a locating or placing of ideas made substantial: light may be "wound," thread-like, or "hung"; it has dimensions, position, so that nature, tortured on Judgment Day, is some oddly cathedral-like structure, built, demolished and rebuilt again within the life-span of the poem. Images of roundness run through the first stanza: "wound," "overbend," "round"; and the emotion in response to the event is rendered, potentially at least, in the terms or shape of the event itself, "Óur évening is over us; óur night ' whélms, whélms / ánd will end us." "Whelming," as something partial, attracts its natural partner "over"; and our emotion, "overwhelming" takes on the literalness of enclosure. Evening seems to move literally, mechanically, into night. And structuring seems to be remembering, "spooling" in contrast to the unstructuring or architectural "dismembering" and "disremembering." Nature acts on what is man-made, on definition or "thinging," on light which is "tool-smooth":

Only the beakleaved boughs dragonish ᴵ damask the tool-
        smooth bleak light; black,
Ever so black on it. Óur tale, O óur oracle!

If definition is a way of rendering and making accessible what is abstract, so, too, is winding a kind of organizing what is random and disordered. The poem's end seems enclosureless: the Last Judgment, what amounts to "undoing," is imaged by the absence of peripheries, night being no longer a "hearse" but now "sheatheless" and "shelterless." That final night cannot be enclosed or have perceptual limits suggests that it cannot therefore be grasped, worded, or defined. Instead, we have an image of sacrifice on a torture rack, but no saint, not even Christ, is being tortured: "self" is. And, crucially, "self" is defined, figured forth, "selved," as thought substantialized or concretized. Hopkins, though, goes still further: even torture is, in a sense, potentially generative. In the poem's end, thought retains its substance and, therefore, its mechanical capabilities: "thóughts agaínst thoughts ín groans grínd" as if thoughts have weight, direction, position. And grinding, while a wearing down, also suggests a productive and generative friction: metaphor pruned, worn down, shaped, releases the intellectual and poetic energy of probing, defining, rendering or transposing. In this way, the end of the poem is almost affirmative: thoughts have taken on the architectural, physical characteristics that syllables had in Hopkins's "Rhythm and other structural parts," and we have the sense that although all else may be destroyed in the end, the artist, perhaps Hopkins as artist, can create poems so long as thoughts can generate other thoughts, syllables other syllables, poems other poems.

Some of Hopkins's poetic terms, such as *pitch* and *stress*, are both musical and architectural, and as much may be said of the images in "Spelt from Sibyl's Leaves" and in another poem, "On a Piece of Music."

(On a Piece of Music)

How all's to one thing wrought!
The members, how they sit!
O what a tune the thought
Must be that fancied it.

Nor angel insight can
Learn how the heart is hence:
Since all the make of man
Is law's indifference.

[Who shaped these walls has shewn
The music of his mind,

Made known, though thick through stone
What beauty beat behind.]

Not free in this because
His powers seemed free to play:
He swept what scope he was
To sweep and must obey.

Though down his being's bent
Like air he changed in choice,
That was an instrument
Which overvaulted voice.

What makes the man and what
The man within that makes:
Ask whom he serves or not
Serves and what side he takes.

For good grows wild and wide,
Has shades, is nowhere none;
But right must seek a side
And choose for chieftain one.

Therefore this masterhood,
This piece of perfect song,
This fault-not-found-with-good
Is neither right nor wrong.

No more than red and blue,
No more than Re and Mi,
Or sweet the golden glue
That's built for by the bee.

[Who built these walls made known
The music of his mind,
Yet here he has but shewn
His ruder-rounded rind.
His brightest blooms lie there unblown,
His sweetest nectar hides behind.]
					(Poem 148)

Here the same concretizing takes place that occurred in the other poems; and
"mind" itself looms an architectural structure such that inside and out seem to
define self and not-self:

> Who shaped these walls has shewn
> The music of his mind,
> Made known, though thick through stone
> What beauty beat behind.

So, too, definitions of values, aesthetic and ethical, hinge on an architectural image. Harmony, or discord for that matter—the mind's character and the artist's—are revealed by an architectural analogue, the artifact or structure, either as mind or as product.

> What makes the man and what
> The man within that makes:
> Ask whom he serves or not
> Serves and what side he takes.

It is not surprising if, on reflection, the mind as structure, so imaged in "On a Piece of Music," makes us think that God's mind, gigantic yet structural or architectural, was also figured forth in "Spelt from Sibyl's Leaves," a mind extending into nature the way God's mind does in "The Wreck of the Deutschland." Just so, order in "On a Piece of Music" is imaged by architectural members, and that order testifies to divine or ethical control:

> How all's to one thing wrought!
> The members, how they sit!
> O what a tune the thought
> Must be that fancied it.

We may well recall Robert Browning's "Abt Vogler" where, in the same way, music takes the form of a piece of architecture; but for Hopkins, the artifact, not only as an extension of the artist, but as an emblem of him, is imaged by construction. We sense both an internal and an external pressure, man shaped and shaping; and "what side he takes" assumes a literalness of actual position. By contrast, that over which the artist exerts no control is imaged as organic growth, defined not as the tree-steepled Oxford was but as was modern Oxford and her shapeless suburbs.

> For good grows wild and wide,
> Has shades, is nowhere none;
> But right must seek a side
> And choose for chieftain one.

Architecture may embody nature, but more important, it should offer structure to nature, not miming a structureless opulence and variety. Here again Hopkins's value system reminds us of that in his schoolboy poem, "The Escorial," in which poet-architect rejects Gothic forms with their "engemming rays," their "foliag'd crownals" all "in a maze of finish'd diapers" (Poem 1) of a nature untended. We also have the sense that, for Hopkins, structure protects; while soul may be imaged organically, as flower, as nectar, the creating and created mind walls it in, over-bending the flower of soul or idea, that it be safe from destruction.

> Who built these walls made known
> The music of his mind,
> Yet here he has but shewn
> His ruder-rounded rind.
> His brightest blooms lie there unblown,
> His sweetest nectar hides behind.

Stress, grind, and density of syllables are notably absent from the neatly mellifluous stanzas of "On a Piece of Music," so that it is *more* obscure than the strenuously mannered "Sybil's Leaves."

It should not surprise us, after looking at these three poems, to find that Hopkins, when doubting his own generative, creating capacity, images that capacity or lack thereof architecturally. In one of his most personally poignant poems, the structure, built from nature, the stuff of nests and twigs, is architecturally laced and fretted:

> Oh, the sots and thralls of lust
> Do in spare hours more thrive than I that spend,
>
> Sir, life upon thy cause, See, banks and brakes
> Now, leavèd how thick! lacèd they are again
> With fretty chervil, look, and fresh wind shakes
>
> Them; birds build—but not I build; no, but strain,
> Time's eunuch, and not breed one work that wakes.
> Mine, O thou lord of life, send my roots rain.
>
> (Poem 74)

While the imagery suggests the procreative, it seems more the fathering forth of an artifact-child that Hopkins so desires. The sought-for rain almost suggests a need for growth in order to build, the need for sustenance in order to create rather than sustenance of which the direct product is the artifact. For Hopkins the nest, the structural home for offspring, suggests that poems house ideas, that they are constructed nature monuments; and we have the sense that, for Hopkins, his recasting of nature constitutes a survival or preservation effort. For this purpose, as poetic metaphors, art, science and nature, music, architecture, mechanics and optics, are all potentially compatible. Throughout his oeuvre, Hopkins varies the theme, but for the most part, in all he images construction—whether of body, artifact, created world of human mind—as architectural structure. Man's body not only houses but grounds, substantiates, his spirit: in "The Caged Skylark," we find both ideas, momentarily perhaps, compatible: potentially, the bird's nest is no prison.

> As a dare-gale skylark scanted in a dull cage
>   Man's mounting spirit in his bone-house, mean house,
>   dwells—
>
> Man's spirit will be flesh-bound when found at best,
> But uncumberèd: meadow-down is not distressed
>   For a rainbow footing it nor he for his bónes risen.
>   (Poem 39)

So, too, does Hopkins figure mind as structurally limited and delimiting: in "The Lantern out of Doors," he writes,

> Death or distance soon consumes them: wind
>   What most I may eye after, be in at the end
> I cannot, and out of sight is out of mind
>
> Christ minds: Christ's interest, what to avow or amend
>   There, éyes them, heart wánts, care haúnts,
>   foot fóllows kínd,
>
> Their ránsom, théir rescue, ánd first, fást, last friénd.
>   (Poem 40)

Here again, mind is defined by the literal peripheries of perception, distance. We have, in a sense, a double idea, that projection is out of the mind, "out" meaning from out of, generated from inside and projecting out; that which is deduced, understood from sight is also "from" the mind, and sight itself is an act of the mind. To "eye after," to sight—we are prepared for what happens in the poem: the mind is defined by and becomes its own action, and appropriately is transformed from noun into verb.

MARYLOU MOTTO

Dramas of Time and Loss

Deeply concerned with human loss, the poems of Hopkins will the redemption of loss, directing human experience toward the saving grace of future
time. For as the poet bids man to know direction within the world's space, he
bids him too to know direction in time. Hopkins' Christian sense of time is
always in evidence, reminding us that however unique a given phenomenon
may appear, it yet proceeds from time past and foreshadows time future. The
design through time gathers the seemingly unique event into enduring
principle; the discrete occurrence is reseen in its truer form as a manifestation
of recurrence in a Christ-informed world.

That is the represented time of the poem, what the poem says of time.
But any poem exists in many times—in the time of its author's making of it
and in the time of its reader's reading of it, and both those times in experiential, representational, and historical dimensions. In Hopkins, not the least of
these is the experiential time of the speaker and reader. Hopkins enacts his
sense of Christ-informed time by using recurrence as a poetic means as well as a
thematic element in the poem: For the reader, Hopkins' bold recurrence of
sound and rhythm creates known patterns, recognizable design in the temporal experience of the saying. But just as interesting is the speaker's own
experiential or enacted time, which sometimes rises up to tense against the
recurrence of represented time, creating complex drama indeed.

Hopkins fosters our awareness of experiential time in his determination
to be heard and not merely read. "To do the Eurydice any kind of justice," he
instructs Bridges, "you must not slovenly read it with the eyes but with your

From "Mined with a Motion": The Poetry of Gerard Manley Hopkins. © 1984 by Rutgers, The State
University. Rutgers University Press, 1984.

127

ears, as if the paper were declaiming it at you . . . Stress is the life of it."
Elsewhere, he repeats the exhortation: "but take breath and read it with the
ears, as I always wish to be read, and my verse becomes all right." Such
comments make explicit a demand inherent in the poetry itself. Filled with
recurrent sound, filled with explosive and stressed sound, Hopkins' verses
nearly leap off the page in their eagerness to be heard aloud. Indeed, the
poetry's adamant and individual sound patterns compose no small part of its
power to bid us. The poem is to be read "as if the paper were declaiming it *at*"
us. We are forcefully confronted by sound, the poetry's orality signaling its
'reality' and spontaneity.

Any poem read aloud, heard rather than seen, engenders a distinct
experience for the reader. Sound makes us aware of time because sound
happens only in movement through time; in Walter J. Ong's phrase, sound
tells us that something is "going on." Spoken aloud, the poem comes off the
page and ceases to be the still icon of a timeless urn; spoken aloud, the poem is
a durational happening with beginning and end.

Because it has a defined beginning and end in time, lyric poetry speaks to
the sustaining of meaning: What is said resurrects for a moment what has been
and what has been said. For a while, too, it further succeeds in delaying the
end, in foreclosing on silence. But by its very nature, the poem said aloud also
reminds us of loss: What is said is lost in the time of its saying, the beginning
implying the end, the moment of silence or non-saying which succeeds all
sound. When the poem is sounded aloud, the tension between lastingness and
passing, between the continuity of experience and its loss, becomes explicit. In
this sense, it may be that the printed page or space of the poem preserves only
the possibility of recreation and loss, preserves only the time we must relive
and lose. And Hopkins insists that his poems be lifted off the page to become
that temporal experience: "My verse is less to be read than heard, as I have told
you before."

The openings of Hopkins' poems, we have seen, are often abrupt intrusions on consciousness that proclaim their difference from the time that
preceded the saying: "Thou mastering me / God!" or "No worst, there is
none." Not so, his endings. The closures of the poems typically seek to prevent
a sharp line of demarcation; many poems seem to want to continue, however
impossible that may be, after the sounds cease. So the poem's *process* often
echoes or underlies the idea of the poem as loss.

"Pied Beauty," for example, seeks at its end to "Praise him" beyond the
limits of the poem, and perhaps beyond the limits of language as well:

> All things counter, original, spare, strange;
>   Whatever is fickle, freckled (who knows how?)
>   With swift, slow; sweet, sour; adazzle, dim;

He fathers-forth whose beauty is past change:
            Praise him.

The poem tries to break through the natural constraints of its own medium as
the structure forces the reader to prolong the closing words. The concluding
clause, "Praise him," is startlingly concise, a forceful summary command, but
the clause emerges quietly, the sounds of the words' ends linger, and the
poem's structure and meaning lead us to dwell on and in the final words. The
reader's impulse is to prolong those two syllables, "Praise him," to protract the
sounding of them so that their duration in time matches that of the other lines.
Through structure, through meaning, and through sound, Hopkins attempts
to sustain the experience of assent, to make it lasting.

That so many poems end in the suggestion of incipient flight prolongs
the experience of the poem into the time that succeeds the saying. These
endings glimpse and so start the reader toward something "yonder" in both
space *and* time. The images of bird and flight suggest all their traditional
Romantic connotations, the longed-for freedom from earth's mortal pull,
although now, in Hopkins, that freedom is to be used to soar to a specific,
directed end. That is, flight in Hopkins enacts the directions of assent. The
poem's image begins to soar into seemingly limitless space as it moves out and
up toward an immortal future:

            —Where kept? do but tell us where kept, where.—
Yonder.—What high as that! We follow, now we follow.—
      Yonder, yes yonder, yonder,
Yonder.

                                    ("The Golden Echo")

                                    let joy size

      At God knows when to God knows what; whose smile
      's not wrung, see you; unforeseen times rather—as skies
      Betweenpie mountains—lights a lovely mile.

                                    ("My own heart")

      The heart rears wings bold and bolder
      And hurls for him, O half hurls earth for him off under his
            feet.

                                    ("Hurrahing in Harvest")

      Because the Holy Ghost over the bent
      World broods with warm breast and with ah! bright wings.

                                    ("God's Grandeur")

After the hard bidding of the opening, declaiming itself at us, the poems typically end in something soft and melting, gesturing upward and outward in space *and* time as they hint at the yet greater wonder:

> Man's spirit will be flesh-bound when found at best,
> But uncumberèd: meadow-down is not distressed
> For a rainbow footing it nor he for his bónes rísen.
>
> ("The Caged Skylark")

Half realization, half anticipation, the endings direct us as the sounds of language fade away. The poet relies on the hush of a final unstressed syllable or on final consonants that linger to suggest that there is more than what has been (or possibly ever can be) articulated:

> The thunder-purple seabeach plumèd purple-of-thunder,
> If a wuthering of his palmy snow-pinions scatter a colossal
>   smile
> Off him, but meaning motion fans fresh our wits with
>   wonder.
>
> ("Henry Purcell")

> For Christ plays in ten thousand places,
> Lovely in limbs, and lovely in eyes not his
> To the Father through the features of men's faces.
>
> ("As kingfishers catch fire")

In such endings, the sounds die, slowly, but the experience, ascending, yearns to continue. The image is flying away, just barely at the edge of sight, lighting "a lovely mile." In their attempts to sustain vision and meaning and to prolong the time of the poem, such endings proclaim the fact of loss in their very resistance to losing.

Even when the poem's end is not beginning to soar, it is often countering loss or possible loss with an openly said and enacted effort to forestall what has to come. The repetitious ending of "Inversnaid" may well be like this; that of "Binsey Poplars" surely is:

> Ten or twelve, only ten or twelve
> Strokes of havoc únselve
> The sweet especial scene,
> Rural scene, a rural scene,
> Sweet especial rural scene.

The speaker here dwells in a memory of that which no longer exists. His words cherish the memory and try to sustain it by repeating themselves in time. In

"Brothers," the closure's repetition would similarly hold on. But here it is the idea of Nature's kindness, the boy's effortless goodness, that wants remembering in days to come:

> Ah Nature, framed in fault,
> There's comfort then, there's salt;
> Nature, bad, base, and blind,
> Dearly thou canst be kind;
> There dearly thén, deárly,
> Dearly thou canst be kind.

These endings dramatize the problem posed in "The Leaden Echo and the Golden Echo," where the speaker explicitly asks how to stop time and hold on to beauty. In all these poems, the pointed repetition of language serves as an external sign of the interior process that tries to prevent loss. In a language elsewhere so motionable and dynamic, the repetition shapes a moment strikingly still—and one which by its very nature is always reminding us that it is doomed to pass.

Hopkins makes us aware of loss in any number of other ways. Although he does not, for instance, use more than an average number of present-tense verb forms, the ones he does use make sharp intrusions into the experience of the poem, again lending the sense of spontaneity that bids. The present-tense verbs make us highly conscious of fleeting time, for they are prominently placed, stressed, and often syntactically uncomplicated by modifiers intervening between them and their subjects. In excitement, the speaker points at himself, says "I walk, I lift up, I lift up heart, eyes"; or he points at the world and says, "Summer ends *now; now*, barbarous in beauty, the stooks rise" ("Hurrahing in Harvest," [italics added]). The aim is to say the thing that is, to catapult the reader into the instant, but the instant so abruptly and forcefully immediate inevitably suggests its own transience.

Through the transient immediacy of the experiences recorded, through the self-proclaiming sound patterns that insist that we read "with the ears," Hopkins' poetry is always making us aware of loss. As I. A. Richards was first to point out, Hopkins' poems are *about* loss—loss of humanity, loss of grace, loss of self, beauty, and life. And all loss happens in time, through time, because of time:

> The telling time our task is; time's some part,
> Not all, but we were framed to fail and die—
> One spell and well that one. There, ah thereby
> Is comfort's carol of all or woe's worst smart.
>   ("To his Watch")

It is not just "Summer ends *now*" but "Summer *ends* now." In the most excited exuberance of experience and language, in the hurrahing of the happiest of poems, the need is sensed to seize the moment and stave off the loss that has to come.

That motion—from joy to fear of loss—happens over and over again. "Have, get, *before* it cloy," the speaker of "Spring" pleads with Christ, "*Before* it cloud . . . and sour with sinning, / Innocent mind and Mayday" (italics added). And in the midst of his wholehearted joy in the seeming perfection of the bugler's first communion, the speaker abruptly turns in fear: "Let mé though see no more of him, and not disappointment / Those sweet hopes quell." "On the Portrait of Two Beautiful Young People" is rooted in the same fear, for "beauty's dearest veriest vein is tears." In fact, the sharp intake of breath at youth, beauty, or joy so characteristic of Hopkins is just a short step away from his fear of the loss wrought by time. In this sense, the design or argument that follows the image is there to counter loss and the speaker's fear of loss: If indeed the splendid single image is inevitably transient, says the design, it is but one of many, and the principle will endure.

T. S. Eliot's Magus thought that birth and death "were different" until he saw the birth of Christ ("Journey of the Magi"). The idea stands in sharp contrast to Hopkins' speaker, who is never under any such illusion. For him, the moments of splendor in the natural world are the very moments that enfold both phenomena, the moments of beauty in the unselving, of the gold in the fall—or better, of the gold *of* the fall, a goldenfall. Creation is never far from destruction, nor growth from decay.

Thus, what at first appears a fall may be wholly other; if loss is inevitable in the Heraclitean world, the moment of losing is precious. So Hopkins attends to downward motion—the motion of the bird and the leaf and the river, of the man at work, and of the modest boy who stands at the door while his brother performs on stage. Hopkins must seize the day in its transience: If summer ends now, then this is the time when one may find cause to hurrah in harvest.

"Felix Randal" takes its plot from the paradoxical nature of life: Strong in body, the farrier was yet weak in soul; as his body and mind deteriorate, he gradually achieves a stronger spiritual self (the two vectors cross, a *felix culpa* enacted by the sonnet's form, in the sacrament given by the priest). At the last he joins the strength of his soul with the past strength of his body in the transformation and apotheosis of his death. Yet Hopkins makes the sonnet more complex than the neatness of this represented narrative by grounding the whole poem in the speaker's moving relation to the farrier.

At least in its original form, that relation between priest and the farrier is born to die:

Felix Randal the farrier, O is he dead then? my duty all ended,

Separated in time and place, the speaker reacts, springs to the news of the farrier's fall. The rhythm, absolutely colloquial here, seems struck from the speaker at the moment he hears the news. Perhaps it is the "then?" that creates the tone most, stalling for time in a poetry that wastes none. The "then?" seems to figure not loss in poetry but loss in life, the life-loss in which we are at a loss for what to say. If the "O" figures a gathering and catching of self, the "then?" diffuses it, trailing off in a question already answered.

The octave tells the farrier's story, a complexly timed and tensed narrative that ends in the speaker's once again identifiably colloquial voice: "Ah well, God rest him all road ever he offended!" This prayer lends the sense of an ending and exists as a half-dismissal, a willed putting aside of the farrier's life. Indeed, with the particulars told, the sonnet turns, the speaker now free to search out the meaning of his experience with the farrier.

Accordingly, the next words formulate an abstract principle, as if to distance and codify the past relationship with the voice of design: "This seeing the sick endears them to us." The farrier is here one of many, one of "them," the basis for a didactic and dogmatic text. But the speaker cannot sustain this distance. The language begins to repeat itself, but it has turned about and in the same words now refers to the speaker himself: "This seeing the sick endears them to us, us too it endears." Perhaps it is the repetition of "endears" that brings even closer, itself endears, the memory of singular tenderness between the two men, for the distanced generalization now wholly gives way:

This seeing the sick endears them to us, us too it endears.
My tongue had taught thee comfort, touch had quenched thy
      tears,
Thy tears that touched my heart, child, Felix, poor Felix
      Randal;

The speaker moves into an experience unnamed in the narrative octave. He moves into a past intimacy, an I/thou encounter that cherishes the singular, individual man when Felix is seen to have touched and to be yet touching the heart of the priest. The speaker's admission of love comes closest here, when the only distance left is embodied in the past tense of the verb. With the signal event of this intimacy spoken, the third line trails off, now in falling rhythms, repeatedly naming the man. This tender naming of Felix tries to hold on to the experience and to the man; it wants not to relinquish either the remembered intimacy or the remembrance of intimacy. The speaker tries to dwell within this intimacy recreated, newly created, the names stroking the memory and unwilling to release the memory or the man. But the language admits the difficulties of the desire to prolong that intimacy. It admits the difficulties through its falling rhythms, through its repeated pauses, and through the slowing of enacted time that comes with the repeated naming—"child, Felix, poor Felix Randal."

In extended exclamation, the last three lines shake the poem back into narrative movement, directing the experience of loss in the world and in the poem:

> How far from then forethought of, all thy more boisterous
> 　　　years,
> When thou at the random grim forge, powerful amidst peers,
> Didst fettle for the great grey drayhorse his bright and
> 　　　battering sandal!

In their willful confusion of time sense, the lines would have us see an unforeseen persistence through time, a newly found intimation of immortality. The lines move back into chronological time in order to soar forth into a future that escapes time. The named, remembered, and 'visible' past, the physical image, turns symbol; the Christian escape, triumphant, embodied in the representational image of the farrier's early work, is now joyously celebrated by a speaker whom it leaves behind. As always, not intimate human relationships inevitably subject to decay but the symbol, which spans time, spells the future. The glimmer of flight is there, the mythological flying steed in the "bright and battering sandal," and that image gleaned from the far past now directs and determines the future.

The closing image of the farrier forging that sandal tells us of past intimations of immortality at the same time that it is detailing a concrete past long gone. While saying his human joy, Hopkins is again reminding us of its transience. Human life, even at its fullest, perhaps most when at its fullest, is inexorably subject to loss. Countering the endless human loss comes only Christ's design, which allows duration and endurance, and which turns loss into a hint of final gain in a time beyond human time.

The finding of Felix Randal's powerful direction toward heaven within an image of what had seemed an undirected life is a finding of recurrence, the only holding possible in a Christian, linear ontology. Exact repetition of event and being are possible only within a primitive, cyclical world view where "through . . . repetition, time is suspended, or at least its virulence is diminished." Christianity restores time and progress because the original fall, the coming, and the second coming are singular events—the only truly singular events—

and so create discernible time. They give direction and force to Christian time; they give history meaning. All the stress felt by man, writes Hopkins, "dates from day / Of his going in Galilee" (*Deutschland*). Because it ceases to be random, time within the Christian world is irreversible, irreplaceable, and unrepeatable. Thus, in the Christian world view, exact repetition of consciousness or happening is impossible. Man is trapped within the fact of his mortality, and "After-comers cannot guess the beauty been" ("Binsey Poplars").

In an undergraduate essay, Hopkins defines beauty as a tension between sameness and difference, and uses the device of rhyme to illustrate and epitomize the principle. As J. Hillis Miller has indicated, all of Hopkins' poems exist as a tour de force of rhyme, rhyming words, phrases, ideas, and things as well as sounds. Implicitly, rhyming is omnipresent in Hopkins because "Christ plays in ten thousand places"—because what is fathered forth rhymes with the fatherer.

Recurrence is the rhyming—the sameness with difference—that happens in time. It partially compensates for inevitable loss in that it partially stays time in its looking backward, in its overt connection or rhyming of human experience. The event of Christ's coming gives direction to history and in so doing creates the possibility of symbol in the world: Inherent in every physical event is its representational, recurrent meaning. Iconographically, Hopkins captures and recaptures that coming and so recovers meaning for otherwise disconnected events. If the *haecceitas* of every being is inescapable, reccurence constitutes a kind of earthly salvation, a continuity of grace and purpose in worldly time.

Furthermore, Hopkins seems always to be confirming or validating the thematic recurrence he speaks of by what is happening in his language. The motionable, chiming language enacts a poetic recurrence for the speaker and reader in their experience of time in saying the poem. Hopkins is hardly alone in using mimetic, suggestive sound and rhythm, but the degree to which he makes us aware of them, stresses them, is unusual. It is largely because of its recurrent sounds that his language seems meant to be read aloud. And read aloud, the poetry proclaims the principle of recurrence all the more strongly, making us know the sameness-with-difference as a dramatic experience in sounded time as well as on the space of the page. Theme is made process again, the dogma turned into a way of seeing.

When, in "The Blessed Virgin compared to the Air we Breathe," the speaker finds the sound of the word "air" in "Mary," he is finding linguistic recurrence that would confirm principle in the world. Indeed, the speaker frequently appears to confirm thought with language—as if sounds closely related to one another were there to convince us that the things and events they name are closely related:

As *kingfishers* catch *fire*, *dragonflies draw flame*;

Each animal's name contains, at the beginning of a stressed syllable, a sound that recurs at the beginning of its verb or action, and another that recurs at the beginning of the verb's direct object. Each animal, then, is closely identified with what it does. But the analogy between the two actions is also stressed by recurring rhythm:

kíng	físh	ērs ⏐	cátch	fíre
drág	ōn	flíes ⏐	dráw	fláme

The spondees draw the weight of the line's stress into the beings' actions (where Hopkins obviously wants it), but they also make known a second rhythmical configuration that is strongly analogous to—but not exactly like—the first. The rhyming of the two actions in the space of the world becomes a recurrence in sounded time for the reader.

The force of boldly recurrent sound and rhythm is felt repeatedly, in all of Hopkins; the speaking voice is always experiencing in the event of the poem a recurrence not unlike what the speaker is reporting in the world. "Now burn, new born to the world, / Double-naturèd name" (*Deutschland*), the speaker implores Christ, and the reader may be the more ready to assent to the "Double-naturèd name" because of the previous doubling in sound and rhythm: "Now burn, new born."

Similarly, the end of "That Nature is a Heraclitean Fire" leads us to assent to the seemingly impossible recurrence it names by the way it apprehends the idea:

In a flash, at a trumpet crash,
I am all at once what Christ is, ⏐ since he was what I am, and
This Jack, joke, poor potsherd, ⏐ patch, matchwood, immortal
diamond,
Is immortal diamond.

In the next to last line, all of time is collapsed into the two 'timeless' focal points of Christian time. In the speed of the rhythms and monosyllabic words—a speed suggestive of the instantaneous transformation—the first verses strain against the temporal nature of their own medium. The verbs "am . . . is . . . was . . . am . . . / . . . Is" mirror the reciprocity of the two moments, the rhymed interchange, in an explanation of absolute simplicity.

Christ's mortal existence ("he was") is at the center, making the whole recurrence possible.

In the last line, the accumulation of stressed, rhymed things that together spell man results in the reader's increasing attention to the ungainly, recurring sounds. The "immortal diamond" at the end of this swollen line is almost lost in the long list of trivial objects and demeaning names that precedes it. Thus the poem's last words, direct repetition on the page, intend and achieve a stunning surprise. The reader accepts, assents to, and trusts this 'shock' because of its antecedent. In the verbal repetition, the full import of what was there before flashes out into meaning. When the concealed diamond emerges, Hopkins succeeds in rhyming perfection, immortality, and transcendent beauty—"in a flash"—with the very mankind that the poem had almost despaired of. Here, the fact of the recurrence *is* the meaning, and the stunning repetition on the page would stop man for all time.

The pattern is familiar. In Hopkins, although it may at first appear to come from nowhere, the revelation always emerges from obscurity, from where it was hiding. In retrospect, we see it anew, now recognizing the anticipatory hint, the seed or symbol, for what it always was. It is in fact the continuity of recurrence that makes design or abstraction existent and intelligible. Good or bad, good and bad, "From life's dawn it is drawn down" (*Deutschland*). And we return in order to know the place for the first time: "Over again I feel thy finger and find thee" (*Deutschland*).

Always assenting to something anterior, something that was once a presence, recurrence locates its own present in relation to another time and space, sound and place. So, in affirming the past, recurrence attempts to store a self, a sighting, and thus deny a fearful fragmentation. If exact repetition is impossible in this world view, so too is absolute isolation, the still death. While recurrence points backward to resay a saying, it also points to itself in its saying that this is *not* the same, for it is another saying, and now is not then. That which is new in recurrent experience validates difference, selfhood, and change; it mocks the dying of the light. Exact repetition, were it possible, would annihilate time and difference; recurrence creates the vitality and intensity of the felt continuous.

In two poems especially—"Felix Randal" and "Spring and Fall"—the explicit subject of recurrence and even the recurrence of sound and language pales before the experience of a speaker who dramatically reenacts recurrence. The speaker of "Felix Randal," perhaps against his own expectations, brings the past to life, which allows a kind of redemption to happen in the poem; the speaker of "Spring and Fall" undergoes an experience in the poem that, in its affirmation of recurrence, contradicts or at the least profoundly tempers the sense of the design.

We return to "Felix Randal," where not only do ideas and language recur, but recurrence itself becomes a temporal experience for the speaker as he speaks. The poem is a study of loss and gain through interior mental and emotional processes that turn loss into continuing presence. We know, first of all, the chronological time of the speaker's speaking, and this ongoing chronological time of the speaker plays against other experiential times that are discovered within the self or are created by the drama of the poem. These fuller experiences of time are realized and become dominant as they emerge out of and counter the speaker's chronological time. Chronological time thus informed by the speaker's inner experience is instressed, and it is this compounding of time senses which creates experiential time and meaning for the speaker; it makes possible unforeseen discovery in the poem as it reenacts intrinsic revelatory and redemptive design in the world.

The poem begins with loss and gain—gain because Felix Randal comes into the speaker's mind so markedly after an absence unthought of, loss because the news of his death makes the farrier's absence present. The paradox goes further as the poem becomes a testing of whether that absence, death, is a real absence. The knowledge of Felix Randal's death fills the speaker's consciousness, starts it on a quest toward assent as he tries to fill the absence with a past made present through memory. The poem, in fact, lives the past over twice, once in the octave and once in the sestet. And these retrograde motions of retrospection play against the continuing, ongoing linear dimensions of the speaker speaking.

At the same time, there is not only the farrier's absence, which must be filled within the speaker, but an absence in the speaker himself. The two are yoked together, each pulling the other toward assent and ascent: "O is he dead then? my duty all ended . . . ?" The quest to make good the absence of Felix is also a quest to make good an absence of self.

The octave is largely a narrative of memory, of linear time within the present, ongoing time of the speaker speaking. Here, memory rediscovers the farrier, but only barely. Although the voice approaches a lyrical dimension in its physical description of Felix, the octave is essentially a recitation and not an evocation:

> Felix Randal the farrier, O is he dead then? my duty all
>   ended,
> Who have watched his mould of man, big-boned and hardy-
>   handsome

Pining, pining, till time when reason rambled in it and some
Fatal four disorders, fleshed there, all contended?

Sickness broke him. Impatient, he cursed at first, but mended
Being anointed and all; though a heavenlier heart began some
Months earlier, since I had our sweet reprieve and ransom
Tendered to him. Ah well, God rest him all road ever he
  offended!

The linear sequence of the processes of retrospection is similar to the linear sequence of the speaker's speaking. But simultaneously, for all its sameness, the voiced experience of retrospection begins to mount from the speaker's speech as if it might overcome that ongoing voice and veer beyond clear chronicle toward empathy, as in the very recurring sounds and words of "Pining, pining, till time when reason rambled." Later, the clear chronology is shaken again when the speaker qualifies his statement of fact and, in so doing, doubles back to reconsider and expand on the summary already offered: "though a heavenlier heart began some / Months earlier." The drama of the voices of time begins to reconstitute the presence of both Felix and the speaker, and hints at a more real fullness of time and experience to come.

 The narrative octave of memory, then, partially recovers the physical image, recalls the strength of Felix, but moves on to the loss of that strength and the priest's blessing, a blessing that occurs both in the past and now in the present moment at the edge of memory: "Ah well, God rest him all road ever he offended!" With that, the poem seems to return to the single dimension of the chronological time of the speaker speaking. The blessing offers an easy assumption of ending, of memory returning to the present tense. Yet the return distances the speaker from Felix and himself, the immediate present holding a greater absence because of the failure to make either the self or Felix, glimpsed in the octave, a real and sustained presence. The blessing as blessing is formulaic, yet the slight distortion of syntax may suggest a slight hesitation within the self rather than a complete resolution.

 Memory does return in the sestet but not to narrative recitation and sequentiality. Rather, after a momentary deflection, it returns to a lyricism that immerses itself in a moment of experience and dwells in that experience:

This seeing the sick endears them to us, us too it endears,
My tongue had taught thee comfort, touch had quenched thy
  tears,
Thy tears that touched my heart, child, Felix, poor Felix
  Randal;

Chronology is lost, and the loss is gain. The momentary deflection, the generalization on the text of the first half of the first line, bends back into the self as the speaker realizes his own gain in ministering to Felix. The past empathy between the speaker and Felix recurs then, is made both present and presence—compounded because existing both now and then. It is the same empathy yet different and multiple because, more than empathy in memory recounted, it is held in slow time, reflected upon and reflecting back: "endears . . . us, /us . . . endears"; "child, Felix, poor Felix Randal."

Duty then is not ended. As Felix and the speaker "touch" one another, all the doublings touch and converge, flowing into assent:

> How far from then forethought of, all thy more boisterous
>   years,
> When thou at the random grim forge, powerful amidst peers,
> Didst fettle for the great grey drayhorse his bright and
>   battering sandal!

Assenting to the touch and because touched, the speaker in the final tercet moves deeply into a now more deeply known past. The motion is an assent to the intimacy reknown. The self once known is no longer absent. Nor is Felix. Although the farrier's power is presented once more, it is no longer physical power but metaphorical power. The past has become a continuously active presence, the imaged flight of the "battering sandal." Touched by "touch" and "tears," the self merges into the real river of time and, as it emerges in one of its recurrent surfacings, overtakes and suspends the chronological voice of the speaker. The speaker's final motion into the past becomes his assent as well as a mode of rising to what has now been revealed as a previously unseen, unknown, unforethought of assent and ascension.

It is, ironically, the poet who has gained for the priest what the priest had lost. And it is in all senses the poet who realizes the gain. The poet's ministering rediscovers through the recurring dramas of the speaker in the poem the recurring dramas of redemptive presence. And this is not, as is more usual in Hopkins, gleaned from without, from the world, but from within—not from the Holy Ghost coming in revelation as the morning emerges from obscurity of darkness, nor even the direct assent of the heart in hiding, stirring outward in instinctual response. But with greater difficulty and through labyrinthine currents of the interior made real, made felt, by language as sign of that interior, the hiding and shifting centers of recurrent experience emerge to displace chronological time and to speak of, and in speaking fill, a continuous presence.

More consciously, more directly than "Felix Randal," "Spring and Fall" reaches into the past to find a future. It reaches back to origins—to our origins and to its own origins, to the ontological and epistemological sources of being—to find recurrence through time. Uncharacteristically for Hopkins, the poem names no ultimate redemption. It leaves us instead with pathos, with a saying of human loss in life and of death as the mortal direction of all. At the same time, the speaker's temporal experience in the poem would gainsay that pathos and find a more human and hopeful event. As in "Felix Randal," in "Spring and Fall," the speaker's experience of recurrence revises the explicit saying of the poem.

"Spring and Fall" is motivated by Hopkins' characteristic 'Why?'—the question which precedes the finding of an anterior, the 'before' and 'behind' of phenomena. Perhaps the poem is able to go as far as it does toward that anterior because it discovers location and definition of what is anterior in visible time and space—the child, Margaret, who sits in front of and outside the speaker. The speaker implicitly modifies the didactic 'answers' he finds by grounding them in the moving relationship between himself and the child. That is, the poem formulates with clarity the answers to the questions it raises, yet as in "Felix Randal," the experience of the poem resides just as strongly in the more problematic and complex motions of the speaker toward the other person. (It is not just "Spring and Fall" but "Spring and Fall: to a young child.") As age reaches back to its origin in youth, the motion of the speaker toward the child itself finds a source, a spring of being, within the poem.

Faced with her first experience of fall, Margaret reacts in a way that the speaker cannot. Thus the poem's rhetorical situation dramatizes from the start the blight that man was born for: For the first time the young child sees the unleaving of life, and she weeps; the older man sees it for the thousandth time, and he speaks.

The speaker's words seek out the child's response and, in so doing, seek out a beginning of time in which words themselves were unnatural:

> Márgarét, áre you gríeving
> Over Goldengrove unleaving?

The leaves fall down, the leaves fall down and die. Margaret's tears fall down *over* (in space and 'because of') the leaves; her tears, too, will die. The rhyming begins as both the leaves and the child appear to advantage in their falling. The leaves are golden—beautiful, valuable, rare—at the moment when they un-selve, fall, and die. But "unleaving" also suggests 'not leaving'—staying, lasting, permanency. And 'golden' also suggests long-lastingness or time-lessness. Thus, the speaker's words intimate the original "Goldengrove unleaving," the "Eden garden" ("Spring") that haunts mankind by its absence, and the poem widens to carry the implications of the original fall of man as well as the immediate and recurrent one. The first fall, original, causes all the others.

The second question is a revision of the first, the tone of wonder growing even as it is defined:

> Leáves, líke the things of man, you
> With your fresh thoughts care for, can you?

The simplicity and directness of the first couplet have yielded to a more complex syntax, an order of thought disjuncted and difficult. In their repetition and rhyming, the 'you's' are stressed, in effect repeating the meaning of the syntax and further differentiating the child from the speaker.

"Leaves" are foliage, of course, but by now they must also be 'leave-takings'—which *are* the "things of man." Margaret, her fresh thoughts undissociated from emotion, can care. The speaker sounds affectionate, bemused, fatherly, and already aware of his own loss of fresh thoughts, of care, in marking his separation from the child. Yet if the syntax is fragmented, disjuncted, and intellected, and if it so marks a separation from the lack of similarity to the child, Hopkins' sense units betray a rhyming of motion and rhythm:

> Leáves | līke the thíngs | of mán
> yóu | With your frésh | thoúghts cáre

That is, the child's weeping makes the speaker aware of another 'leave-taking' —her tears evoke an awareness of his own lack of tears—yet at the same time, his own phrases subtly rhyme. The springs of a sympathetic remembrance of feeling stir even as he suggests that, for him, they will no longer flow.

In the lack of rhyming between Margaret and himself, the speaker finds his transition:

> Áh! ás the heart grows older
> It will come to such sights colder
> By and by, nor spare a sigh
> Though worlds of wanwood leafmeal lie;

As she approaches her own winter in age, Margaret, the speaker says, will be sighless and sightless, colder and uncaring. The speaker's "By and by" with its echo of resigned leave-taking ('bye and bye') posits time, careless time, as well as space, removed space, all in contrast to Margaret's present weeping "over" the fallen leaves.

The speaker seems to be growing older in front of us. His statement explaining the difference between youth and age, child and self, is didactic, an apparent retreat from earlier sympathy. But his tone is quiet, almost meditational, and the lines in their motion betray more of the speaker than the speaker himself seems aware of.

We have seen the leaves turn out to *be* the things of man (instead of being analogous to or "líke" them). "Such sights" works in the same way: In her rhyming with the leaves, Margaret herself is such a sight. That is, the speaker's larger point of view sees Margaret as well as the leaves in the flowering of the fall, in the flowering that *is* the fall. Her tears spring and fall, and in her weeping Margaret 'leaves' with the leaves. Her expression of innocence is inevitably a loss of innocence; she is, all unknown to her, moving closer toward the speaker. Meanwhile, the speaker is saying that age cannot react so sympathetically to "such sights," but the poem rebukes the whole idea, and nowhere does it do so more than in these lines.

For "such sights" is not the only indistinction of statement here. The "Áh!"—that open syllable held, the exclaimed interjection so characteristic of Hopkins—seems born for this poem, this place. In that open syllable held, the highly articulated consciousness that speaks the poem retreats to let the speaker breathe out, just once, all that his verbal awareness would guard against. And it is as if the suspension of "Áh!" does not want to end, as if the speaker would dwell there if he could, wanting not to be born out of that sympathy breathed, nor borne forward from it. In the "Áh!" Margaret's tears find the form of sound in the speaker, his exclamation barely escaping the self even as it discovers a self that the speaker does not wholly recognize. An instinctive exclamation of pity for the future unweeping Margaret and for the speaker himself who is supposed to be like the future unweeping Margaret he projects, the "Áh!" arrests the poem. The lines speak of a future disconnection, speak to a failure of recurrence, but as that syllable is held in its slow falling, it catches and reenacts the bright wings: The "Áh!" *is* recurrence because the "Áh!" subsiding and ascending at once is the *speaker's* spring and fall. The syllable responds emotionally to the imaginative connection made, and it so belies by its very existence the statement that the grown cannot spare a sigh. It *is* a sigh—if only a sigh—and it so spells his—and Margaret's—salvation. The child's sympathy is not wholly lost in the man. (And having said that, one begins to wonder if that disembodied world, that "wanwood leafmeal," does not "lie" in another sense—the leaves lie, perhaps, because to the voice behind the speaker's voice the afterlife exists.)

The next line, a structural surprise, forms a triplet at the center of the poem:

> And yet you *will* weep and know why.

The verse pulls the speaker out of himself and back into the world, out of the
hypothetical future and back into the present falling. In effect, the line returns
the poem "to a young child." It is not enough, the speaker consciously realizes,
to tell the child that her sorrow will pass. "*Will*" may be future tense, but as
I. A. Richards first pointed out, the line may also be read as the emphatic
present: 'And yet you insist in weeping and on knowing why.' Since Hopkins
italicized the "*will*," the second reading may well be the intended one. Even
so, the line remains ambiguously simple, gathering up all human seeking after
the cause for suffering.

All the sadness in the world comes together as the poem's implications
widen:

> Now no matter, child, the name:
> Sórrow's springs áre the same.

The word, the name—like her name here—does not matter because the
emotion and the fact do matter now. Sorrow springs from the blight man was
born for, from his dying, from the dying of his heart. But the poem does not
name this cause yet. The second line in particular achieves a simplicity and
even sureness in its syntax, sound, and meaning, all of which seem to be
leading toward the answer named, the explanation given.

Once again, however, the explanation is forestalled, and the poem is
momentarily deflected:

> Nor mouth had, no nor mind, expressed
> What heart heard of, ghost guessed:

The expressions of age, we are told, cannot begin to approximate the intuitive
responses of the soul, the springs of feeling. The spirited rumors of mystery
and emotion are uncatchable in language or conscious thought. After the
child-directed simplicity of the previous statement, these lines move back to
complex abstraction. The syntax is as contorted as any in the entire poem, and
the verses again work at a level of intellect the child could not understand. It is
as if the speaker has stepped back, fearful of seeming to say it all, fearful of the
simplicity of the word he has come upon.

But again, even here, we catch the echoes come from a farther room. If
the syntax is mature, the meaning harks back to the remembrance of youth. To
reaffirm, as these lines do, the primacy of that mysterious heart sympathy, the
speaker has had to have felt that sympathy and must now remember—under
the child's tutelage—something of what that experience was. The very contor-
tion of the language seems a willed defense against the experience, the heart's

hearing. The didacticism of these lines, the disjunction they say so absolutely, is yet open to question because those rhyme words—"expressed" and "guessed" (also heard as 'guest')—do come together in rhyme.

At the end the speaker returns to "sorrow's springs" to answer grandiloquently all the questions asked:

It ís the blight man was born for,

Man was born for blight—sickness, devastation, disease, the failure of the human crop, the fall of worlds, the fall of man. All of this, Margaret mourns in its inescapable recurrence. But "It" in this line must also refer to the previous couplet: "It" is also that man cannot make his words mean what he wants them to, cannot fit words to feeling, logic to emotion, sense to mystery; that as he grows greater in word power, he grows increasingly impotent in the power of his feelings to respond.

And the speaker's words have grown great indeed. "It ís the blight man was born for" tolls down at its audience, all impressive and all-encompassing. The tragic didacticism sounds good, but it is all futile to alleviate, console, or perhaps even to explain Margaret's weeping to man or child. As impressive as these words sound, they exist almost completely as sign, as object, as the hardest otherness and the one farthest from Margaret's tears. They are in sharp contrast to the "Áh!," that unformulated word, all indistinction, that bends the sign back into the self. "It ís the blight man was born for" is almost pure sign, the harsh motion of unforgiving otherness.

At the very end, the speaker's thought 'buckles,' plunging from that encompassing universal to the individual child:

It is Margaret you mourn for.

Her name does matter, and it matters because his words fall from his own recurring spring. Like leaves, like the things of man, his words must fall and fail; and yet they have sprung from a source that thought had lost, beyond saving and caring, and even in their falling are hardly guessed at. The harshness, the hardness of pronouncement, is tempered by the humanness. Margaret mourns her spring, which is her fall. Her dawn, her morning, her spring, intimates her even-ing, her fall, her death. They are all one, and they are all subject to that blight: the spring, the fall, Margaret, the wood, mankind. That this, the last line, glances back to gather in the previous line and temper that hardness and show it all one is evident in the interchangeable homonyms of the rhyme words—"born" may be heard as 'borne,' and "mourn" as 'morn.' The verses would so exchange meanings, yet the couplet's meaning would remain the same. The phenomena are one, the child's springing the same as her falling.

Thus, the closure of the poem is as complete in rhyme as in rhythm as in sense; poetic closure is, in fact, as complete as is imaginable, and the end is memorable. The end affects us because of the strength of the closure; because of the strength of "blight" and "Margaret" within the simplicity of the diction and sense; and because, most of all, of what happens between the two lines, the connective fall enacted, the forgiveness arrived at. Yet this revision, as powerful and as memorable as it is, affirms some of the separation of man and child spoken of. The child cries in assent to the sadness; the man's words assent to the fact that the world has to be so; that it has to be so posits the acceptance of the hardness of age, assents in spite of its sense to the loss of sympathy in age. For all its mercy, for all its human-directed tenderness, "It is Margaret you mourn for" yet looks down at the child, consciously bending the sign and the voice saying it toward the object, the other.

It is much earlier, in the "Áh!" that the speaker *is* the child, re-enacting the child's act, which is itself an age-old recurrence. The poem centers and lives in its dying, springs in its own fall. The ripeness is all: the grove golden and dying, the child's tears, and the "Áh!" breathed in empathy for the child, for the self, and for the unselving of both. The child responds to the unselving of trees, the speaker responds to the unselving of child, the reader responds to the unselving of speaker. And all responses in their springing forth may at the same time reach back to re-enact and re-sound the original and recurring unselving of self.

J. HILLIS MILLER

The Linguistic Moment

Gerard Manley Hopkins begins in the human and poetic situation I have sketched with the help of Pater, Hegel, and Nietzsche. Hopkins' often negative comments in his letters on the English Romantic poets and on the Victorians corresponds, somewhat surprisingly, to those by Matthew Arnold— for example, in Arnold's letters to Clough. For both Arnold and Hopkins Romanticism seeks "fulness without respect of the means" and claims to have an ontological grounding it lacks. In this both Arnold and Hopkins agree with Hegel's characterization of Romanticism as the perhaps irrevocable splitting apart of nature, consciousness, God, and language. Both Arnold and Hopkins found this splitting apart intolerable, and both, in quite different ways, attempted to use language to bring the fragmented pieces back together, to revoke the irrevocable, with indifferent success, in Arnold's case at least, . . . Hopkins' parallel attempt to reintegrate the disintegrated proposes a chiming of nature, man, and God as it may be affirmed in what he called the "inscapes" of language.

The primary motive for Hopkins conversion to Roman Catholicism from his native Anglicanism was the absence in the latter of any genuine belief in the "Real Presence" of Christ in the bread and wine of the Sacrament of Communion. In that Presence nature, God, self, and Word come together. Poetry, if it is to have value, must repeat that magical assimilation of the dispersed into one. Like the words of the priest in the Communion, poetry must not describe things as they are but make something happen. This presupposes that the initial situation in poetry is the dispersal Hopkins inherited from the Roman-

From *The Linguistic Moment: From Wordsworth to Stevens*. © 1985 by Princeton University Press. Originally entitled "Hopkins."

tic and Victorian poets, just as his situation in religion was the lax Anglicanism, as he saw it, of his family and of his native land.

That this situation of separation was Hopkins' starting place is indicated
in the melancholy eloquence of the celebrated opening of his commentary on
the *Spiritual Exercises* of Saint Ignatius: "And this [my isolation] is much more
true when we consider the mind; when I consider my selfbeing, my consciousness and feeling of myself, that taste of myself, of *I* and *me* above and in all
things, which is more distinctive than the taste of ale or alum, more distinctive
than the smell of walnutleaf or camphor, and is incommunicable by any means
to another man (as when I was a child I used to ask myself: What must it be to
be someone else?)." Selfhood, each man's consciousness of himself, is incommunicable by any means to another man (a terrifying thought) because, just as
Hegel said, it has no kinship with those things in nature all men share, for
example, the taste of ale or alum or the smell of walnutleaf or camphor. This is
true in spite of the fact that, for the man himself, the taste of "*I* and *me*" is "in
all things," as well as "above" them. If I borrow figures from nature to attempt
to express my sense of myself to others, I shall communicate not my taste of
myself but what other people already know: the taste of ale or alum, the smell
of walnutleaf or camphor. This conspicuously happens in the passage just
quoted. The passage does not tell the reader anything at all about what it was
like to be Gerard Manley Hopkins, except that it was a state of desolate solitude. His state was like that of a man who has been shipwrecked in a country
where no one knows his language. He was like Conrad's Yanko Goorall, for
example, already invoked here apropos of Browning's "The Englishman in
Italy." Or Hopkins' situation was like that of Dante's Nimrod, who can only
babble in an utterly private language: *Raphel maì amècche zabì almi.* As Virgil
explains to Dante, Nimrod is the one "through whose ill thought one language
only is not used in the world [*per lo cui mal coto / pur un linguaggio nel mondo non
s'usa*]," and there is no use talking to him, "for every language is to him as his
is to others, which is known to none [*ché così è a lui ciascun linguaggio / come 'l suo
ad altrui, ch'a nullo è noto*]."

If Hopkins' isolation is like that of Yanko or Nimrod, it has a special
twist, for Hopkins is a master of many languages, a teacher of Latin and Greek,
a skilled translator, able to write poems in Latin, Greek, and Welsh. This is to
say that Hopkins is a comparatist, engaged in the repair of the disaster of Babel,
Nimrod's folly, according to the tradition Dante follows. Nevertheless, for
all his linguistic skill Hopkins is unable to communicate "by any means," that
is, by means of any language or sign system, his taste of himself. If he speaks
or writes in any language, he will communicate only what that language already
says. If he speaks adequately of his self-taste, he will, like Nimrod, speak
a private language and so communicate nothing: *Raphael maì amècche zabì almi.*

The Wreck of the Deutschland, that first great burst of poetic language of Hopkins' maturity, speaks from such a condition of desolation and attempts to escape it. The wreck is Hopkins' own, incarnated in his own flesh, blood, and self-taste, and it is at the same time the wreck he inherited from his immediate predecessors in poetry. Hopkins' attempted repair of the disaster of Babel had long been preparing, for example, in his early diaries and journals. It continues, of course, in all the poems written after *The Wreck*. Hopkins' poetic problem was to find a way to communicate the incommunicable. It was an attempted rescue of the self and of language through language.

Kenneth Burke, in remarks about an earlier version of this essay, argued that I should add something about the multiple meaning of the word *wreck* in the title. *The Wreck of the Deutschland*, he said, is about Hopkins' wreck, as indeed in this present essay I am also affirming in my own way. Burke's statement was a powerful plea to relate the linguistic complexities, or tensions, back to their subjective counterparts. Much is at stake here. That the poem is a deeply personal document there can be no doubt. Its linguistic tensions are lived, not mere verbal play in the negative sense. It has always been Kenneth Burke's great strength, as opposed to some present-day structuralists or semiologists, never to neutralize literary language, never to make it into a tame conundrum or trivial crossword puzzle. For Burke literature is always incarnated in the flesh and blood and nerves of its writer or reader. In this he is true to his great exemplar, Sigmund Freud.

Nor can there be any doubt that in *The Wreck of the Deutschland* Hopkins is speaking of his own wreck in the sense of personal disaster, fragmentation, or blockage (with the pun, elsewhere used by Hopkins, on *reck* as *beware of, take warning from*). Hopkins' experience of himself as a wreck was associated with his sense of impotence, with his inability ever to finish anything or to "breed one work that wakes," as in a moving late letter: "And there they lie and my old notebooks and beginnings of things, ever so many, which it seems to me might well have been done, ruins and wrecks" [*Further Letters of Gerard Manley Hopkins*; all further references to this text will be abbreviated *FL*].

The movement to resurrection and salvation in *The Wreck of the Deutschland* does not, I agree, fully counterbalance the extraordinary expression of unresolved tension. Resolution, in the sense of the final untying of a blocking knot, always remains a future event in Hopkins' writing, and necessarily so, on the terms of his own theology. The danger in Burke's suggestion, however, is, as always in such cases, the possibility of a psychologizing reduction, the making of literature into no more than a reflection or representation of something psychic that precedes it and could exist without it. Hopkins' personal wreck is rather his inextricable involvement, in flesh and blood, in a net of signs, figures, concepts, and narrative patterns. The exchanges, permu-

tations, contradictions, latent aporias, untyings and tyings of these elements
he had the courage and the genius to live through in his writing and in his
experience. Subjectivity, with all its intensities, is in this case, too, more a
result than an origin. To set it first, to make an explanatory principle of it, is,
as Nietzsche says, a metalepsis, putting late before early, effect before cause.

Hopkins' attempt to rescue himself from language through language
begins with a linguistic assumption, an assumption about the relation of individual words to the Logos—Christ the Word. Hopkins' religious thought is
centered on an ultimately acentric analogy: the parallelism between the structure of language and the structure of the creation in relation to the creator.
The most obvious way in which this analogy appears is in the systematic and
of course wholly orthodox use of a metaphor drawn from language to describe
the relation of the world to God. Christ, the second person of the Trinity, is
the Logos, the word or utterance of God. The world with all its multitude of
creatures, including man, is spoken into existence in the name of Christ,
modeled on Christ, just as all the multiplicity of words in a language might
be considered as the product of an increasingly elaborate differentiation of a
primal word, an ur-word. The structure of language is the vehicle of the metaphor that is the irreplaceable means by which Hopkins expresses his conception of God in his relation to the creation. One might say that his theological
terminology is logocentric. Language itself, however, is also a primary theme
in Hopkins' writings, not only in the brilliant etymological speculations in
the early diaries or in the early essay on words, but also in the mature poetry
itself, for example, in "That Nature is a Heraclitean Fire and of the comfort
of the Resurrection," and in "I wake and feel the fell of dark, not day." The
theme of language is most elaborately developed in Hopkins' masterpiece, *The
Wreck of the Deustchland*. This motif runs all through *The Wreck*, not just as a
metaphor but as a theme treated directly, for itself.

Hopkins affirms three apparently incompatible theories of poetry. Each
is brilliantly worked out in theory and exemplified in practice. Poetry may be
the representation of the interlocked chiming of created things in their relation
to the Creator. This chiming makes the pied beauty of nature. Poetry may
explore or express the solitary adventures of the self in its wrestles with God or
in its fall into the abyss outside God. Poetry may explore the intricate relationships among words. These three seemingly diverse theories of poetry are
harmonized by the application to all of them of a linguistic model. This model
assumes that all words rhyme because all are ultimately derived from the same
Logos. Nature, for example, is "word, expression, news of God" [*The Sermons
and Devotional Writings of Gerard Manley Hopkins*; all further references to this
text will be abbreviated *SD*] because God has inscribed himself in nature. The

structure of nature in its relation to God is like the structure of language in relation to the Logos, the divine Word. Christ is the Logos of nature, as of words. The linguistic model also applies to the changes within the self. The permutations of language, as in the final two lines of "That Nature is a Heraclitean Fire," mime the permutations of the self as it is changed by grace from a Jackself, steeped in sin, turned from God, to a more Christ-like, Logosimilar, self. The lines solve a linguistic puzzle. How to get from "Jack" to "immortal diamond" with the smallest number of changed or added sounds. The solution to the puzzle corresponds to Hopkins' escape from the incommunicable solitude of his self-taste. He escapes from it in the only way possible, by the transformation of what is altogether particular, his self-taste, to the altogether general—Christ the ubiquitous Word. He makes this change without ceasing to be himself, as carbon may be changed, with enough fire and pressure, into its allotropic form, diamond, though it is still carbon:

I am all at once what Christ is ¹ since he was what I am, and
This Jack, joke, poor potsherd, ¹ patch, matchwood, immortal diamond,
                    Is immortal diamond.

Since the structure of language is the indispensable metaphor by means of which Hopkins describes nature or the self, the nature of language is a matter of fundamental importance to him. From his early diaries to the last poems, Hopkins shows his fascination with language as such. One can see why, since everything else, his vision of nature and of the self in their relations to God, hangs on the question of the nature of language and of the adequacy of the linguistic metaphor.

In all three realms—language, nature, and self—the notion of rhyme, the echoing at a distance of entities that are similar without being identical, is essential. The exploitation of rhyme in this extended sense may be seen operating throughout *The Wreck of the Deutschland* as its fundamental organizing principle. Rhyme operates in *The Wreck* both on the microscopic level of local poetical effect and on the macroscopic level of the large structural repetitions organizing the whole.

On the local level there are repetitions with a difference of word sounds, word meanings, and rhythmical patterns. As is indicated by the etymological speculations in Hopkins' early diaries, the basis of Hopkins' interest in the labyrinth of relations among the sounds of words is the assumption that if words sound the same they will be similar in meaning. Each sequence of words with the same consonant pattern but with different vowels—for example, *flick*, *fleck*, *flake*—is assumed to be a variation on a single ur-meaning from which they are all derived. All words whatsoever, all permutations of all the letters

of the alphabet, are assumed to have a common source in the Word, "him that
present and past, / Heaven and earth are word of, worded by," as Hopkins puts
it in *The Wreck* (lines 229—230). This attention to sound similarities in their
relation to similarities of meaning is perhaps most apparent in the emphatic
use of alliteration throughout the poem (breath/bread; strand/sway/sea; bound/
bones); but there are many other forms of sound echo—assonance, end rhyme,
internal rhyme, recurrences of vowel sequences, and so on—which the attentive reader will follow as threads of embodied meaning in the tapestry of the
poem. In all these cases the underlying assumption is theological as well as
technical. The fact that Christ is the Word, or Logos, of which all particular
words are versions, variations, or metaphors, allows Hopkins even to accomo-
date into his poem words that are similar in sound though opposite in meaning. Christ underlies all words and thereby reconciles all oppositions in word
sound and meaning: "Thou art lightning and love, I found it, a winter and
warm" (line 70).

The same assumptions ground the various forms of repetition with difference of word meaning in the poem. The complex fabric of recurring metaphors is not mere verbal play to unify the poem. This pattern is based on
the assumption that metaphorical comparisons reflect ontological correspondences in the world. Such correspondences are placed there by the God whom
heaven and earth are word of, worded by. Fire, water, sand, and wind are the
primary elements of this "metaphorology." To the recurrence of metaphors
may be added the repetition of metaphorical elements by thematic motifs that
exist on the literal level of narrative in the poem. It is no accident that the
poet's experience of grace in the first part of the poem is described in terms of
figures of fire, sand, and water. These anticipate the elements literally present
in the lightning, sandbar, and ocean waves of the shipwreck.

Hopkins' frequent use of puns assumes that a single sound may be a
meeting place, crossroads, or verbal knot where several distinct verbal strands
converge. This convergence is once more evidence of ontological relations
among the various meanings layered in a single word. Man's condition as
sullenly fallen, stubbornly "tied to his turn" away from God ("Ribblesdale,"
line 11), for example, may be expressed by calling him "dogged in den" (line
67). Here, *dogged* is a quadruple pun meaning sullenly determined, doglike,
twisted down (as a *dog* is a kind of bolt), and hounded (as a wild animal is
chased by dogs into its den and kept at bay there). There may also be an
expression of the mirroring of God by man in the fact that *dog*, man's epithet
here, reverses the letters that spell *God*.

Hopkins' use of sprung rhythm, a distinctive feature of *The Wreck of the
Deutschland* is discussed in a letter of October 5, 1878, to R.W. Dixon.

Hopkins' prosodic practice is a complex matter, since most of his verse combines sprung rhythm with elements from the ordinary accentual rhythm of English poetry, but the basic principle of sprung rhythm is simple enough. Each foot or measure has a single strong beat, but there may be "any number of weak or slack syllables" ("Author's Preface," [*The Poems of Gerard Manley Hopkins*]), so that a foot may have only one syllable or many, though the time length of all feet is the same. This gives the great effect of tension, or "springing," to such verse. Hopkins insisted that sprung rhythm is the "rhythm of common speech and of written prose, when rhythm is perceived in them." Hopkins expected his poetry to be recited aloud with the emphases and rhythms of common speech. A note written apropos of *The Wreck of the Deutschland* makes explicit the way Hopkins wanted the poem to be spoken out:

> Be pleased, reader, since the rhythm in which the following poem is written is new, strongly to mark e beats of the measure, according to the number belonging to   of the eight lines of the stanza, as the indentation guides the eye, namely two and three and four and three and five and five and four and six; not disguising the rhythm and rhyme, as some readers do, who treat poetry as if it were prose fantastically written to rule (which they mistakenly think the perfection of reading), but laying on the beat too much stress rather than too little, nor caring whether one, two, three, or more syllables go to a beat, that is to say, whether two or more beats follow running—as there are three running in the third line of the first stanza—or with syllables between, as commonly, nor whether the line begin with a beat or not; but letting the scansion run on from one line into the next, without break to the end of the stanza: since the dividing of the lines is more to fix the places of the necessary rhymes than for any pause in the measure. . . . And so throughout let the stress be made to fetch out both the strength of the syllables and the meaning and feeling of the words.

The rhythmical complexities in *The Wreck* are not ends in themselves. They are another form of repetition with variation. They are another way to set down or to specify a given sound pattern, which is then differentially echoed in later units of the poem, according to the fundamental principle of all poetry, which Hopkins identified in "Poetry and Verse" (1873 or 1874) as "repetition, *oftening, over-and-overing, aftering*" [*The Journals and Papers of Gerard Manley Hopkins*; all further references to this text will be abbreviated *JP*].

The sprung rhythm of *The Wreck* has as much a theological basis as any of the other forms of rhyme. As Hopkins says in the letter to Dixon of 1878, he "had long had haunting [his] ear the echo of a new rhythm which now [he] realized on paper" [*The Correspondence of Gerard Manley Hopkins and Richard Watson Dixon*]. The strategic use of the metaphor of music in *The Wreck* makes it clear that the rhythm echoed in the poet's ear and then embodied in the words of the poem is no less than the fundamental rhythm or groundswell of the creation—the ratio, measure, or Logos that pervades all things, as a fundamental melody may be varied or echoed throughout a great symphony. This rhythm is not "*I* and *me* above and in all things" but God above and in all things. The long Platonic and Christian tradition connecting the notion of rhythm to the Logos or underlying principle of things, "Ground of being, and granite of it" (line 254), as Hopkins calls it here, is subtly integrated into the texture of thought in this poem as well as into its rhythmical practice. When the poet is at the point of affirming the attunement of the tall nun with the name of Christ, worded everywhere in the creation, he affirms that His name is "her mind's" "measure" and "burden" (lines 215—216), where *measure* is musical measure and *burden* is fundamental melody, as in Shakespeare's "Come Unto these Yellow Sands"; "and, sweet sprites, the burden bear." The sprung rhythm of *The Wreck* is not merely a device for achieving a high degree of tension and patterning in the poem. It is based on the belief that God himself is a rhythm that the poet may echo in his verse. The poet's breath in its modulations and tempo may answer God's "arch and original Breath" (line 194).

To these small-scale forms of organization corresponds the way in which the large-scale dramatic or narrative structure of the poem is put together. If the poem is an ode, it is also an elegy for the dead, part of the long tradition of elegies in English stretching from "Lycidas" to *The Waste Land* and "The Owl in the Sarcophagus." Like "Lycidas," "Adonais," or *In Memoriam*, *The Wreck of the Deutschland* is only nominally about the dead whom it memorializes. The poet's response to the death of another is the occasion for a personal affirmation about the poet's inner life and his sense of vocation.

Once again repetition with variation is the basis of Hopkins' poetic practice. The key to the overall structure of *The Wreck of the Deutschland* is given in stanza 18. There the poet describes his tears when he reads of the death of the nuns in his safe haven "away in the loveable west, / On a pastoral forehead of Wales" (lines 185—186): "Why, tears! is it? tears; such a melting, a madrigal start!" (line 142). The poet's tears are a madrigal echo or rhyme of the nun's suffering, that is, an echo of the same melody on a different pitch, as in the basic musical structure of a Renaissance madrigal, canon, or round. This canonlike response leads the poet first to re-enact in memory an earlier experience in which he felt God's grace, then, in the second part of the poem, to re-enact in his imagination the death of the nuns. The narrative doubling, the memory of his own experience doubling his vivid picture of the shipwreck, causes a redoubling in a new experience of God's presence to the poet. This new experience of grace occurs within the poem itself and is identical with the writing of it. The poem is addressed directly to God in the present tense, and this immediate reciprocity between the poet and the God who "masters" him is the "now" of the poem generated by its doubling and redoubling of the two earlier "nows" that it iterates.

The various techniques of "rhyme" in *The Wreck of the Deutschland*, though perhaps based on methods Hopkins had learned from Pindar's odes, from Old English verse, or from the complex Welsh system of poetry called *cynghanedd*, are in fact a magnificent exploitation of the general properties of language as they may be put to a specifically poetic use. This use Roman Jakobson calls the set of language towards itself. This formulation occurs in an essay in which Jakobson quotes with approval Hopkins' expression of the same idea. In the passage in question Hopkins defines poetry as repetition. As he puts it, "poetry is in fact speech only employed to carry the inscape of speech for the inscape's sake," and "in this light poetry is speech which afters and oftens its inscape, speech couched in a repeating figure" (*JP*).

Hopkins' exploitation of the manifold possibilities of repetition in language is based then throughout on the theological notion that God is the Word. The divine Word is the basis of all words in their relations of similarity and difference. The play of phonic, verbal, and rhythmical texture in *The Wreck of the Deutschland* is controlled by the idea of a creator who has differentiated himself in his creation. The world is full of things that echo one another and rhyme. The same God is also the Word behind all words, the "arch and original Breath" that modulates itself into all the words that may be said. The branches and twigs of the tree of language are divided and derived forms of the initial Word. Word and world in this happily correspond because they have the same source.

This theory of poetic language is not only exemplified in *The Wreck*. It is one of the chief thematic strands in the poem. Repeatedly, in one way or another, throughout *The Wreck*, the question of language comes up, for example, in "I did say yes" and "truer than tongue" as early as the second stanza (lines 9, 11). One theme of the poem is its own possibility of being. *The Wreck of the Deutschland*, like many great poems of the nineteenth and twentieth centuries, is, in part at least, about poetry. In this, in spite of Hopkins' Catholicism, he may be seen as a poet in the Romantic tradition, a poet who belongs in the great line leading from Wordsworth, Blake, and Hölderlin through

Baudelaire, Tennyson, and Rimbaud to poets of our own century like Yeats, Rilke, and Stevens. All in one way or another make the powers of poetry a theme of their poems.

In exploring this aspect of *The Wreck*, however, the reader encounters what is most problematic about it, both in its form and in its meaning. In a letter to W. M. Baillie of January 14, 1883, Hopkins develops a theory that in classical literature—for example, in Greek tragedy—the overt meaning may be matched by a covert sequence of figures or allusions constituting what he calls an "underthought." This will be an "echo or shadow of the over-thought . . . an undercurrent of thought governing the choice of images used." "In any lyric passage of the tragic poets," says Hopkins, ". . . there are—usually; I will not say always, it is not likely—two strains of thought running together and like counterpointed; the overthought that which everybody, editors, see . . . and which might for instance be abridged or para-phrased . . . the other, the underthought, conveyed chiefly in the choice of metaphors etc used and often only half realized by the poet himself. . . . The underthought is commonly an echo or shadow of the overthought, something like canons and repetitions in music, treated in a different manner" (*FL*). If the overthought of *The Wreck of the Deutschland* is the story of the tall nun's salvation and the story of the musical echoes of that salvation both before and after by the poet's parallel experiences of grace, the underthought of the poem is its constant covert attention to problems of language. This linguistic theme is in a subversive relation of counterpoint to the theological overthought.

One important thematic element in *The Wreck of the Deutschland* is the image of a strand, rope, finger, vein, or stem. This image is Hopkins' way of expressing the link between creator and created. One form of this motif, "ton-gue," is present in the poem in "truer than tongue" (line 11), in "past telling of tongue" (line 69), with its reference to the gift of tongues, which descended at Pentecost on the Apostles in tongues of flame (Acts 2:1ff.), in "a virginal tongue told" (line 136), and in the conflation of God's finger and the tongue which rings the tall nun as if she were a bell (stanza 31). The creative "stem of stress," in Hopkins' phrase, between God and his creatures is a tongue that speaks by modulating or dividing the arch and original breath, the undiffer-entiated word that is Christ, as the tongues of fire at Pentecost were "cloven."

Christ, the second Person of the Trinity, the link between God the Father and the creation, is a principle of unity. He is the only means by which man may return to the singleness of the Godhead. At the same time He is the prin-ciple of differentiation. Christ is the model for the multiplicity of individ-ual things in the world, including that most highly individuated creature, man. This is one meaning justifying Hopkins' epithet for Christ in stanza 34: "double-naturèd name" (line 266). Christ is both God and man, both one and many. He is the avenue by which man loses his individuality in God, in imitating Christ or, like the tall nun, in reading Christ as the single word of the creation. At the same time Christ is the basis of puns in language. He is also the explanation of the fact that God manifests himself as both lightning and love, as winter and warm—that is, in things named by words that sound alike but have opposite meanings. The devil is in this diabolical imitation of Christ, as Abel and Cain are brothers, or as Deutschland is "double a desperate name" (line 155), the name both of the ship and of a country, a country that is itself double. Germany has given birth both to a saint, Gertrude, lilylike in her purity, and to Luther, the "beast of the waste wood" (lines 157−158).

The theme of language in *The Wreck* moves toward the ambiguous vision of a God who is single but who can express himself in language and in his creation only in the multiple. Though it takes a "single eye" to "read the unshapeable shock night" (lines 226−227)—that is, to see the unitary presence of God in the storm—this insight must be expressed by the poet in multiple language. There is no masterword for the Word, only metaphors of it, for all words are metaphors, displaced from their proper reference by a primal bifurcation. When the tall nun "rears herself" (line 150), like "a lioness . . . breasting the babble" (line 135), she is moving back through the multiplicity of language (by way of the pun on *Babel*) to the Word—Christ. But what the nun says must be interpreted: "the majesty! What did she mean?" (line 193). Ultimately her word must be moved back into the babble, the confusion of tongues introduced by Babel and confirmed as well as repaired by the gift of tongues at Pentecost.

In the same way the straightforward linear narrative of Hopkins' poem is continuously displaced by all the echoes and repetitions that turn the language of the poem back on itself in lateral movements of meaning. These lateral relationships proliferate in multitudinous echoes. If Hopkins' basic poetic strategy, as Geoffrey Hartman has noted, is a differentiation of language that attempts to say the Word by dividing the word, these divisions are controlled by no central word that could be enunciated in any language.

Striking evidence of Hopkins' awareness of this tragic eccentricity of language appears in two crucial places in *The Wreck* where the poet presents an ornate series of terms or metaphors for the same thing. In one case, significantly enough, the series names the act of writing, that act whereby God's finger inscribes his own name on those he has chosen, "his own bespoken" (line 173). The stanza (22) presents a series of metaphors for the act of stamp-

ing something with a sign, making it a representation or metaphor for something else, as grace makes man a metaphor of Christ. These are metaphors for
metaphor:

> Five! the finding and sake
> And cipher of suffering Christ.
> Mark, the mark is of man's make
> And the word of it Sacrificed.
> But he scores it in scarlet himself on his own bespoken,
> Before-time-taken, dearest prizèd and priced—
> Stigma, signal, cinquefoil token
> For lettering of the lamb's fleece, ruddying of the rose-flake.

Finding, sake, cipher, mark, word, score, stigma, signal, cinquefoil token, lettering—
each is only one more word for the act of wording, in the physical sense of carv-
ing and inscription. The series of terms is controlled by no unmoving word in
any human language that would be outside the play of differences.

The other such list appears at the climax of the poem, the appearance of
Christ to the nun at the moment of her death. It comes just after a passage in
which the poet's syntactical control breaks down (the ellipses are Hopkins'):
"But how shall I . . . make me room there: / Reach me a . . . Fancy, come
faster—" (lines 217–218). Then follows a list of names for Christ. Significantly, this is the only place in the poem, and one of the few places in all
Hopkins' English poetry, where the poet speaks with tongues himself and in-
serts a word not in his native language: "There then! the Master, / *Ipse*, the only
one, Christ, King, Head" (lines 220–221). The tragic limitation of poetic
language lies in the fact that the Word itself cannot be said. Far from having
a tendency to fall back into some undifferentiated ground of phonemic similarity (as Hartman affirms), a word by the very fact that it is just that pattern
of vowels and consonants which it is, cannot be the Word. The words of human
language, for Hopkins, seem to have been born of some primal division, a fall
from the arch and original breath into the articulate. This fall has always already
occurred as soon as there is any human speech. Words have therefore a tendency to proliferate endlessly their transformations by changes of vowel and
consonant, as if they were in search for the magic word that would be the Word.

In the example already given of the permutations of vowels and consonants in the series turning a mere "Jack" into Christ in "That Nature is a Heraclitean Fire," the endpoint is not some triumphant uttering of the Word as
such. It is only another metaphor, and a metaphor tautologically repeated at
that: "immortal diamond, / Is immortal diamond." It seems as if such a series
can only be arbitrarily ended by being turned back on itself in a locution that in

its punning doubleness confesses to its inadequacy as a name for the Word. "Immortal diamond," uttered as an epithet for the hardest and most indestructible of natural substances, is then thrown out as a figure for what has no literal name, the self turned into supernatural brilliance, transparency, hardness, and permanence: "Immortal diamond / Is immortal diamond." The language remains still as far as it was when it began with "Jack" from speaking the Word literally.

In the same way, the dramatic climax of *The Wreck of the Deutschland* is also the climax of its treatment of the theme of language. Its dramatic climax is the tall nun's saying the name of Christ and thereby being saved, transformed into Christ at the moment of her death. The linguistic climax is the implicit recognition, in stanzas 22 and 28, that there is no way of speaking of this theological mystery except in a cascade of metaphors whose proliferation confesses to the fact that there is no literal word for the Word. Since these "metaphors" do not replace a literal term, they are, strictly speaking, not metaphors but catachreses, names thrown out toward the unnamable Word and more covering it in human noise than revealing it or speaking it out.

A confirmation of the eccentricity, or irremediable distance from the center, of natural language is the fact that the original meaning lying behind most of the word lists in Hopkins' early diaries is one form or another of the gesture of dividing or marking. Hopkins' insight into the nature of language is a complex matter, but here, as in other areas of his thought, he had the insight of genius. The center around which Hopkins' linguistic speculations revolve, the unsettling intuition that they approach and withdraw from, is the exact opposite of his theological insight. It is the notion that there is no primal word, that the divisions of language have always already occurred as soon as there is language at all. If this is so, there is no word for the Word, only displaced metaphors of it. In the word lists in Hopkins' early onomatopoetic etymological speculations, each list goes back to an ur-gesture, action, or sound. In each case this is an act of division, marking, striking, or cutting. Here are examples of these lists: "grind, gride, gird, grit, groat, grate, greet," "flick, fleck, flake," "skim, scum, squama, scale, keel," "shear, shred, potsherd, shard." Of the first list Hopkins says, "Original meaning to *strike, rub,* particularly *together*." Of the second list, "*Flick* means to touch or strike lightly as with the end of a whip, a finger etc. To *fleck* is the next tone above flick, still meaning to touch or strike lightly (and leave a mark of the touch or stroke) but in a broader less slight manner. Hence substantively a *fleck* is a piece of light, colour, substance etc. looking as though shaped or produced by such touches. *Flake* is a broad and decided *fleck*, a thin plate of something, the tone above it. Their connection is more clearly seen in the applications of the

words to natural objects than in explanations." The third list involves the
notion of "the topmost flake what [sic] may be skimmed from the surface of a
thing," and the fourth list is of words playing variations on the act of division,
as "the *ploughshare* [is] that which divides the soil." For Hopkins, "the onomatopoetic theory has not had a fair chance" (*JP*), and all these word lists
lead back to an original sound or sound-producing act of differentiation. For
Hopkins, as for modern linguistics, the beginning is diacritical. Even the
intimate life of the Trinity, in which Hopkins was much interested, is
characterized, for him, by the act whereby God divides himself from himself,
goes outside himself, "as they say *ad extra*" (*SD*).

   The metaphor of language, moreover, has a peculiar status in Hopkins'
poem. It seems to be one model among others for the relation of nature to
Christ or for the relation of the soul to Christ. A chain of such metaphors exists
in Hopkins' poems and prose writings: music, echo, visible pattern or shape as
figures for nature's interrelations of "rhyme" in the connection of one item in
nature to another and of each item to its model, Christ; cleave, sex, threshing,
pitch (with a triple pun) for the action of grace on the soul. Along with the
other items in the first sequence is the metaphor that says nature is interrelated
in the way the words in a language are interrelated. This is one reason why
Hopkins is so insistent that words should be onomatopoetic in origin. The
second sequence includes the metaphor that says the transformations of grace
are like the changes from one word to another in the chain that goes from *Jack*
to *diamond*. Christ is the Word on which all other words are modeled.

   The difficulty raised by these figures of language is double. In the first
place there is something odd about using as a model what in other cases has to
be assumed to be a transparent means of naming. Language about language
has a different status from language about pomegranates being cloven, about
threshing, or about sexual intercourse. Insofar as language emerges as the
underthought of *The Wreck of the Deutschland*, language in general and figure in
particular are made problematic. They no longer can be taken for granted as
adequate expressions of something extralinguistic. Second, this metaphor,
like the others, asks to be followed as far as it can be taken. When this happens
in Hopkins' case, the whole structure of his thought and textual practice—
theological, conceptual, or representational—is put in question by the fact
that there is no master word, no word for the Word, only endless permutations
of language. For Hopkins these permutations are not based on an emanation
from a primal unity. The "origin" of language is a nonorigin, a bifurcation.
This bifurcation has always already taken place as soon as there is language at
all. This split, not unity, is reached by a backward movement to the origin of
language, as in Hopkins' etymological speculations, just as it is not "the Word"

that is reached in *The Wreck of the Deutschland* or in "That Nature is a Heraclitean Fire," but only another word or a tautology.

There are indeed two texts in Hopkins, the overthought and the underthought. One text, the overthought, is a version (a particularly splendid
version) of Western metaphysics in its Catholic Christian form. In this text the
Word governs all words, as it governs natural objects and selves. Like Father,
like Son; and the sons, all the particular words, are a way back to the Father.
"No man cometh to the Father but by me" (John 14:6). On the other hand,
Hopkins' underthought is a thought about language itself. It recognizes that
there is no word for the Word, that all words are metaphors. Each word leads
to another word of which it is the displacement, in a movement without origin
or end. Insofar as the play of language emerges as the basic model for the other
two realms (nature and the effects of grace within the soul), it subverts the
theological harmony of both nature and supernature. The individual natural
object and the individual self, by the fact of their individuality, are incapable
of ever being more than a metaphor of Christ—that is, split off from Christ.
They are incapable by whatever extravagant series of sideways transformations
from ever becoming more than another metaphor. On the one hand, then, "No
man cometh to the Father but by me," and on the other hand, to vary John's
formulation, in accordance with Hopkins' darker insight, "No one comes to
the Father by imitating me, for I am the principle of distance and differentiation. I am the principle of a splitting or punning which is discovered to have
already occurred, however far back toward the primal unity one goes, even
back within the bosom of the Trinity itself."

If the tragedy of language is its inability to say the Word, the mystery of
the human situation, as Hopkins presents it, is parallel. The more a man affirms himself, the more he affirms his eccentricity, his individuality, his
failure to be Christ, or Christ-like, an "AfterChrist," as Hopkins puts it (*SD*).
It is only by an unimaginable and, literally, unspeakable transformation, the
transformation effected by grace, such as the nun's "conception" of Christ at
the moment of her death in *The Wreck of the Deutschland*, that the individual
human being can be turned into Christ. The fact that this transformation is
"past telling of tongue" in any words that say directly what they mean is indicated not only by the fact that the action of grace (both in this poem and
throughout Hopkins) is always described in metaphor, but also by the fact that
such a large number of incompatible metaphors are used: forging (lines 73,
74), sexual reproduction, speaking, eating and being eaten, threshing, rope-
twisting, armed combat, change of pitch or angle ("she rears herself," line
150).

To put this in terms of the linguistic metaphor: if Hopkins' poetic theory and practice are everywhere dominated by wordplay based on a recognition that the relation of rhyme is the echoing at a distance of entities that are similar but not identical, the change of man through grace into Christ is a transcendence of that distance and difference into identity, a change of play into reality in which the image becomes what it images. "It is as if a man said," writes Hopkins, "That is Christ playing at me and me playing at Christ, only that it is no play but truth; That is Christ *being me* and me being Christ" (*SD*). *The Wreck of the Deutschland*, like all the great poems of Hopkins' maturity, turns on a recognition of the ultimate failure of poetic language. Its failure is never to be able to express the inconceivable and unsayable mystery of how something that is as unique as a single word—that is, a created soul—may be transformed into the one Word, Christ, which is its model, without ceasing to be a unique and individual self.

Rather than being in happy correspondence, Hopkins' theological thought and its linguistic underthought are at cross-purposes. They have a structure of chiasmus. The theological thought depends on the notion of an initial unity that has been divided or fragmented and so could conceivably be reunified. The linguistic underthought depends on the notion of an initial bifurcation that could not by any conceivable series of linguistic transformations, such as those that make up the basic poetic strategies of Hopkins' verse, reach back to any primal word. There is no such word. Hopkins' linguistic underthought undoes his Christian overthought.

After all his efforts, Hopkins remains as far as language goes, where he was in the beginning, imprisoned within a self-taste that can be communicated by no means to another man, not even when it undergoes that transformation by grace which turns it into an AfterChrist, that is, into another utterance of the aboriginal Word. Though Hopkins seems so different from Pater, Hegel, or Nietzsche, and though he makes every effort to escape the poetic and personal impasse of Romanticism, he is forced, in his linguistic insight and in his linguistic practice, to express another version of the detachment from one another of self, nature, God, and language that Pater, Hegel, and Nietzsche in their different ways express. For Hopkins, too, language is a medium of separation, not of reconciliation. For Hopkins, too, all things come together within language only to disperse.

Chronology

1844   Born to successful middle-class Anglican family.

1854   Begins boarding at Sir Robert Chomondeley's Grammar School in Highgate.

1859   Hopkins's poem "The Escorial" wins school poetry prize.

1860   Hopkins wins second Highgate prize for "A Vision of Mermaids."

1863   Goes up to Balliol College, Oxford.

1863–67   At Oxford. Friendship with members of the Oxford Movement.

1864   Meets Christina Rossetti. Writes "Heaven-Haven" and "A Voice from the World."

1865   Begins correspondence with Robert Bridges. Writes "Easter Communion," "The Alchemist in the City," and "See How Spring Opens."

1866   Received into the Roman Catholic Church by John Henry Newman.

1867   Graduates from Oxford with a double first in Greats (Classics).

1868   Enters Jesuit novitiate at Roehampton. Burns his poems. In the next seven years, he writes only two new poems.

1870   Studies philosophy at St. Mary's Hall, Stonyhurst.

1872   Discovers Duns Scotus.

1873   Teaches classics at Manresa House, Roehampton.

1874   Studies theology at St. Bueno's College, North Wales.

1875   Begins *The Wreck of the Deutschland*.

1876   *The Wreck of the Deutschland* rejected by *The Month*.

1877   Ordained as a priest. Moves to Mount St. Mary's College, Chesterfield, where he teaches, and serves as a subminister. Writes "The Windhover."

1878   Returns to Oxford as a preacher at St. Aloysius's Church. Writes "The May Magnificat."

1879   Writes "Binsey Poplars," "Duns Scotus's Oxford," and "Henry Purcell." Teaches at St. Francis Xavier Church, Liverpool.

1880   Writes "Felix Randal."

1881   Writes "Spring and Fall."

1882   Teaches classics at Stonyhurst College.

1883   Writes "The Blessed Virgin Compared to the Air We Breathe."

1884   Becomes Professor of Greek at University College, Dublin. Writes "Spelt from Sybil's Leaves."

1885   Writes "Carrion Comfort" and other "terrible" sonnets.

1887   Writes "Henry Ploughman" and "Tom's Garland."

1888   Writes "That Nature is a Heraclitean Fire and of the Comfort of the Resurrection."

1889   Falls ill of typhoid fever. Writes "Thou Art Indeed Just." Dies of typhoid on June 8.

1918   First edition of Hopkins's collected poems, edited by Robert Bridges, is published.

Contributors

HAROLD BLOOM, Sterling Professor of the Humanities at Yale University, is the author of *The Anxiety of Influence*, *Poetry and Repression*, and many other volumes of literary criticism. His forthcoming study, *Freud: Transference and Authority*, attempts a full-scale reading of all of Freud's major writings. A MacArthur Prize Fellow, he is general editor of five series of literary criticism published by Chelsea House.

AUSTIN WARREN was one of the most influential of the Kenyon critics. In addition to his *Elder Henry James* and *Rage for Order*, he co-authored, with René Wellek, *The Theory of Literature*.

GEOFFREY H. HARTMAN is Karl Young Professor of Comparative Literature at Yale University. His books include *The Unmediated Vision*, *The Fate of Reading*, *Criticism in the Wilderness*, and most recently *Easy Pieces*.

ELISABETH W. SCHNEIDER is Professor of English Emeritus at Temple University. Her books include *Aesthetics of William Hazlitt*, *Coleridge, Opium and Kubla Khan*, and *The Dragon in the Gate*.

PAUL L. MARIANI is Professor of English at the University of Massachusetts, Amherst. His books include *William Carlos Williams: A New World Naked*, *A Commentary on the Complete Poems of Gerard Manley Hopkins*, and *A Usable Past*.

JAMES MILROY is Senior Lecturer in Linguistics and Director of the Language Centre at the University of Sheffield. He is the author of *The Language of Gerard Manley Hopkins*.

ELLEN EVE FRANK has taught literature and the visual arts as Assistant Professor of English at the University of California, Berkeley, and is now a full-time painter and writer.

165

MARYLOU MOTTO is Assistant Professor of English at Rutgers University. Her study, *"Mined with a Motion": The Poetry of Gerard Manley Hopkins*, was published in 1984.

J. HILLIS MILLER, Frederick W. Hilles Professor of English and Comparative Literature at Yale University, is author of *Charles Dickens: The World of His Novels*, *The Disappearance of God: Five Nineteenth-Century Writers*, *Poets of Reality: Six Twentieth-Century Writers*, and most recently *The Linguistic Moment*.

Bibliography

Bergonzi, Bernard. *Gerard Manley Hopkins*. New York: Macmillan, 1977.

Bottral, Margaret, ed. *Gerard Manley Hopkins's Poems: A Casebook*. London: Macmillan, 1975.

Boyle, Robert. *Metaphor in Hopkins*. Chapel Hill: University of North Carolina Press, 1960.

Bump, Jerome. *Gerard Manley Hopkins*. Boston: Twayne, 1982.

Christ, Carol T. *The Finer Optic: The Aesthetic of Particularity in Victorian Poetry*. New Haven: Yale University Press, 1975.

Cotter, James Finn. " 'Hornlight Wound to the West': The Inscape of Passion in Hopkins's Poetry." *Victorian Poetry* 16 (1978): 297−313.

———. *Inscape: The Christology and Poetry of Gerard Manley Hopkins*. Pittsburgh: University of Pittsburgh Press, 1972.

Dickey, James. "Hopkins: *The Wreck of the Deutschland*." In *Master Poems of the English Language*, edited by Oscar Williams, 842−44. New York: Washington Square Press, 1967.

Dilligan, Robert J. and Todd K. Bender, comps. *A Concordance to the English Poetry of Gerard Manley Hopkins*. Madison: University of Wisconsin Press, 1970.

Downes, David A. *Gerard Manley Hopkins: A Study of His Ignatian Spirit*. New York: Bookman, 1959.

———. *Victorian Portraits: Hopkins and Pater*. New York: Bookman, 1965.

Dunne, Tom. *Gerard Manley Hopkins: A Comprehensive Bibliography*. Oxford: Clarendon Press, 1976.

Eble, Joseph. "Levels of Awareness: A Reading of Hopkins's 'Felix Randal.' " *Victorian Poetry* 13 (1975): 129−35.

Fulweiler, Howard. *Letters from the Darkling Plain: Language and the Grounds of Knowledge in the Poetry of Arnold and Hopkins*. Columbia: University of Missouri Press, 1972.

Gardner, W. H. *Gerard Manley Hopkins (1844—1889): A Study of Poetic Idiosyncrasy in Relation to Poetic Tradition*. 2 vols. 1949. Reprint. London: Oxford University Press, 1966.

Gerard Manley Hopkins, By the Kenyon Critics. New York: New Directions, 1945.

Grigson, Geoffrey. *Gerard Manley Hopkins*. London: Longmans, Green, 1955.

Harris, Daniel A. *Inspiration Unbidden: The Terrible Sonnets of Gerard Manley Hopkins*. Berkeley and Los Angeles: University of California Press, 1982.

Heuser, Alan. *The Shaping Vision of Gerard Manley Hopkins*. London: Oxford University Press, 1958.

The Hopkins Quarterly, 1974— .

Johnson, Wendell Stacy. *Gerard Manley Hopkins: The Poet as Victorian*. Ithaca: Cornell University Press, 1968.

Keating, John E. " 'The Wreck of the Deutschland': An Essay and Commentary." *Kent State University Bulletin* 51, no. 1 (1963).

MacKenzie, Norman H. *A Reader's Guide to Gerard Manley Hopkins*. Ithaca: Cornell University Press, 1981.

Martin, Philip M. *Mastery and Mercy: A Study of Two Religious Poems*. London: Oxford University Press, 1957.

McChesney, Donald. *A Hopkins Commentary: An Explanatory Commentary on the Main Poems*. London: University of London Press, 1968.

Milroy, James. *The Language of Gerard Manley Hopkins*. London: Andre Deutsch, 1977.

Milward, Peter. *A Commentary on G. M. Hopkins's "The Wreck of the Deutschland."* Tokyo: Hokuseido Press, 1968.

———. *Readings of "The Wreck": Essays in Commemoration of the Centenary of G. M. Hopkins's "The Wreck of the Deutschland."* Chicago: Loyola University Press, 1976.

Moore, Michael D. "Newman and the Motif of Intellectual Pain in Hopkins's 'Terrible Sonnets,' " *Mosaic* 12 (Summer, 1979): 29—46.

Motto, Marylou. *"Mined with a Motion": The Poetry of Gerard Manley Hopkins*. New Brunswick, N.   itgers University Press, 1984.

Ong, Walter J., S. J. "Voi   ummons for Belief." In *Literature and Belief*, edited by M. H. Abrams, 80—105. English Institute Essays, 1957. New York: Columbia University Press, 1958.

Peters, W. A. M. *Gerard Manley Hopkins: A Critical Essay Towards an Understanding of His Poetry*. London: Oxford University Press, 1948.

Phare, Elsie. *The Poetry of Gerard Manley Hopkins: A Survey and Commentary*. Cambridge: Cambridge University Press, 1933.

Pick, John. *Gerard Manley Hopkins: Priest and Poet.* 2d ed. New York: Oxford University Press, 1966.

Robinson, John. *In Extremity: A Study of Gerard Manley Hopkins.* Cambridge: Cambridge University Press, 1978.

Schneider, Elisabeth W. *The Dragon in the Gate: Studies in the Poetry of G. M. Hopkins.* Berkeley: University of California Press, 1968.

Sherwood, H. C. *The Poetry of Gerard Manley Hopkins.* Oxford: Blackwell, 1969.

Sprinker, Michael. *"A Counterpoint of Dissonance": The Aesthetics and Poetry of Gerard Manley Hopkins.* Baltimore: The Johns Hopkins University Press, 1980.

Storey, Graham. *A Preface to Hopkins.* London: Longman, 1981.

Sulloway, Alison G. *Gerard Manley Hopkins and the Victorian Temper.* London: Routledge and Kegan Paul, 1972.

Thornton, R. K. R. *Gerard Manley Hopkins: The Poems.* London: Edward Arnold, 1973.

———. *All My Eyes See: The Visual World of Gerard Manley Hopkins.* Sunderland, England: Sunderland Arts Centre. Ceolfrith Press, 1975.

Walhout, Donald. *Send My Roots Rain: A Study of Religious Experience in the Poetry of Gerard Manley Hopkins.* Athens: Ohio University Press, 1981.

Walliser, Stephen. *"That Nature is a Heraclitean Fire and of the Comfort of the Resurrection": A Case Study in G. M. Hopkins' Poetry.* Berne: Francke, 1977.

Weyand, Norman, S. J., ed. *Immortal Diamond: Studies In Gerard Manley Hopkins.* London: Sheed and Ward, 1949.

Winters, Yvor. *The Function of Criticism.* London: Routledge and Kegan Paul, 1957.

Acknowledgments

"Introduction" (originally entitled "Gerard Manley Hopkins") by Harold Bloom from *Victorian Prose and Poetry* (*The Oxford Anthology of English Literature*) edited by Lionel Trilling and Harold Bloom, © 1973 by Oxford University Press, Inc. Reprinted by permission.

"Instress of Inscape" by Austin Warren from *Gerard Manley Hopkins* by the Kenyon Critics, © 1944 by The Kenyon Review, © 1945 by New Directions. Reprinted by permission of the publisher.

"The Dialectic of Sense-Perception" by Geoffrey H. Hartman from *Hopkins: A Collection of Critical Essays* edited by Geoffrey H. Hartman, © 1966 by Geoffrey H. Hartman. Reprinted by permission of the author.

"The Dragon in the Gate" by Elisabeth W. Schneider from *The Dragon in the Gate: Studies in the Poetry of G. M. Hopkins* by Elisabeth W. Schneider, © 1968 by The Regents of the University of California. Reprinted by permission of the University of California Press.

"The Dark Night of the Soul" (originally entitled "The Dark Night of the Soul: 1885"; and " 'Summertime Joys' and 'Winter World': 1886–1889") by Paul L. Mariani from *A Commentary on the Complete Poems of Gerard Manley Hopkins* by Paul L. Mariani, © 1970 by Paul Mariani. Reprinted by permission of the author.

" 'The Weeds and the Wilderness': Local Dialect and Germanic Purism" by James Milroy from *The Language of Gerard Manley Hopkins* by James Milroy, © 1977 by James Milroy. Reprinted by permission.

"The Poetry of Architecture" (originally entitled " 'The Poetry of Architecture': Gerard Manley Hopkins") by Ellen Eve Frank from *Literary Architecture: Essays Toward a Tradition* by Ellen Eve Frank, © 1979 by The Regents of the University of California. Reprinted by permission of the University of California Press.

"Dramas of Time and Loss" by Marylou Motto from *"Mined with a Motion": The Poetry of Gerard Manley Hopkins* by Marylou Motto, © 1984 by Rutgers, The State University. Reprinted by permission of Rutgers University Press.

"The Linguistic Moment" (originally entitled "Hopkins") by J. Hillis Miller from *The Linguistic Moment: From Wordsworth to Stevens* by J. Hillis Miller, © 1985 by Princeton University Press. Reprinted by permission of the publisher.

Index

178 INDEX

Redemption, 141; as effect of thing, 21—22; in interior world, 140; and loss, 127
Rhetorical figures, 16, 24—25, 35, 39—40
Rhyme: internal, 11; as organizing principles, 151; recurrence and, 135; substitutes for, 10; universality of, 150
Rhythm, sprung. *See* Sprung rhythm
Richards, I. A., 131, 144
Richardson, Charles, 86
Ritualistic Movement, 5
Ritz, Jean-Georges, 51
Romanticism, 78, 147; defined, 147; freedom as theme in, 129. *See also* Hopkins, Gerard Manley: romantic sensibility of
Romantics, German, 77—78
Ruskin, John, 1, 7, 30, 52; aesthetics of, 30; influence on Furnivall, 11; influence on Hopkins, 7, 30, 78, 104

Saint Ignatius. *See* Loyola, Saint Ignatius of
Saint Thomas Aquinas. *See* Thomas Aquinas, Saint
Samson Agonistes (Milton), 3, 5
Self: ascent through time of, 140; in the child, 143, 146; explored in poetry, 150; in "Felix Randal," 139, 140; and Hopkins's search for opposites, 8—9; as "Jack-self," 57, 69, 74, 151; loss of, 131; relation of, to Christ, 162; seen in natural objects, 78; as unique to each individual, 148
Shelley, Percy Bysshe, 35, 154
Shipwrecks, 32—33. *See also Wreck of the Deutschland, The*
Skeat, W. W., 86
Society for Pure English, 81
Sonnets, 71, 76; as Hopkins's last work, 76; *volta* in, 73, 75. *See also* "Terrible Sonnets, The" *and individual titles*

Sources of Standard English, The (Oliphant), 84—85
Speechcraft (Barnes), 12
"Spelt from Sybil's Leaves," 124; "disremembering" in, 119; God in, 123; "hell" in, 58; images of enclosure in, 120; night of the soul in, 56; texture vs. structure, 14
Spiritual Exercises (Loyola), 35, 51, 71, 148
Spring and Fall": aging as motif in, 142, 144—45 complex syntax in, 142; diction in, 141—46; "leaves" as double entendre in, 142, 146; loss of innocence in, 143; recurrent language in, 137—38, 143, 145; speaker and "other" in, 141; unleaving as death in, 141—42
Sprung rhythm: defined, 153; roots in early English of, 3; in sonnets, 55—56, 60, 67; in *The Wreck of the Deutschland*, 34—35, 36, 40, 43—44, 50, 152
Stress, Hopkins's system of, 115—16
Structuralism, 149
Structure, as construction, 110, 112—13
Survey of English Dialects, 87
Symbolists, French, 29
Syntax, 17, 55, 114, 117, 142. *See also individual titles*
Sweet, Henry, 84

Tennyson, Alfred, Lord, 85
"Terrible Sonnets, The," 51—76; death in, 61—62, 64; God in, 64, 65, 69; influence of Dryden and Milton on, 55; night as symbol in, 56; patience as theme in, 66—68; religious metaphors in, 65; as prayer, 55; self in, 64, 68; sequence of, 51; subjective elements in, 68—69; syntax in, 55; *volta* in, 57, 64
"That Nature is a Heraclitean Fire,"